Suspects' Rights in India

This book examines the procedural, cultural and institutional framework of custodial interrogation in India. It explores theoretical and practical perspectives on custodial interrogation practices in India, which have been in urgent need for reform, and critiques the systemic failure on the part of the police in India to implement suspects' rights uniformly.

This volume

- Analyses the Indian framework of custodial interrogation to identify its fundamental flaws and emphasises on the need for having a lawyer present during custodial interrogation.
- Demonstrates significant evidence on state of suspects' rights in India through comparative law methodologies with a focus on common law scholarship and jurisprudence, more particularly England and Wales, and supplemented by vital empirical research through key interviews with related institutional parties.
- Discusses emerging, seminal jurisprudence of the European Court of Human Rights on applications of the right to fair trial at the custodial interrogation stage, especially shedding light on modern applications of the right to legal assistance in England and Wales, and radical Strasbourg-inspired reforms in other European jurisdictions.
- Highlights the right to legal assistance as one of the viable solutions to break the culture of police lawlessness at this critical stage of the criminal process.

An invigorating study, this book is aimed at enriching data and hypothesis for academics, policymakers, civil society organisations and students working in the area of law and legal studies, police and policing, citizenship and political science.

Prejal Shah is working as Lecturer in Law at the University of Lincoln, UK. Her current research involves custodial legal assistance during police interrogation during COVID-19 in a comparative perspective.

Suspects' Rights in India

Comparative Law and the Right to Legal Assistance as Drivers for Reform

Prejal Shah

Routledge
Taylor & Francis Group
LONDON AND NEW YORK

First published 2022
by Routledge
2 Park Square, Milton Park, Abingdon, Oxon OX14 4RN

and by Routledge
605 Third Avenue, New York, NY 10158

Routledge is an imprint of the Taylor & Francis Group, an informa business

British Library Cataloguing-in-Publication Data
A catalogue record for this book is available from the British Library

Library of Congress Cataloging-in-Publication Data
A catalog record has been requested for this book

ISBN: 978-0-367-07686-3 (hbk)
ISBN: 978-1-032-08125-0 (pbk)
ISBN: 978-1-003-21302-4 (ebk)

DOI: 10.4324/9781003213024

Typeset in Sabon
by Deanta Global Publishing Services, Chennai, India

Contents

Acknowledgements

Pursuing a PhD was a dream for me, and there are many people who have helped me in making this dream come true. I would like to begin by thanking my lovely parents, Mukesh and Bharti, for helping me believe in myself and making me believe that "no mountain is so big that you cannot climb it." I would like to thank my husband, Kinjal, for his enduring patience and support. A million thanks will not be sufficient for all your efforts and for the patience you've all had in the past few years. I would also like to thank my sister, Shreya, whose wit and humour kept me going through tough times and Praiv, for being brilliant! A special thank you to my entire family for being my guiding light for which I am forever indebted.

I would also like to express my gratitude to my supervisor, teacher, guide and mentor Dr Dimitrios Giannoulopoulos; thank you for all your help and guidance from the initial days of my research to the completion of this volume.

Lastly, but by no means the least, I would like to thank God for everything. A huge thank you to my numerous friends who kept me going regardless of the circumstances and helping me through all times.

I would like to dedicate this monograph to my daughter, Drisana. You make everything almost perfect!

Abbreviations

AHRC	ASIAN CENTRE FOR HUMAN RIGHTS
CPS	The Crown Prosecution Services
CRPC	The Code of Criminal Procedure, 1973
ICCPR	International Conventional on Civil and Political Rights
IEA	The Indian Evidence Act, 1872
IPC	The Indian Penal Code, 1860
NGOS	Non-Governmental Organisations
NHRC	National Human Rights Commission
PACE	The Police and Criminal Evidence Act, 1984
RCCP	The Royal Commission on Criminal Procedure
SHRC	State Human Rights Commission
UDHR	United Declaration of Human Rights
UNCAT	The United Nations Convention Against Torture

1 Introduction

1.1 Nature and scope

Manning and Hawkins note:

> In discussing legal decisions, the world outside is never fully screened out, for the personal values, ideologies, and beliefs of individuals are the "background" against which they are able to order the "foreground" of facts that cohere in the decision field.[1]

Policing is rooted in the particular contexts of authority and the maintenance of law and order. This is reflected in police interrogation, which is a crucial element in gathering evidence in order to advance further towards a fair trial.[2] According to Baldwin,

> It is evident ... that the idea that police interviewing is, or is becoming, a neutral or objective search for truth cannot be sustained, because any interview inevitably involves exploring with a suspect the detail of allegations within a framework of the points that might at a later date need to be proved.[3]

This volume is an attempt to analyse whether the custodial interrogation framework in India is neutral and whether it indeed provides for an objective search for truth. Instead, it may be more realistic to see interviews as mechanisms directed towards building a case and finding evidence.[4] This volume aims to identify the factors which make this construction of proof possible, focusing on police questioning as an evidence-gathering mechanism par excellence. This analysis proceeds against the background of suspects' rights operating at the custodial interrogation stage in India. The perennial issue of abuse of police power at the custodial interrogation stage, which manifests itself through the use of force, threats to use of force and even resorting to torture and degrading and inhumane treatment and the concerning divide between the law in theory and the law in action provide the backdrop against which these enquiries are undertaken.[5]

DOI: 10.4324/9781003213024-1

1.2 Aim

This volume revolves around a detailed examination of the procedural, cultural and institutional framework of custodial interrogation in India, from a theoretical and practical perspective, and is informed by a strong empirical element in the form of interviews with related institutional parties. The intuition that underpinned this research was that custodial interrogation practices in India were in urgent need for reform, and significant evidence in the form of appellate jurisprudence, criminal law scholarship and empirical research will be presented to support that. Adopting an outward-looking frame of mind, the research concentrates on the use of comparative law methodologies as the most appropriate means for effectively seeking reform, with an emphasis on common law scholarship and jurisprudence and the law of England and Wales in particular and on the emerging, seminal jurisprudence of the European Court of Human Rights on applications of the right to fair trial at the custodial interrogation stage.

More specifically, this volume aims to address the flaws inherent in the Indian framework for custodial interrogation and the use of confessional evidence obtained at this stage as well as the recurrent use of force and even torture by the police. The English custodial interrogation framework, as exemplified by the detailed provision of the Police and Criminal Evidence Act 1984, is examined from a comparative perspective and suggestions are made for the incorporation of particular solutions that derive from it, although note is also taken of continuing concerns with the practical implementation of some of its key guarantees including the right to custodial legal assistance and the right to silence.

This research sets out with the hypothesis that there exist vast differences between the custodial interrogation regimes of India and England and Wales, and particular attention is paid to adopting a contextual approach to the incorporation of potential 'foreign' solutions. The cultural, procedural and institutional obstacles to reforming custodial interrogation in India cannot be underestimated, and suggesting that the mere adoption of solutions that *may* have worked in England and Wales would be legal fiction.

1.3 Structure of volume

The volume explores the relevant substantive issues in four chapters (Chapters 3–6), while a chapter is dedicated to methodological perspectives. The comparative methodology informs discussion in all chapters, with the first part in each chapter highlighting aspects of the Indian framework and the second looking for what has worked, and what has not, for England and Wales. Differences and similarities are critically analysed, while the discussion is enriched by the empirical reflections deriving from interviews with police officers and other institutional parties.

It also discusses the methodology used in this volume. A triangulation of research methods combines comparative research, doctrinal analysis and empirical research. This chapter also explains the use of comparative methodology between the two countries highlighting its implication and limitations. Excerpts from interviews conducted are used to demonstrate the continuing problems with the law in action in India.

Chapter 2 undertakes an analysis of police interrogation frameworks in India and England and Wales locating attention on police powers, training and accountability, public perceptions about the police and law commission efforts to strengthen the rule of law in this critical area of the criminal process. Supreme Court jurisprudence is central to this discussion. While analysing police interrogation in England and Wales, the pre-PACE and post-PACE positions are compared and contrasted, with a view to highlighting the dramatic impact of PACE upon improving police interrogation practices. Various law commission reports that have contributed to the enactment of PACE are also analysed. The conclusion that derives from these analyses is systemic failures in India that underline an urgent need for reform.

Chapter 3 then locates the right to custodial legal assistance as potentially the most powerful driver for future reform. A detailed discussion assists in establishing the relevant stipulations under the Constitution of India and the institutional interpretation of the right to legal assistance. An enquiry is made into the impact international conventions have had on the provision of custodial legal assistance. The implementation of the right to legal assistance in England and Wales is analysed in parallel with seminal ECHR jurisprudence; both are seen as capable to provide the Indian criminal justice system with a useful compass when seeking reform.

Chapter 4 concentrates on India's idiosyncratic ban on admitting in court any confessions made before a police officer, and much attention is paid to sketching the dire state of affairs as to the credibility of the police as an institution capable of protecting suspects' rights, as illustrated by the existence of such a rule.[6] Consideration is then given to the effect of a potential enhancement of the right to legal assistance for this exclusionary rule; the argument is developed that the lawyer's presence during custodial interrogation would automatically reduce the need for an absolute ban on confessions made to the police, with the focus being on the lawyer's capacity to act as a safeguard against abuses of suspects' rights by the police rather than on having an absolute ban precisely because the system places no faith on the police to obtain confessions without abusing the rights of the suspect.

Chapter 5 takes further the line of reasoning developed in the previous chapter, exploring the main reasons underpinning abuse of power at the police station. The excessive use of force in India has resulted in custodial violence and at times even custodial death. This chapter tests the impact of the ratification of international conventions and their application in domestic legislation and practices in the comparator countries. While investigating into the use of force and torture in India, the role of the National Human Rights Commission and State Human Rights Commission is analysed. Similar provisions are analysed surrounding the use of force in England and Wales, particularly the impact of the ECHR and relevant provisions.

The volume concludes with a discussion of practical recommendations ensuing from the preceding theoretical discussion. India has traditionally given little attention to the right to custodial legal assistance. This is the fundamental flaw that this volume sets out to address, inspired by contemporary transformations of the right to legal assistance in England and Wales and in the jurisprudence of the European Court of Human Rights.

1.4 Research methods and methodology

1.4.1 Research methodology: comparative Law

A study of any given legal system involves the study of law as a system of norms and law as a system of social behaviour.[7] The main research methodology used in this volume is a comparative textual analysis between India and England and Wales that aims to discover the similarities and differences between the practices of police interrogation in the two countries. Maintaining the orthodoxy of comparative law, this volume considers the functionality of the comparison. There are certain similarities and differences between the procedures and methods involving police interrogation. For the purpose of considering this specifically, this volume uses the system in England and Wales to ascertain the potential for change in India. This volume aims to address the disparity between the procedures concerning police interrogation and associated practices. This will assist in ascertaining what can be done to identify and fill in the gaps in the Indian criminal justice system to make it a more rights-based system. The right to legal assistance plays a key role in this comparative scheme.

This researcher had the advantage of studying the English Criminal Justice system at a postgraduate level and hence has an insider-outsider approach to the English legal system.[8] This provides a two-dimensional view: a participant and a critic for both the compared countries, to adopt Riles' approach.[9] Orucu rightly mentions that comparative law is still an underutilised research methodology even in the twenty-first century.[10] Comparative law assists in widening the knowledge of the researcher and obtaining a broader and in-depth understanding of the comparative institutions. This critical extraction of legal knowledge is the primary aim of the present volume. The present research falls under the classification of "descriptive and analytical" noted by Kothari.[11]

1.4.2 Why compare India and England and Wales?

Kahn-Freund observed that lawmakers look abroad for a fresh perspective and new ideas to resolve issues.[12] India and England and Wales share a political and legal history resulting in the adoption of common law. Historically, legal regulation entailed borrowing and adopting laws during both colonial and post-colonial times. Among these are the criminal law codes, which contain the provisions relating to police interrogation and practices such as the right to custodial legal assistance and the admissibility of confessions. These codes are still effective today, virtually unchanged since their inception. But in recent years these outdated codes have invited criticism from various authors, highlighting the need for urgent police reforms to respond to what are perceived to be systemic violations of suspects' rights during police interrogation in India. The Supreme Court itself has highlighted this need, and various other courts, at appellate and first instance level, have emphasised the need for safeguarding the suspect at the time of police interrogation.

This research aims to identify the flaws inherent in the police interrogation regime in India, including the impact that the inability to implement the right to legal assistance has on obtaining confessional evidence and the continuous use of force in custodial interrogation. It does so through a comparative examination of the law of England and Wales, which have emerged as leaders in the field of the suspects' rights and police interrogation, as well as modern jurisprudence of the European Court of Human Rights. This volume refers to the ECtHR jurisprudence owing to its recent developments highlighting the importance of the right to legal assistance. This also assists in providing an outward perspective to other jurisdictions and what lessons they might learn from the Indian criminal justice system. It also does so against the backdrop of a lack of comparative scholarly work contrasting Indian and English approaches to criminal justice matters, which is an observation that merits attention in itself, considering the substantial colonialist influences leading to the adoption of the common law legal culture in India. This volume aims to offer a cosmopolitan understanding of other systems and jurisdictions and a wider approach to the ECHR by providing the current situation in the Indian criminal justice system. Using the Indian criminal justice system, this volume aims to inform the above-mentioned systems the importance of the right to legal assistance as a part of the wider debate sparked by the ECHR. This is clearly evident from the various cases discussed by the ECHR demonstrating how jurisdictions are now waking up to reform the right to legal assistance. The timeliness of this volume is consistent with what is happening in Europe concerning the above topics.

This comparative study is therefore essential as India is required to understand the importance of giving effect to suspects' rights during police interrogation. As will be fully demonstrated later on, England and Wales have been successful in implementing custodial interrogation reforms and thus offer a useful comparative prism through which to evaluate the need for reform.[13] Even where England and Wales have *not* been successful in implementing reforms, investigating the reasons for this could be instructive for the Indian legislator; in his efforts to avoid mistakes, he would surely be keen to learn from the "mistakes" of others.[14]

1.4.3 *Drawbacks of using comparative law*

The idea of comparing two countries with very little in common was expected to be called "naive" according to Graziadei,[15] bearing in mind that it was still thought necessary to compare the police interrogation systems and factors associated with it. The major difference between legislation and police culture between the comparative countries might be subject to criticism. However, despite cultural differences in the police interrogation techniques, precedents are always taken from England and Wales. This has been highlighted in various Indian law reports.[16] However, the comparative nature of the methodology used has tried using the philosophy of "all things are comparable even if unique,"[17] hence justifying the use of comparing apples with oranges.[18] This also enhances the chances of providing legislative reforms based on existing legal systems. This comparison was made possible with the use of functional elements, both common and different. The cultural element contains both these elements, hence making the comparison convenient and possible.

1.4.4 *Legal transplant*

A comparative study often leads the researcher to provide practical solutions to rectify the gaps identified during research. The present research attempts to enquire if there is any merit in legal transplant, specifically of statutory rules concerning police interrogation and suspects' rights from England and Wales.[19] Legal transplants of one system into another may not always work, hence any recommendations being made will be subject to testing in practice.[20] Legal regulation in India has been known to "adopt" and "borrow" laws from other systems in order to endeavour to comply with international norms.[21] Transplantation from Western Law such as England and Wales may not result in full-scale rejection as predicted by Legrand[22]—one of the speculated reasons being the colonial history for borrowing laws especially criminal laws. The volume also aims at finding the balance between the crime control and due process systems in the Indian criminal justice system, and the use of legal transplant is thought in the best interest to attain this. Comparative law as a precursor to legal transplantation may help achieve this balance. While culture may restrict the application of this legal transplant, this volume is aimed at providing legal reforms legislatively, which is thought to have little impact on culture. The application of legal transplant is therefore speculated and requires further investigation into the practical application of this matter.

1.4.5 *Research method*

Research methods are the tools, processes and ways by which data is obtained. In order to ascertain the criminal justice efficiency issues, existing data is examined on the subject of the right to legal assistance, the use of force and the inadmissibility of confessions made to police officers. The value of evidentiary material obtained by interrogation has a major impact in many countries such as England and Wales. This adversarial aspect assists in the smooth running of a criminal justice system.[23] Typically, an empirical research is conducted when there is a gap in the research or the literature is wrong or incomplete. In the present circumstances, it would appear that the literature is incomplete with regard to the above-mentioned provisions in India.

Officials from different police ranks were chosen for the interview.[24] In order to make the research diverse and geographically proportionate, police officers were chosen from different states in India. In order to facilitate the timings of the availability of police officers, most of them were approached from various cities and a few others were approached from rural villages. Most empirical scholars use legal history in their empirical research. Typically this uses hypothesis based on data based on historical information. This has not been employed in the present research as it does not assist in hypothesis surrounding the research. This research employs traditional analysis of legal documents, court decisions and legislative materials. This research combines traditional legal analyses with additional empirical research undertaken to fill the gaps in previous research on the topics undertaken here.

In this research of "police organisation" in India, and the comparative perspectives from England and Wales, the researcher has an outsider's approach and studies the past practices.[25] It would have been invaluable to be able to gain the experience as an outside-insider or an insider perspective towards policing.[26] In order to ensure that the recommendations can be applied to future policing, this extends to research "for the police" as well. In order to provide a practical account, this research extends to being "with the police," as it involves interviewing police officers from different ranks and geographical areas. A combination of these methods may assist in studying both: the police force as an organisation and the police officer as an individual, who carries out the duties representing the organisation.

Every research requiring practical implementation of a reformative structure, which aims at filling the gaps left by previous research, requires a transition from doctrinal research to empirical research.[27] Empirical research is no longer a relic enjoyed exclusively by social scientists alone. Growing need for empirical studies in the legal realm has been highlighted by upcoming empirical research in the past few years. This could also assist in educating legal scholars to adopt an outward-looking approach towards legal literature.

Empirical work employs statistics and other qualitative methods among other things. While there is very little training on empirical research in the United Kingdom,[28] there is even lesser leverage given to it in India. Empirical research requires the systematic collection of data and carrying out analysis according to generally accepted methods. For the sake of the present research, data has been collected by way of interviews only. All the participants were assured of confidentiality and anonymity in accordance with Brunel University ethical guidelines and procedures.

1.4.6 Primary data: legal cases and legislation

At the start of this project, research was carried out with a view to forming a working hypothesis. The parts where there were significant gaps in the present literature have been identified and aimed to be filled in by further research. Doctrinal analysis of related legal provisions and jurisprudence forms the major part of the methods for this volume. The empirical survey of the opinion of institutional parties was aimed to facilitate an examination of the law in action that would run parallel to doctrinal analysis.

1.4.7 Triangulation method

This research relies on the combination of various methods. This is used while triangulating data from doctrinal or library-based research and empirical research. Triangulation, as explained by Valentine, is as follows:

> Often researchers draw on many different perspectives or sources in the course of their work. This is known as triangulation. The term comes from surveying, where it describes using different bearings to give the correct position. In the same way researchers can use multiple methods or different sources to try and maximise their understanding of the research question.[29]

By using a triangulation method, this research aims to provide a clear and practical picture relating to the right to legal assistance, use of force and admissibility of confession. Previous research in India confines itself to the role of a lawyer at the trial stage, is very limited on the topic of inadmissibility of confession and almost takes for granted the use of force at the police station. Despite these provisions being listed in the Fundamental Rights chapter of the Constitution of India, they have a different effect in practice. In order to ascertain the extent to which these provisions are being implemented by police officers, an empirical research was carried out with a range of different actors of the criminal justice. This methodology will assist in testing the hypothesis: whether the role of a police officer in investigating can be assisted by the presence of a lawyer in order to avoid the abuse of police powers during interrogation and the impact of these reforms on the admissibility of confessions given to a police officer.

1.4.8 Empirical research

Like legal theory, empirical research aims to help the observer understand law and legal systems.[30] Essentially, it is a means of obtaining information about the social implications of law. Empirical data provides a practical approach to the elements, which are examined using the primary sources of data. For the present study, it was observed that many police officers were reluctant to participate in the survey. While a considerable number of participants were approached initially and followed up, in the end most of them seemed hesitant to be interviewed. A total of 25 participants were interviewed, of which 16 were police officers, 4 were defence lawyers and 5 were public prosecutors. These participants were selected from different regions and states in India. While this small group does not represent a unanimous section of the population, it is used as a sample group. A consistent country-wide approach would have perhaps facilitated wider participation and a more representative sample but lack of funds did not allow extending the scope of the survey in that way.

These interviews are used to voice the current situation in India and aim at depicting the "law in practice" element of this research. They do not represent any group or are not considered a sample to represent any part of the population.

1.4.8.1 Qualitative analysis

Documents other than primary legal sources such as cases and statutes are relatively underutilised, even though they provide a rich source of data.[31] Data gathered after using means such as in-depth interviews provide data on the decisions made by the people on a daily basis. These may not relate to a particular event or a particular period and hence fit perfectly with a variety of topics, which form the hypothesis. In the present research, the decisions taken by police officials are examined along with the perspective taken by other criminal justice actors. This will assist in testing the hypothesis and determining the difference between the law in theory and the law in practice. This will also help determine how much reliance can be placed on confessional evidence obtained during interrogation and if a change at the level of procedural guarantees offered at the police station can increase the degree to which we rely on confessional evidence. It must be emphasised that this research aims to provide a contextual study of the relevant provisions mentioned above.[32]

1.4.8.2 Grounded theory

Grounded theory entails developing the theory as the research proceeds rather than testing a hypothesis posited in advance. Here it was essential to identify the practice of providing a lawyer at the police station in India. It was also important to ascertain if the police in India receive sufficient training to carry out an investigation safeguarding the suspects' rights. The empirical research also enquired into the recording of confessions in India.

1.4.8.3 Interviews

In the words of Dunn, interviews are "verbal interchanges where one person, the interviewer, attempts to elicit information from another person."[33] Individual interviews may be conducted face-to-face or via telephone. All forms of individual interviews are used by qualitative researchers examining legal phenomena and the perception of law and legal profession.[34] A face-to-face interview was not possible considering the geographical limitation and the time constraint. All interviews were carried out during 2014–2016 using internet media such as Viber, WhatsApp and Skype and have been recorded and transcribed. Most of these police officers interviewed also preferred to return their answers via email rather than a recorded interview. These interviews were also helpful but were limited in the description of answers, restricting their ample utilisation. In England and Wales, a plethora of empirical studies assists in analysing various factors concerning the workability of the laws relating to policing and suspects' rights. This provided a backdrop for the empirical research in India which could assist in filling the gaps left by previous research. Professor Hodgson's empirical research on the French criminal justice system has provided a good precedent for the structure of present interviews.[35]

1.4.8.4 Groups

The individuals interviewed are divided into three main groups: defence lawyers, public prosecutors and police officers. The lawyers comprise of defence lawyers and public prosecutors specialising mainly in criminal law. Police officers of different ranks were interviewed: police constables, Assistant Commissioner of Police, police officers (retired). Since the hypothesis aimed to test the application of the right to legal assistance and police interrogation in practice, the rank of police officers did have any impact on the data collected. All the police personnel have been classified into one group regardless of their rank and position.

1.4.8.5 Ethical issues

The Ethics Committee were approached and all the relevant paperwork filled out as required by the university's board.[36] Every care was taken to ensure that no question put to the participants would cause them any harm or prejudice. Even when the participants were questioned on the practice at their place of work, they were reminded of the anonymity of their answers. Anonymity was also observed while preparing transcripts of the interviews and they have been labelled accordingly. The transcript has been labelled PO for police personnel interviewed with a distinct number. The transcripts of interviews with public prosecutors are labelled PP with a number and the interviews with defence lawyers have been marked L with a number.

1.4.8.6 *Structure of interviews*

The structure thought most appropriate for this research was a semistructured or loose-structured interview. All of the questions put to the participants were open-ended. This was done mainly with the intent of gaining information based on individual experience. The participants had not been made aware of the questions prior to the interview.

1.4.8.7 *Lack of observation*

No observations were carried out at the police station. Although this would have been appropriate for the research, the lack of uniform implementation of the right to legal assistance at the police stations in India made this impractical. In the absence of continuous availability of lawyers at the police interrogation stage, an observation study was thought to be of little importance. There was also an assumption that the presence of a researcher will alter the behaviour of the interrogating police officer. A new project involving observation at police station at the time of interrogation may be taken up by the researcher after completion of this volume.

1.4.8.8 *Limitations*

Police in India is an institution not easy to penetrate. The majority of police officers approached were reluctant to participate in the survey and so the results should be seen as an additional source of information rather than as providing an accurate representation of police practice in India. On the other hand, useful insights can be gained by the views of those police officers and prosecutors who took part in the survey, in particular about aspects of custodial interrogation not covered by the relevant academic scholarship and jurisprudence.

Notes

1 P Manning and K Hawkins, 'Legal Decisions: A Frame Analytic Perspective' 1990, 209.
2 The Right to a Fair Trial: Part 1: From Investigation to Trial, Chapter 6, available at http://www.ohchr.org/Documents/Publications/training9chapter6en.pdf, accessed on 20 August 2015.
3 J Baldwin, 'Police Interview Techniques: Establishing Truth or Proof?' (1993) 33(3) *British Journal of Criminology* 325–352, 330.
4 Ibid, 333
5 E Orucu, 'A Project: Comparative Law in Action' in E Orucu and D Nelkin (eds), *Comparative Law: A Handbook*, Oxford: Hart Publication, 2007.
6 There are certain exceptions to the admissibility of confessions, which are discussed at length in the chapter.
7 U Baxi, *Socio-Legal Research in India: A Programschrift*, New Delhi: Indian Council of Social Science Research (ICSSR), 1975. Reprinted in S Verma and M

Afzal Wani (ed.), *Legal Research and Methodology*, 2nd edn, New Delhi: Indian Law Institute, 2001, 656.

8 See generally M Graziadei, 'The Functionalist Heritage' in P Legrand and R Munday (eds), *Comparative Legal Studies: Traditions and Transitions*, Cambridge University Press, 2003, and K Zweigert and H Kotz, *An Introduction to Comparative Law*, 2nd edn, trans. Tony Weir, Oxford: Oxford University Press, 1993, R Merton, 'Insiders and Outsiders: A Chapter in the Sociology of Knowledge' (1972) 78(1) *American Journal of Sociology* 9–47.

9 A Riles, 'Comparative Law and Socio-Legal Studies' in M Reimmann and R Zimmerman (eds), *The Oxford Handbook of Comparative Law*, OUP, 2006.

10 E Orucu, 'Critical Comparative Law: Considering Paradoxes for Legal Systems in Transition' (June 2000) 24 Netherlands Comparative Law Association.

11 C Kothari, *Research Methodology: Methods and Techniques*, 2nd edn, New Delhi: New Age International Publishers, 2004.

12 O Kahn-Freund, 'Comparative Law as an Academic Subject' (1966) 82 *Law Quarterly Review*.

13 S Tromans, 'Some Comparative Reflections' in B S Markesinis (ed.), *The Gradual Convergence: Foreign Ideas, Foreign Influences, and English Law on the Eve of the 21st Century*, Oxford: Clarendon Press, 1994.

14 Ibid.

15 M Graziadei, *The Functionalist Heritage*, in P Legrand and R Munday (eds), *Comparative Legal Studies: Traditions and Transitions*, Cambridge University Press, 2003.

16 152nd–244th Law Commission Reports India, available at http://lawcommissionofindia.nic.in/, accessed on 29 July 2016.

17 E Orucu, *The Enigma of Comparative Law*, Leiden/Boston: Martinus Nijhoff Publishers, 2004.

18 E Orucu, 'Critical Comparative Law: Considering Paradoxes for Legal Systems in Transition' (June 2000) 4 Netherlands Comparative Law Association.

19 A Watson, *Legal Transplants*, 2nd edn, University of Georgia Press, 1993.

20 Ibid.

21 Ibid.

22 P Legrand, 'The Impossibility of Legal Transplants' (1997) 4 *Maastricht Journal of European and Comparative Law* 111.

23 J Hodgson, 'Conceptions of the Trial in Inquisitorial and Adversarial Procedure' in *The Trial on Trial (vol 2): Judgment and Calling to Account*, 2006, 223–242.

24 The details of the number of personnel interviewed and the composition is discussed at length later at pp. 11–12.

25 J Brown, 'Police Research: Some Critical Issues' in F Leishman, B Loveday, and S Savage (eds), *Core Issues in Policing*, London: Longman, 1996.

26 Ibid.

27 P Cane and H Kritzer, *The Oxford Handbook of Empirical Legal Research*, OUP, 2010.

28 P Cane and H Kritzer, *The Oxford Handbook of Empirical Legal Research*, OUP, 2010.

29 G Valentine, '"Tell Me About"...: Using Interview as a Research Methodology' in R Flowerdew and D Martin (eds), *Methods in Human Geography: A Guide for Students Doing a Research Project*, Edinburgh: Longman, (1997), 110–127.

30 N MacCormick, *Legal Reasoning and Legal Theory*, OUP, 1978.

31 P Cane and H Kritzer, *The Oxford Handbook of Empirical Legal Research*, OUP, 2010.

32 R Yin, *Case Study Research: Design and Methods*, 2nd edn, Newbury Park, CA: Sage Publications, 1994.

33 K Dunn, *Interviewing in Qualitative Research Methods in Human Geography*, 2nd edn, Oxford: Oxford University Press, 2005.
34 H Sommerlad, 'Researching and Theorizing the Processes of Professional Identity Formation' (2007) 34 *Journal of Law and Society* 190–217.
35 J Hodgson, *French Criminal Justice: A Comparative Account of the Investigation and Prosecution of Crime in France*, Oxford: Hart Publishing, 2005.
36 A copy of this Ethics Committee approval is available on request.

2 Police interrogation
The need for reform

2.1 Introduction

This chapter carries out an analysis of police interrogation with reference to Supreme Court and lower court jurisprudence, and related legislative and institutional framework in India and England and Wales. It concentrates on the factors that shape police interrogation practices such as the wide powers of arrest, quality of police training, public perceptions, accountability and transparency and makes specific enquiries about considerable variations between the law in theory and the law in action. The first half of the chapter deals with the above-mentioned elements from an Indian perspective followed by a discussion of similar elements from the perspective of England and Wales comparing the similarities and differences. The flaws and strengths of the two systems are examined in great detail and a research hypothesis is pursued to the effect that, given its well-documented successes, the English system of police interrogation could potentially function as a model upon which to draw comparative reform of Indian police interrogation practices widely seen as problematic. The wide powers of arrest and interrogation need to be balanced with the protection of fundamental rights of the suspect. This chapter describes the process of police investigation in detail in both the comparative countries.

2.2 The police investigation context: India

Indian policing is regulated by the archaic act of Indian Police Act, 1861 (IPC), originally enacted by the British. Most important provisions are also contained in the Code of Criminal Procedure, 1973 (CrPC),[1] IPC, and each state has its own police act. Indian laws have been largely shaped by colonial British rule.[2] Most of the criminal procedure laws are a result of the drafts constructed during the British regime.[3] From time to time, Indian legislators have looked at English legal systems in order to implement necessary amendments in an attempt to keep abreast with changing times.[4] The Indian police officers are governed by the state and not by the central government as a result of which most of the regulations are

DOI: 10.4324/9781003213024-2

found under the state law and not the central law.[5] In order for the police to carry out an investigation, a complaint has to be filed followed by the police officer making an arrest. Since this precedes a formal police investigation, an analysis of the procedure for arrest is carried out in the next section.

Under the CrPC, offences are classified as cognisable and non-cognisable offences.[6] Section 157 of the CrPC empowers the police officer to start an investigation without the orders of the magistrate and without registering a cognisable offence. The main difference between the two is that a cognisable offence is an offence where a police officer can arrest without a warrant and a non-cognisable offence is one where the police officer requires an arrest warrant.[7] In case of a cognisable offence, the competent magistrate may direct the investigation.[8] If a police officer receives information about an offence, he can visit the place of the commission of the crime and commence an investigation.[9] While the courts do not interfere with the investigative powers of police officers, they may quash the investigation by invoking Article 227 of the Constitution of India.[10] Most of these provisions for quashing the investigation include discrepancies and irregularities of the First Information Report, but also include an "abuse of power" by the police.[11] These provisions are discussed in this section to highlight the importance of the police powers to arrest and record information given by the suspect.

2.2.1 *First Information Report (FIR): cognisable offences*

When a cognisable offence is reported, an investigation can commence immediately after the police receive the information of the crime.[12] The FIR is a written document containing the information received by the police officer in charge of a police station about the commission of a cognisable offence.[13] An FIR may be created on receipt of a complaint or on the police officer's own initiation. The CrPC does not define the FIR, but this explanation is the usual practice reflecting the provisions of Section 154 of the CrPC.[14] Ordinarily, an officer in charge of the police station and above the rank of a constable is authorised to register an FIR. It is the duty of the police officer to record an FIR in every cognisable case. The FIR is the initiation of any criminal case and sets the process of criminal justice in motion. It should record all the details: the name and addresses, true facts of the incidents and names and description of the persons involved. The FIR is signed by both the police officer recording it and the person lodging the complaint. A copy of this FIR is given to the person making the complaint. The importance of an FIR is also highlighted under Section 74 of the Evidence Act, 1872, which refers to an FIR as a public document. The suspect is entitled to get a free copy of the FIR at a much earlier stage than that described under Section 207 of the CrPC.[15] This is the only written confirmation that the suspect receives throughout the investigative process. Thus, although the FIR is not in itself a proof of crime, it is a corroborative evidence for the prosecution's case.[16]

Under certain circumstances, the police officer may refuse to carry out further investigation but they are required to record the FIR.[17] This gives police officers wide powers to exercise their discretion to refuse an investigation, but not to register the FIR. As a result, it is not an unusual practice for police officers to deny recording of the FIRs.[18] In such an event of refusal to register an FIR, one may approach the Superintendent of Police in the concerned area as observed in the case of *Sakiri Basu v. The State of UP*.[19] It is argued here that approaching a Superintendent of Police is not an effective solution as he belongs to the same police station. Needless to mention, this might dissuade the suspect from approaching the officers of the same police station, presuming that there might be an internal acquaintance.

Almost all the police officers interviewed for this research affirmed the notification of the FIR and making entries required by the police station diary. But very few of them confirmed that they were expected to provide the suspect with a copy of the FIR.[20] It is therefore essential to enquire into the procedure of FIR.

2.2.1.1 Failure to register FIR

One of the common complaints against police officers, which exists since the 1980s and has been called pervasive and a malpractice, is the failure of the police to register FIRs.[21] Failure to register an FIR does not automatically vitiate a trial.[22] This may also condone the police officer's action to avoid registering the FIR. As observed in the interview,

> It is a culture (among the police officers) that most of the FIRs will not be recorded. There are many reasons.[23]

It is suggested here that stringent measures need to be taken legislatively for the non-registering of the FIR.

Each state may also vary in the practices of registering an FIR and the failure may have a different impact in each state.[24] This makes the regulation of compliance open to interpretation, in case of a conflict brought before the Supreme Court by a high court of any state. It is a common practice that most police officers will refrain from registering the FIR in order to avoid an investigation.[25] Some studies have acknowledged that police officers may refrain from registering an FIR to keep the crime rate low.[26] This is also due to political interference from the state government.[27] This is just one of the drawbacks of the impact of political interference in policing duties. The absence of a national survey to determine the actual number of complaints not registered as FIRs makes it difficult to determine the gravity of this issue. However, as observed in a study undertaken, the Lucknow (an Indian state) police recorded only 4.5% of the complaints they received.[28] Senior Police

Officers usually justify the non-registration of crimes due to the pressure from the political leaders to show a reduction in crime.[29] At times, the junior police officers also face the fear of reprimand or suspension if they register too many FIRs.[30] In an interview, a police officer from New Delhi also noted that police officers would avoid registering an FIR saving them any hassle to pursue an investigation.[31]

The CrPC authorises the police officer to decline an investigation, but it requires the police officer exercising this power to prepare a report after filing an FIR. This inadvertently instigates the police officer to avoid registering the FIR altogether. It is not difficult in the present circumstance therefore to imagine this practice being unusual for police officers in rural areas. In the absence of an effective monitoring system of the FIR, it is not surprising that this failure for police officers to abide by their duty has been a common practice. The Supreme Court has made several efforts to illustrate the importance of registering an FIR and its effect on fundamental rights. As observed in *Mohindro v. The State of Punjab*, the registration of the FIR is the most imperative step for the recording of the crime.[32] The Supreme Court also held that there can be no enquiry without initial registration of an FIR.[33] Authors like Vadackumchery observe that police officers fail to register "all" the FIRs.[34] Vadackumchery also questions the sincerity of police officers in recording the FIRs and the mandate on the manipulation on the part of these officers.[35] Law commissions have also been critical of this issue in their reports, criticising the wide powers of arrest and discretion given to police officers to record the FIR.[36] This is a misinterpretation of police powers as the code requires them to record an FIR and does not empower a police officer with the discretion to do so. The lack of awareness among police officers about the mandatory provision of recording an FIR results in the non-recording of the FIR.

The Supreme Court while providing guidelines to arrest an individual observed the existence of the "abuse of power" by the police officer.[37] The Supreme Court expressed concern about the violation of police duties as it is committed by the same people who are supposed to be the protector of the citizens.[38] Section 154 of CrPC confers a statutory obligation on the police officer to enter substantial information in an FIR and failure to do so would mean breaching the mandate of Section 154(1) of the CrPC.[39] The Code also fails to provide punitive measures for the breach of police duties. The Delhi High Court interprets the non-compliance of these police duties would amount to a breach, but does not clarify any punitive measures for this breach.[40] As observed above, it is clear that an FIR is the only written evidence of the details of the police investigation for both the suspect and the police officer. However, one may observe the absence of a consistent and mandatory practice throughout all the states. It is suggested here that the lack of legislation implementing the jurisprudence has resulted in such an inconsistent practice. Also, the lack of punitive measures towards the police officers failing to record an FIR results in the continuation of such a practice. It is argued here that because of the non-registration of FIRs, the code provides for a magistrate's order for certain offences.

2.2.1.2 *Use of discretion*

Police officers are vested with the power to use their discretion for registering the complaint and record it in the FIR, as observed above.[41] It is beyond doubt that the use of discretion would depend on the nature of the crime reported and the experience the police officer has had in conducting an investigation. Despite clear provisions for mandatory preparation of a full report stating the reasons for the use of discretion for non-registration of FIR, this provision is hardly complied with in practice.[42] It is argued here that this use of discretion to carry out an investigation should not overlap with the power to file an FIR. In any case, there should be a written proof of complaint received and a copy of this should be served to the suspect. Merely noting this in the report at the police station does not ensure transparency. The police also use their discretion to pre-empt the filing of the FIR in order to altogether avoid the investigation.

The police also exercise their discretion for not recording the FIR due to the reliability of the informant. This is evident from the empirical research as one personnel observes:

> Call it power abuse or use, police officers use decision making power (discretion) for a lot of things such as recording FIRs.[43]

The Supreme Court has condoned this in its judgement in the case of *State of Haryana v. Ch Bhajan Lal*.[44] This extends the power of discretion by the police officer to carry out an investigation.

Many reports suggest the existence of other problems with the use of discretion in areas such as the attitude of the police officer and the most commonly used excuse of jurisdiction issues.[45] This determination of jurisdiction power used by police officers should be mandated and documented.[46] This non-registration of the FIR owing to the lack of jurisdiction has caused serious problems in the criminal justice system.[47] Mathur describes the misuse of discretionary power by "police arresting a man, not showing the arrest in the registers, not informing the court, keeping the man in illegal detention," as an "organisational crime."[48] He further adds that these organisational crimes are "condoned, connived, or even expected" of the police.[49] It may be deduced here that in the absence of strict protocol to follow these guidelines, these acts of police officers go unnoticed and unaccounted for.

2.2.2 *Magistrate's order: non-cognisable offences*

A non-cognisable offence is an offence under Section 2(1) of the CrPC where the police officer has no authority to arrest without a warrant from the magistrate. The police officer is not competent to record an FIR and carry out an investigation pertaining to any non-cognisable offences, unless he obtains permission from the magistrate.[50] Non-cognisable offences are also less serious in nature and are generally "private wrongs."[51] Most police officers use this as an excuse to avoid registering an FIR.[52] Further, if it appears to the magistrate that an offence can be tried exclusively by the Court of Sessions, the magistrate may not make any direction for investigation under Section 202(1) of the CrPC.[53] This provision under Section 202 of the CrPC does not apply to a fresh case initiated by the police report but only to assist already existing proceedings before the magistrate.[54]

This provision requires the magistrate to act in his own capacity and issue an order. This procedure of obtaining a warrant from the magistrate is criticised for "the non-application of mind by the magistrate."[55] In the case of *Anil K Khandelwal v. Maksud Saiyed*, the magistrate failed to assess the complaint made by the police officer and allow further investigation.[56] It is, as it may seem, the responsibility of the police officer to distinguish a complaint to be cognisable and non-cognisable. As a result, there have been cases of misclassification later identified by the courts.[57] This not only prevented the police officer from registering the FIR and carrying out investigation but also caused delay. The courts have repeatedly held that matters initially thought to be non-cognisable were later identified to be cognisable requiring no permission from the magistrate.[58] The magistrate has to be convinced that the person holds potential evidence and hence an arrest and investigation thereafter is justified.[59] This dilemma between the classifications of offences allows the police officer to carry out an investigation first and later record an FIR. This results in an investigation being carried out undocumented and unrecorded.

Following the FIR and warrant, in both cognisable and non-cognisable offences, respectively, the police officer has to carry out further formalities such as confirmation of jurisdiction, ensuring the well-being of the complainant and giving information to the superiors.[60] Depending upon the nature of the offence which is reported to the police officer, the subsequent steps follow: collection of evidence, search and seizure, or arrest. In case of a warrant issued by the magistrate, the police officer has the power to arrest and detain a suspect for carrying out the interrogation. For the next steps of discussion, this volume moves on to the procedure of arrest.

The Justice Malimath Committee Report came up with the suggestion that the period of police remand be extended from 15 to 30 days for grave offences (where punishment is more than five years), given that "It is not possible to fully investigate serious crimes having interstate ramifications in this limited period."[61] The recommendation also allows the transfer of detainees from judicial custody back into police custody if further investigation is necessary. This recommendation has been criticised by both academic scholars like Mehra and Amnesty International.[62] The main concern expressed by both these groups is that this extension from 15 to 30 days leaves detainees more vulnerable to torture or ill-treatment.[63] However, the presence of a lawyer at the time of interrogation would reduce this risk, putting less pressure on the magistrate.

2.3 Arrest

Following the report made after the FIR or the warrant obtained from the magistrate, it is entirely a matter of the police officer's discretion to proceed to make an arrest. Sections 41–60A of the CrPC describe the powers of the police officer to arrest, the duties and the rights of the detainee. Section 151 of the CrPC contains the provisions relating to preventive detention. It is important to consider the provisions of arrest as different stages of arrest assist in identifying the flaws in the later process, which is the police interrogation stage. Once an arrest is made by the police, recording of data and details of the suspect marks the beginning of an investigation. As observed above, this information is recorded in the FIR or a magistrate's order. Under the CrPC, police investigation includes all the proceedings under this code for the collection of evidence conducted by a police officer or by any person (other than a Magistrate) who is authorised by a Magistrate on this behalf.[64] Since an arrest by the police deprives the suspect of his rights guaranteed under Article 21 of the Constitution of India, it should be according to the procedure established by law. Therefore, the arrest must be constitutionally justifiable as it restricts the rights and freedom guaranteed under Article 19 of the Constitution of India.[65] It is essential that the police follow each stage of evidence collection as the procedure entails and in a fair and rational manner. The aim of this descriptive narrative is to find the drawbacks during this procedure for arrest, which has an impact on the investigation.

2.3.1 Difference between arrest and investigation

At this stage it is important to point out that the CrPC uses the terms "custody" and "arrest" almost interchangeably. It is therefore important to study if the procedural safeguards apply to both of these stages. It is essential to investigate whether there is a mechanism to ensure a balance between the wide police powers of investigation and recording and if the suspect is ensured a fair investigation. The clarification was provided by the Supreme Court, saying that both these terms *can* be used interchangeably, as the police officer is the custodian of the suspect.[66] Reiterating earlier judgements of *Niranjan Singh v. Prabhakar*, the courts held that "this word is of elastic semantics but its core meaning is that the law has taken control of the person."[67] As a result of this, the maximum period of detention without judicial sanction is 24 hours.[68] It is mandatory that the arrest has to be within the parameters of the constitutional provisions and must stand the grounds for constitutional justifications. These constitutional provisions are in place to ensure procedural safeguards and prevent the abuse of arrest powers. The courts have provided the exact description of the duties of a police officer at the time of the arrest.[69] The Supreme Court has also explained that the scope of investigation by the police also includes the power to arrest, and there is no dispute about this.[70] This may be interpreted as when a police officer upon investigating feels the need to arrest, he may do so. This somehow makes the procedure of arrest and investigation ambiguous to the public and also facilitates the police officer to arrest immediately following an investigation, if he thinks it is reasonable. This is demonstrated by one personnel interviewed for this research as follows:

> So we don't know if we should interrogate as soon as we arrest them or as soon as we bring them to the lock-up (police station).[71]

It is an assumption that Supreme Court jurisprudence has not addressed the issue of what differentiates an arrest and an investigation. Thus, it raises the issue of whether the police interrogation commences at the time of the arrest, or can the investigation precede an arrest. Inferring from the above that the police officer may use discretion in order to make an arrest, this allows him to interrogate without an arrest. In the absence of any legislation mandating an arrest before an investigation may result in the suspect's rights not being safeguarded. It may be argued at this point whether there are enough safeguards between the time the suspect is arrested and investigated. There are legislative duties on the police officer and the courts have interpreted these duties also updating them periodically.

2.4 Duties of the police officer

The duties of the police officer while and after arresting an individual are enlisted under Sections 42–60 of the CrPC and Sections 23 and 24 of the Indian Police Act. Along with these legislative provisions, Supreme Court decisions emphasised the importance of provisions relating to the duties of the police officer during investigation. In the case of *Jogindar Kumar v. The State of UP*, the Supreme Court issued the following requirements for the effective enforcement of the fundamental rights:

1. An arrested person being held in custody is entitled, if he so requests to have one friend, relative or other person who is known to him or likely to take an interest in his welfare told as far as is practicable that he has been arrested and where he is being detained.
2. The police officer shall inform the arrested person when he is brought to the police station of this right.
3. An entry shall be required to be made in the diary as to who was informed of the arrest. These protections from power must be held to flow from Articles 21 and 22(1) and enforced strictly.[72]

These requirements were to be read along with the state police manuals. It was also entrusted upon the Magistrate to ensure that these requirements had been complied with. However, ensuring such a duty with the Magistrate alone is not a sufficient compliance mechanism. Despite these enumerations, there are continued instances of abuse of police duties at the time of interrogation. This was recognised by the Supreme Court in the case of *D K Basu v. The State of West Bengal*. *D K Basu*, the Executive Chairman of the Legal Aid Services, wrote a letter to the Chief Justice of India highlighting the issues of custodial deaths and violence in police custody. This letter also urged the court to develop "custody jurisprudence" among other provisions to award compensation for the victims of custodial death or violence. The court treated this letter as a writ petition and decided to investigate into this as a result of continuous custodial deaths.[73] The Supreme Court in this case recommended an exhaustive list of provisions to be followed in all cases of arrest or detention:

1. The police personnel carrying out the arrest and handling the interrogation of the arrestee should bear accurate, visible and clear identification and name tags with their designation. The particulars of all such police personnel who handle interrogation of the arrestee must be recorded in a register.
2. That the police officer carrying out the arrest of the arrestee shall prepare a memo of arrest at the time of arrest and such memo shall be attested by at least one witness, who may either be a member of the family of the arrestee or a respectable person of the locality from where the arrest is made. It shall also be countersigned by the arrestee and shall contain the time and date of arrest.
3. A person who has been arrested or detained and is being held in custody in a police station or interrogation centre or other lock-up shall be entitled to have one friend or relative or other person known to him or having interest in his welfare being informed, as soon as practicable, that he has been arrested and is being detained at the particular place, unless the attesting witness of the memo of arrest is himself such a friend or a relative of the arrestee.
4. The time, place of arrest and venue of custody of an arrestee must be notified by the police where the next friend or relative of the arrestee lives outside the district or town through the Legal Aid Organisation in the District and the police station of the area concerned telegraphically within a period of 8 to 12 hours after the arrest.
5. The person arrested must be made aware of this right to have someone informed of his arrest or detention as soon as he is put under arrest or is detained.
6. An entry must be made in the diary at the place of detention regarding the arrest of the person which shall also disclose the name of the next friend of the person who has been informed of the arrest and

the names and particulars of the police officials in whose custody the arrestee is.

7. The arrestee should, where he so requests, be also examined at the time of his arrest and major and minor injuries, if any present on his/her body, must be recorded at that time. The "Inspection Memo" must be signed by both the arrestee and the police officer effecting the arrest and its copy provided to the arrestee.
8. The arrestee should be subjected to medical examination by a trained doctor every 48 hours during his detention in custody by a doctor on the panel of approved doctors appointed by Director, Health Services of the State or Union Territory concerned. Director, Health Services should prepare such a panel for all tehsils and districts as well.
9. Copies of all the documents including the memo of arrest, referred to above, should be sent to the Illaqa Magistrate for his record.
10. The arrestee may be permitted to meet his lawyer during interrogation, though not throughout the interrogation.
11. A police control room should be provided at all district and State headquarters, where information regarding the arrest and the place of custody of the arrestee shall be communicated by the officer causing the arrest, within 12 hours of effecting the arrest and at the police control room it should be displayed on a conspicuous notice board.[74]

One would readily assume that investigating police officers would be familiar with the seminal *D K Basu* jurisprudence. However, in the present research, when interviewed, only 8 out of 16 police officers made reference to the case of *D K Basu* and the guidelines, and only 5 of them had the knowledge of the guidelines, although not in-depth knowledge. *D K Basu's* pronouncements on legal assistance are discussed in Chapter 3. The other important duties arising from the judgement are analysed in the following section.

2.4.1 *Duty to inform the suspect of the grounds of arrest*

According to Article 22(1) of the Indian Constitution, "no person who is arrested shall be detained in custody without being informed, as soon as may be, of the grounds for such arrest." Initially, the police were supposed to provide the information of arrest by an FIR or a chargesheet "before the enquiry or trail."[75] But a chargesheet is a report prepared by the police officer containing the list of the charges, which he files in the court before a magistrate.[76] However, the preparation of the chargesheet could involve many investigations and might take a long period of time. In the absence of an FIR, the suspect would have to wait for the chargesheet to be submitted to the Magistrate and this could take up to six months in some cases.[77] This would leave the suspect without any written proof of the investigation during this period. This anomaly was later changed to comply with the safeguards assured by the provisions of Article 22 (1) of the Constitution of India by way of Section 50 of the CrPC.[78] This provision is the partial result of the recommendation made by the 152nd Law Commission Report, 1994. Among several recommendations, the duty to inform the suspect of the grounds of arrest "as soon as may be" was incorporated into the legislation.[79] The question that arises is whether a mere verbal as opposed to detailed written notification of the investigation report suffices. This issue has been dealt with by the High Court of New Delhi in *Vikram v. The State.*[80] The court held that the investigating police officer has to record in the police papers the exact grounds of arrest. While the court mentions recording of the grounds of arrest, it does not specify the mode of communication. It is argued here that there is little importance attached to the notification of the details of the investigation to the suspect. This is also demonstrated by the account narrated by the police officer interviewed for this research:

> It is common for us to detain him (the suspect) without letting him know why we've detained him.[81]

This brings to light another important issue with regard to the diversity of languages in India and more specifically whether an oral communication would convey the message to the person in the language he understands. This issue was addressed as early as 1972, where the Supreme Court held that the grounds must be communicated to the person arrested in a language he understands.[82] But so far, state police have failed to implement this as they are obstructed by linguistic diversity even at state level.[83] Even if the police officer complies with the provisions, there is no mechanism to ensure or evidence this. This makes it easy for the police officer to ignore this "guideline" given by the Supreme Court. It is suggested here that a nationwide approach needs to be taken on this subject. Recognition of written notification should be implemented by statute and its compliance must be regulated by the state police authorities.

2.4.2 *Duty to inform a relative or a friend*

According to Section 50A of the CrPC, the police officer is under an "obligation" to inform a nominated person about the details of the arrest.[84] The nominated person usually is a member of the family or a friend. This interpretation echoes the provision of "one phone call" after being arrested in European jurisdictions, and has been observed by Indian courts in many instances to have similar bearing.[85] In *Joginder Kumar*, the Supreme Court also held that the suspect was entitled to have a friend or family member informed if the suspect requests so.[86] It is, however, highly unlikely that the suspect would be aware of such a provision and would initiate such a request where illiteracy is higher, especially in the rural parts of India.[87]

The Supreme Court has on several occasions recognised that it is easy for the police officer to deny that the suspect has made such a request.[88] In the absence of any supervision or other provision of safeguard, police officers are likely to prevent the suspect from informing his family.

In one of the interviews I conducted, one police personnel acknowledged that the provisions of Section 50A were not followed in practice:

> The Indian police will stop any communication. They will also stop the communication with the family. The family is also told no communication for 24 hours.[89]

2.4.3 *Duty to have the suspect examined by a medical practitioner*

The relevant provisions concerning examination by a medical practitioner are contained under Sections 53 and 54 of the CrPC. These are a wide range of provisions covering examination by a medical practitioner at the request of a police officer in order to collect evidence, on the charge of or related to rape, and at the request of the arrested person before a Magistrate.[90] It may be pointed out that an examination by a medical practitioner is not an absolute duty of the police officer. Thus, the well-being of the suspect is not yet guaranteed even by this provision. The Supreme Court held in *D K Basu v. State of West Bengal* that the arrestee should be subjected to a medical examination every 48 hours during his detention in police custody.[91] The implementation of this was also endowed with the state police, but no consideration has been given to regulating or monitoring this practice. The mandated practice of medical examination seems to lack a consistent application as most police officers in the cities are more likely to offer the suspect this privilege, whereas those in the rural areas would not.[92] This was displayed in the interview when one personnel observed as follows:

> While most of the cities have the compulsory practice of having the suspect examined by a medical practitioner, I don't think it is compulsory in villages.[93]

2.4.4 *Duty to be presented before a Magistrate within 24 hours*

Article 22(1) of the Indian Constitution provides procedural safeguards for the arrested person in the form of ensuring his attendance before the Magistrate within 24 hours of his arrest.[94] This provision was put in place to safeguard the well-being of the suspect. However, this excludes the time it takes for the police officer to get the suspect to the nearest court. This provision reflects the requirement of Article 9 of the International Convention on Civil and Political Rights (ICCPR). If the investigating police officer feels that he requires more than 24 hours for interrogating the suspect, he can approach the Magistrate to obtain a further 24-hour custody. The

Magistrate may authorise an extension after referring to the grounds of the application made by the police officer. The Constitution similarly provides that no person shall be detained for a period longer than 20 hours without the authority of the magistrate.[95] Whether this time limit is effective in controlling the state power to arrest an individual is a subject of debate. Uma Devi argues that in giving a magistrate the power to extend the custody of the suspect, the Constitution invests him with a *carte blanche*.[96] From this angle, it may be argued that the constitutional mandate in this area does not protect the suspect, but merely provides for the application of a judicial mind.[97] Sections 56 and 57 of the CrPC provide for producing[98] the person arrested before a magistrate. Section 56 of the CrPC provides for the person arrested to be brought before a magistrate "without further delay."[99]

Law commission reports have gone so far as to observe that the issue of jurisdiction is used as an excuse, which inevitably delays producing the suspect before the magistrate.[100] Police officers often benefit from alleged conflicts of jurisdiction in justifying a delay to produce the suspect before a magistrate.[101] The 152nd Commission Report also emphasised the duty of the Magistrate to verify certain facts confirming the well-being of the arrested person and complacency in the procedure of arrest.[102] This recommendation has not been taken on board and hence this provision can be criticised for not fully implementing the safeguards guaranteed under Article 21. It may be pointed out here that the Magistrate plays a role of an enquirer and may also perform his duties of investigations.

2.4.5 Interpreter

In a linguistically diverse country such as India, it is possible that at the time of the arrest a suspect may not speak the same language as that of the police officer. Even before the investigation, it may be the case that the suspect may fail to understand the reason of his arrest. One of the most fundamental issues which are either neglected or overseen in the debate over the suspects' rights is the issue of interpretation or translation. In the absence of a written notification of the grounds of arrest, it is possible that the suspect may fail to understand the grounds of his arrest. This is in contravention to fundamental rights guaranteed to the suspect under the Indian Constitution. The lack of reports or studies shows how under-researched this key topic is.

With every state having a different state language and each area having a different dialect, language always poses a problem in communication. While this may not be a big issue in metropolitan cities, it remains a question to be considered in rural areas. The researcher's interviews with police personnel in India provide a useful illustration. Participants were categorical that the state does not provide an interpreter. As there is no provision in any legislation about the right to interpretation or the provision of an interpreter if a linguistic dilemma arose, the police are left to come up with impromptu solutions. As one police officer notes:

> The state doesn't provide any interpreter. In India there are many languages and we often know only about the main ones. We don't consider looking into the colloquial languages and they don't even have a script sometimes. In that case we have to get somebody who knows that language so we can proceed with the interrogation. Now you have to depend on the honesty of the interpreter. It is possible that the interpreter may misguide both the suspect and the police. Who knows? Officially there are no interpreters. There is no state appointment.[103]

There should be provision of interpreters at the police station or at least there should be a roll of interpreters available for police officers in the form of a ready reference available to them.

2.4.6 *Consequences of failure to comply with guidelines*

The provisions for failure to comply with the directions of the Courts issued in the case of *D K Basu and Joginder Singh* are contained in Section 217 of the IPC.[104] These cases provided an exhaustive list of the police duties with an aim to balance the rights of the suspect with the investigative powers of the police. In order to understand the institutional approach taken by the Supreme Courts in relation to non-compliance of the provisions surrounding interrogation, the landmark cases have been analysed. Both these authorities are analysed bearing in mind the application of provisions guaranteed under Articles 21 and 22(1) of the Indian Constitution.

In *Joginder Kumar v. State of UP*, the Supreme Court made non-compliance a subject matter for the state department to ascertain. The head of the department in the police station was entrusted to take the necessary action.[105] Later in 1997 in the case of *D K Basu*, the Supreme Court took proactive steps towards non-compliance. The Supreme Court suggested a list of "actions" to be followed by an arresting police officer, failure of which could lead to contempt of court.[106] But the supreme jurisdiction in India did not at the same time specify the means to oversee its compliance and regulate the contempt proceedings. No measures were taken to follow up on these contempt proceedings thereafter.

In 2013, amendments were made to the CrPC and Section 166A(c) was introduced. It provided that failure to record information under Section 154 could lead to imprisonment for a maximum of two years and a fine. Implementation of this provision is far from being satisfactory though, as very few cases have been registered so far. In addition, in the absence effective monitoring process, potential dereliction of duty by the police officer would be difficult to prove. In 2014, the Supreme Court emphasised that failure to comply with the safeguards and provisions suggested in the previous cases would invite departmental action.[107] This direction is left open to interpretation by each state and is governed by their police manual. It is therefore easy to infer that while the Supreme Court makes the provisions for contempt, the process of its application is not explained. It is also observed here that these contempt provisions are not appropriate as these failures continue to exist.[108] A more stringent procedure may be adopted in order to demonstrate the gravity of this situation. A nationwide legislative approach needs to be adopted in order to ensure transparency of proceedings and the use of discretion by the police. As observed above, the police exercise wide powers such as use of discretion to arrest and investigate. It is also argued here that the legislation confers wide powers on an investigating police officer. In order to ensure the fair use of these powers, the police must receive sufficient training.

2.5 Police training

Police training in India is mandated by the Indian Police Act. Police officers are trained by the state government and not under the national law. Investment in training of police officers is critical and is most necessary in the compliance towards the principles of the rule of law in a democracy. Police training has always been an issue of concern for the drafters of various law commissions. The Committee on Police Training, 1971, found evidence that there is substantial political interference in the administration and operation of the police force. Current police training seems to have the following drawbacks: state-regulated training, lack of training for investigation, senior officers training junior officers, knowledge of human rights, lack of technology and lack of funds. These provisions will be discussed in this section.

2.5.1 State-regulated training

Each state mandates its own training of police officers. This makes for a highly variable practice across different states. While the state laws borrow from the Indian Police Act, the latter act mentions very little on training for investigating or interviewing. However, each state gives authority to the executive state government to "interfere" with police work.[109] It has also been observed by law reports that state police training provides very little in terms of investigation.[110] Discrepancies between the Indian Police Act and the CrPC cause confusion for police officers. For instance, a Director General of the Karnataka Police told Human Rights Watch that "The police guidelines say that a station should investigate 60 cases (per year), but it's actually 300."[111] One of the police officers attributed this problem of state-regulated training as follows:

> I think this problem of the different states regulating their own training procedures causes confusion. Some reform may allow this to change.[112]

2.5.2 Lack of specific training for interrogation

Police officers are given no specific training for interrogating the suspects.[113] Training related to conducting an interrogation cannot be done using a general method, which seems to be the current practice. The idea of applying the principle of "one size fits all" for training police officers for investigation and interrogation can be questioned. This lack of specific investigative training has been criticised by the courts in the case of *State of Gujarat v. Kishanbhai*:

> The Home Department of every State Government will incorporate in its existing training programmes for junior investigation/prosecution officials course-content drawn from the above consideration. The same should also constitute course-content of refresher training programmes, for senior investigating/prosecuting officials. The above responsibility for preparing training programmes for officials should be vested in the same committee of senior officers referred to above. ... Judgments like the one in hand (depicting more than 10 glaring lapses in the investigation/prosecution of the case), and similar other judgments, may also be added to the training programmes. The course content will be reviewed by the above committee annually, on the basis of fresh inputs, including emerging scientific tools of investigation, judgments of Courts, and on the basis of experiences gained by the standing committee while examining failures, in unsuccessful prosecution of cases. ... We further direct that the above training programme be put in place within 6 months. This would ensure that those persons who handle sensitive matters concerning investigation/prosecution are fully trained to handle the same. Thereupon, if any lapses are committed by them, they would not be able to feign innocence, when they are made liable to suffer departmental action, for their lapses.[114]

This was also demonstrated by one personnel who observed as follows:

> Yes, among other things there needs to be specific training relating to police investigation. How much expertise will you get crammed in 24-month training?[115]

It is no surprise that no steps to implement this judgement have been taken by the state or the central government. While the National Human Rights Commission tried to address this by providing a draft bill for investigative training, it was never considered by either the central or any state government.[116] This lack of action to reform from the central and various state governments despite Supreme Court jurisprudence is a repetitive phenomenon.

2.5.3 Senior officers training junior officers

Within every state, senior officers are responsible for the training of junior police officers. The High Court of Delhi in 2014 expressed concerns about the competence of the police personnel in carrying out investigation, either due to lack of training or due to lack of competence.[117]

> With utter disgust and dismay we express our utmost displeasure with regard to the manner of investigation, as was carried out by the investigating officer in this case. ... With the kind of investigation as has been carried out in this case, we have no hesitation in saying that this Police Officer has no basic knowledge or competence for conducting investigation in any crime. ... This is not a solitary case where we find the failure of the Investigating Agency to commit such serious lapses. This is primarily due to the incompetency of many such police officers who are entrusted with such a sensitive job of carrying out investigation into any crime and secondly because of lack of willingness on the part of the government to separate the investigation from the law and order, despite being directed by the Hon'ble Supreme Court many a times, right from the authoritative pronouncement in Prakash Singh vs. Union of India reported in (2006) 8 SCC 1; 2006 Indlaw SC 514 and various recommendations made by Law Commission of India in this regard.[118]

While the senior officer's intervention during an investigation may be legitimate to clarify certain doubts, it cannot be used as a sole method for providing investigative training. Vadackumchery relates the art of questioning during investigation to the police officer's academic background and their social background.[119] This sole reliance cannot be expected to suffice for the upholding of constitutional standards by an interrogating police officer.

When a complaint is made, very often police officers record the FIRs with an intention to fit it in with the legal provision of the ambit of law. When a complaint is outside the said ambit, the investigating police officer resorts to means like not recording the complaint altogether.[120] In situations such as these, a senior officer may advise according to his experience and the best of his knowledge. The junior officer following such orders may confuse this procedure as a part of the training and may be under the guise of following the law. The court vested the powers to incorporate the training of junior police officers on the senior officers in charge of the state police station. The Supreme Court insisted on recording the reasons for the steps taken pursuant to a senior's consultation, to form a part of the training.[121] This orthodox approach of the senior officers training the junior officers for carrying out an investigation is criticised.

2.5.4 Theory and practice

It is common practice for police officers to use their judgement to apply the training they receive in theory while they interrogate in practice. A personnel demonstrates:

> How much will a police officer remember from his training? On another hand, he will always rely on his seniors for training. So you see, there will always be this interference from the seniors (officers).[122]

However, there seems to be a gap in the training police officers receive before qualifying and the training received at the police station. As observed in a study conducted by Human Rights Watch, one of the newly graduate cadets said that the senior officials at the police station mocked and instructed the junior to forget everything taught during the training.[123] This casual approach towards ignoring the training received by the senior officers is difficult for the juniors to protest.[124] In the absence of elaborate training, there is little that a junior officer can do to improve his investigative skills. This can also be demonstrated by the account given by one personnel interviewed:

> Yes, among other things there needs to be specific training relating to police investigation. How much expertise will you get crammed in 24-month training?

To summarise, in the absence of specific training for investigation and the junior officers relying on senior officers, as demonstrated by the interviewees in the present research, it is imperative that reform steps need to be taken immediately.

2.5.5 Updated technology for investigation

There is little updated technology used for investigation at the police stations in India. For instance, the FIR in many cities and villages is actually handwritten by the police officer.[125] A computerised police station may resolve this issue and also eliminate the flaws caused by human element. The Supreme Court in the *State of Gujarat v. Kishanbhai* held that police training relating to investigation should be updated using the current technology.[126] The court also emphasised that the states must design training programmes to fit in with the changing legal and social scenario. This will in turn assist a welfare state committed to the rule of law and needs to have proper recognition and enforcement of fundamental human rights.

2.5.6 Lack of education of human rights

The investigating police officers face sensitive issues and need to be trained at addressing them while observing the sensitivity of the situation.[127] It is therefore necessary to educate police officers on the subject of human rights and train them to observe the human rights of the accused in all cases. Police officers must be trained to provide the suspect with basic human rights consistently and continuously. Presently, police officers are expected to have this knowledge by perusing the guidelines provided by the courts in the case of *D K Basu*. While this is an initial step towards raising awareness of pretrial human rights standards, much more can be done. Updated and periodic training must be provided and be ensured to be provided to the investigating police officers.

2.5.7 Lack of funds

Factors such as funding allocation for training the officers differ from one state to another and although authors claim uniformity of training throughout the country, this is a practical difficulty.[128] The Indian Police expenditure has a slot under the Non-Plan Budget and includes the budget of other armed forces of the country.[129] But here again a lot depends on the political masters who control critical issues such as training budgets, training grants, granting approvals and organising the training and aspects relative to it. These politicians act in a myopic manner when it comes to allocation of budgets in relation to training.[130] There is no doubt that this shortcoming is actually affecting the general public and can easily be remedied by allocating more funds to police training where required. Needless to mention, this allocation of funds for investigative advancement in a vast country such as India will require willingness from the government.

2.5.8 Is training sufficient?

As observed in the above analysis, the present legislation and practice of police training for interrogation has a few drawbacks. In order to highlight the practical implications of the current process, police officers were approached about their level of satisfaction with their training. Here are some responses from police personnel, who were happy with the level of training they receive:

> The present training is sufficient and apart from that the day-to-day experience helps and sessional courses assist in providing additional training.[131]

> Yes, they have. I won't say for people who would've passed out of the academy 10 years ago. But subsequently yes this has been made available in all the courses.[132]

> Yes (training) is sufficient. Investigation is done well in Mumbai. They are very few but are selected well. They have good knowledge of how to collect info. If someone is not capable then we change them.[133]

> Yes of course. All training is given regarding the law and crime investigation and everything. It is also as per the prevision of the CrPC.[134]

It is argued here that among the above officers who seemed content with the level of training they received, most of them are from cities. Among the others who were dissatisfied with the training mainly discussed similar themes:

> Training is not enough for interrogation, but they can always ask the senior officers or whoever is on duty can be approached.[135]
>
> Of course, the training is not sufficient; we need training and more of it. The way it works around here is "Ask your senior!"[136]

In general, most of these police officers are from villages or small towns. It is argued that police training lacks a uniform approach throughout the country and, as rightly observed by academics, is in urgent need of reform. This analysis provides an updated and practical view of the urgency for police reforms, especially for police training.

2.6 Police reforms

In the light of the above practice, constant efforts were being made by various commissions to provide recommendations to reform police duties, powers and training. This section discusses the important reforms suggested by each committee, the criticisms for its non-implementation and drawbacks, the Supreme Court jurisprudence on police reforms and the need for police reforms.

2.6.1 Commissions

Police reforms have been carried out extensively by various committees and law commissions in India since its independence. The first committee was the Kerala Police Reorganisation Committee in 1949 followed by police commissions appointed in various states. The Working Group on Police by the Administrative Reforms Commission in 1966 was the first national commission, which was set up by the central government. This was followed by the Gore Commission on Police Training in 1971. However, major contributions were made by the following commissions discussed herein.

2.6.1.1 National Police Commission, 1977

The National Police Commission set up in 1977 by the Government of India in order to bring about a fresh examination of the role of a police officer as a law-enforcing agency and as an institution to protect the constitutional rights of a citizen.[137] The first report concentrated on providing training to police officers so that they could discharge their constitutional duties. This report also aimed to find the means to avoid political and executive pressure on the police. It is highlighted that this issue of political interference was identified as early as 1977 and formed a part of this report.

The Fourth Report submitted by this commission aimed at making interrogation a fair and just process. The Eighth Report dealt with issues surrounding police accountability and suggested a draft police bill with all the recommendations.

2.6.1.2 *The Ribeiro Committee, 1998*

The Ribeiro Committee was set up in 1998 on the orders of the Supreme Court following a public interest litigation on police reforms.[138] This Commission presented its first report with major recommendations on police performance and accountability. Among reforms for training for police interrogation, the committee suggested a separation of the investigation wing from the other duties of the police officer.[139] The idea emerged that separation of the "investigation" wing from the "law and order" wing of the police would ensure transparency of investigation.[140] This report highlighted the practice of police officers carrying out investigative duties along with other miscellaneous duties. As a result, the investigative work lacks priority among other tasks. It also recommended setting up a Police Performance and Accountability Commission in each state.

2.6.1.3 *The Padmanabhiah Commission, 2000*

The Padmanabhiah Commission reiterated many of the recommendations previously mentioned by the preceding commissions. This report mentioned recommendations like separation of the interrogation wing, raising the minimum education qualification for police officers, raising the minimum work experience as a police officer, improving the training for investigation and providing better equipment for training.[141] This commission also suggested that existing police officers should be retrained in order to provide a good workplace attitude. It also suggested that those who fail to demonstrate this quality and fail to abide by the norms set by the recommendations should be asked to retire. The most highlighting recommendation made by this commission was the compulsory judicial enquiry into the custodial death and the alleged rape cases. It also suggested setting up of an independent body to enquire into public complaints made against police officers. This Commission also suggested replacing the Indian Police Act 1861 altogether, as the investigative provisions are old and archaic.[142] This committee suggested setting up a Police Station Advisory Council in each state, which will work along the concept of community policing. One of the personnel interviewed for this research notes:

> The Padmanabhiah Commission did have some interesting suggestions; however, we didn't see any being implemented![143]

2.6.1.4 The Malimath Committee Report, 2003

The Malimath Committee wrote extensively about the poor quality of interrogation and urgent need for change in the techniques used for interrogation.[144] The committee stressed on the need for an impartial and fair interrogation. Apart from a different system for the urban and rural areas regarding the training for interrogation, the committee also stressed on having the minimum qualification of police officers and the heads of the police stations. This report also stressed that the investigating police officer should have at least five years of police work experience. The committee also emphasised the need for training the interrogating police officers on the legal provisions.[145] Similar to the recommendations of the previous commissions, this Commission recommended the "insularity and integrity of the investigating agency."[146] This would involve having separate police stations for law and order, on one hand, and investigation on the other hand. It was highlighted by this report that this system already exists in the states of Andhra Pradesh and Tamil Nadu and may be used as precedents.[147]

2.6.1.5 The Sorabjee Commission, 2006

The Sorabjee Commission was set up in 2006 appointed by the central government under the leadership of Soli Sorabjee, former Attorney General. The purpose of this committee was to suggest if the Model Police Act, 2006, drafted by the National Police Commission to replace the Indian Police Act needed any modification.[148] Overall, the report highlighted changing the police service from a feudal force to a democratic service, beginning the change in the interrogatory training. This Commission suggested having a retired police officer on the board of the Police Complaint Authority who would be able to provide insider information. This Committee also suggested the establishment of a State Bureau of Criminal Investigation by the state governments. Along with this, there should be a Public Complaints Authority at district level taking complaints from the public regarding arbitrary arrests, false implications in criminal cases and custodial violence.[149]

2.6.2 Criticisms of commission reports

Despite these elaborate provisions recommended by various commissions, there seemed to be no implementation of these reforms towards better interrogation. Most of the provisions were criticised for being too ambitious, such as the separation of law and order from investigation.[150] Umrishankar refers to this as being too ambitious because of its impracticality due to the political control over police officers who would not want to separate the two for their own interest.[151] The commission reports faced further criticisms discussed herein.

2.6.2.1 Repetitive and lack of depth

The Ribeiro Committee, which was set up mainly to review the actions recommended by the National Police Commission, has been criticised to merely revise them.[152] While some new recommendations were made, a reiteration of previous recommendations could be avoided. However, it may be argued that non-implementations of the previous recommendations could have resulted in the reiteration of those outstanding issues in the Ribeiro report. Baxi criticised the Malimath Committee's empirical research to rely on "common sense" expressed *ad nauseum* instead of adopting appropriate research methodologies.[153] While the Model Police Act, 2006 (a Sorabji Commission Report recommendation), was a welcome step, a lot more needed to be done with regard to police accountability.[154] For instance, the entire chapter on interrogatory training does not address the non-compliance by the police.

2.6.2.2 No regard to suspects' rights

None of the reports address the question of police accountability in the case of an infringement of a suspect's rights during police interrogation. Although the police officer is expected to carry out his duties mentioned in the above section, he is not held accountable for the breach of any duty. Authors have highlighted the need to "humanise" police interrogation by adapting a human rights-based approach, which can be provided during police training.[155] While the Malimath Committee Report discusses this issue, it lacks appropriate intensity to address this issue. This report did not provide any detailed measures that would safeguard suspects' rights.

2.6.2.3 Lack of cooperation from the states

The Sorabjee Commission was criticised by various states for trying to implement the Model Police Act, 2006, at the national level.[156] The states have resisted this reform causing unnecessary delay. Since the states control the police activities and duties, the state actors showed resistance towards national legislation fearing loss of control.

2.6.2.4 Political pressure

This committee is also criticised for being unable to provide mechanisms to insulate the police from illegitimate pressures of politics.[157] Political interference has been highlighted as the cause of non-implementation of police reforms recommended by most of the above-mentioned reports. These reforms depended on the "will of the states" to implement, which was influenced by way of political interference and departmental corruption.[158] While most reports highlighted the need to separate the law and order from the investigation duty of the police, it is speculated by authors that political interference would not allow this.[159]

This is among the many reasons why police reforms and recommendations of these reports have not been implemented in India.

2.6.3 Supreme Court jurisprudence

In *Vineet Narayan and Others v. The Union of India* in 1998,[160] the Supreme Court held that there was an urgent need for state governments to set up the mechanism to pursue police reforms and ensure the selection and appointment of police officers and oversee the transfer of police officers.[161] The Court made a revelation that the tenure of the Superintendent of Police of a particular police station was controlled by political interference. The Supreme Court expressed "shock" at the short tenure of the Superintendent of Police and the whimsical reasons for the transfer.[162] This had an adverse effect on regulating the training of police officers and other policing procedures. The court directed the central government to take prompt measures to urge state governments to eliminate political interference from the police.

2.6.3.1 The seven-point directive

The Supreme Court in *Prakash Singh v. The Union of India* provided a set of guidelines which were referred to as the "seven-point directive"[163] for police reforms. They contained "the appropriate directions for immediate compliance," highlighting the urgency needed for its action.[164] The Supreme Court possesses powers under the Indian Constitution to issue directives to the states to maintain the state of law and order.[165] These seven directives were issued to ensure transparency in police powers and police accountability. The court criticised state governments for taking no action to implement the recommendations of previous commission reports. In providing the guidelines in this case, the Supreme Court made reference to recommendations from all the above Commission reports. Among many useful directives involving police reforms, the most elaborate provisions were setting up the Police Complaints Authority (PCA), National and State Human Rights Commissions and separation of investigation from law and order. The Commonwealth Human Rights Initiative (CHRI) initiated that this provision of having the PCA replaces the practice of internal disciplinary enquiry against police officers.[166] For this to be implemented, the CHRI is right in pointing out that the PCA needs to avoid being vulnerable to external pressures. For facilitating this, some of the following factors are to be considered: independence of members, adequate funding, enabling members to be trained in investigative skills and techniques. While most of the provisions were repetitive, it suggested provisions like setting up a National Security Commission at the Union[167] level and their decisions are binding on state governments.

A majority of the states asked for more time for complying with these directives, while others asked for these guidelines to be reviewed.[168]

However, the Court refused to review its directions and ordered the states to comply with these directions by March 2007.[169] One of the personnel interviewed for this research noted:

> Police reforms are a wide subject but if the Prakash Singh cases reforms are implemented that too will be very useful for bringing about reforms in the police interrogation area. ... But there has been reluctance on the part of the Centre to implement these (reforms), which does not encourage states to implement these reforms.[170]

2.6.3.2 *Action against non-compliance with the directives*

When it was brought to the notice of the court that some of the states were not taking the directions seriously thereby reflecting their attitude, it led to the constitution of a monitoring committee. The main duty of this committee was to oversee the enforcement of the New Police Act. This committee submitted various reports from 2008 to 2009 and observed that many states had deviated from the suggested guidelines of the court.[171] Based on the latest report of this committee on 8 November 2010, the Supreme Court took notice of the lack of compliance by the four major state governments: Maharashtra, Utter Pradesh, Karnataka and West Bengal, ordering their Chief Secretaries to appear before the court in order to clarify why the seven directives have not been complied with. The Supreme Court emphasised the need for action and implementation of these directives as it did not want its judgement to "lie in court."[172] While it may seem that the Supreme Court has provided a practical solution through these seven-step directives, their implementation at the state level seems difficult. Many states have been trying to comply with the seven directives and implement the Model Police Act, but the response has been very slow. This deliberate attempt to allow the states to play against time is also criticised by CHRI.[173]

The PCA may be a way of addressing growing public discontent with policing. An effective mechanism ensuring public complaints redress forum could help fill in the gaps demonstrated by the lack of police accountability.[174] Despite the Supreme Court directives, the states have managed to evade the implementation giving vague reasons.[175] Failure by the state governments to implement these directives may be due to the lack of the Court's authority. Despite these recommendations implying effective implementation "immediately," no follow-up action suggests little or no urgency to implement police reforms.

2.6.4 *Need for reforms: the police perspective*

The police personnel were showing interest in urgently enforcing police reforms after the Prakash Singh judgement. When a few police personnel were approached and asked why the reforms were not implemented, they expressed great concern towards this issue. One of the police personnel blamed the lack of awareness among the public and over interference of external forces.[176] Most others thought that restricting the police from doing "other duties" like "providing security, during festivals, at temples, and to the politicians, would ensure that these reforms are implemented."[177] Almost all the police personnel interviewed felt the urgent need for the implementation of the reforms. While all the police personnel emphasised the need for a nationwide reform, there should be a particular focus on the rural parts of India.[178] One personnel pointed out the reluctance of the central government for implementing these reforms may encourage state governments to be equally reluctant. He observed:

> If you see even the Central Government which administers the Union Territories, there's no reason why they cannot implement these reforms in the right spirit.[179]

This is a valid argument and if the central government starts implementing these reforms, there is a possibility that it might set a precedent for the other states to follow too. A positive step towards police reform taken by the central government will set a good example for the state government.

2.7 Use of CCTV at the police station

With the failure to impose police reform in order to regulate police investigative duties, an important judgement was handed down by the High Court of Bombay. In view of reforming the institutional framework for the supervision of police officers and regulating police behaviour in custodial interrogation, a major step was taken by the High Court of Bombay in 2014. In the case of *Leonard Valdaris v. The Officer in Charge*,[180] the Court directed the state of Maharashtra to install and maintain CCTV. An analysis of the European countries' use of CCTV was also carried out by the court. And it was inferred that the use of CCTV reduced crime in those European countries by 40%.[181] Along with this, the court also reiterated the urgency of incorporation of the guidelines given by the Supreme Court in the case of *D K Basu*. This is a sophisticated action towards regulating the actions of police officers.

However, as the court mentions, "we hope and trust that funds are made available by the state government for installation of video conferencing facilities in all the jails."[182] This factor alone can put doubts in the implementation of the court's order. This is assisted by the fact that this action is at the state level which ideally should be adopted at the national level. This direction clearly lacks authority as no concrete measures for implementation were considered and no penal provisions for non-implementation were suggested. The only assertive step taken by the court was the requirement for the report to be submitted within ten weeks. So far no steps have been taken to install any CCTV in the police station and no report has been filed by any authority. Also, since this is a judgement delivered by the Bombay High Court, it is not binding on other states. The implementation of CCTV at the police station is a good mechanism to monitor the interrogation. In the absence of any other mechanism ensuring the protection of the suspects' rights, CCTV may assist in determining the legitimacy of an officer's action. The use of CCTV may also assist in providing feedback, which can be used for police training.

When the police officers were interviewed in the present research and asked about the impact of CCTV, they responded in a diverse manner. One of the police personnel said:

> So if there is CCTV installed, they would do the formal bit in front of the camera and whatever goes on will be conducted in other rooms.[183]

Two other police personnel suspect the practice of off-camera interrogation in case the use of CCTV is mandated for police investigation.[184]

2.8 Corruption

This section discusses one of the common reasons for non-implementation of the recommendations made by various commissions and Supreme Court guidelines. As discussed by many academics and even acknowledged by the courts, this is due to the high rate of corruption in the police and excessive political interference. Scott mentioned that the concept of corruption owes its origin of the police culture to the British regime. He further alleged that it was a common practice for a Scotsman to accept a bribe as he "spoke the language of the greased palm."[185] Scott portrays a subinspector of the police as a man "who took bribes and stole watches from the men he arrested."[186] In contrast, a lower level English administrator refusing to accept such a gift is a "fool," because he had been taught that any gift from an Indian is a bribe.[187] Corruption in the form of accepting bribery is an ongoing problem, sometimes referred to as an "epidemic," which is "wrecking the country's moral, social, and political fibre."[188] Bailey explained corruption as "misuse of authority as a result of consideration of personal gain which need not be monetary."[189] He also describes that in India corruption amongst the police has become a "byword."[190] Transparency International, India, has carried out extensive work on the issue of corruption and finding ways to reduce it.[191] The CHRI have also highlighted the presence of internal corruption in the police department and have pointed out that this is the main reason why these police reforms have not been implemented.[192]

Palmier's hypothesis for continuing corruption in India is attributed to the low salary of the civil servants, their ample opportunities for corruption and ineffective policing.[193] This is an important fact and although not condoned, there is merit to the argument. The Third Pay Commission in India (1970–1973) addressed the issue about the low wages of police officers. It further mentioned that although higher salaries do not guarantee honesty and integrity, lower salaries invite corrupt behaviour amongst government servants. This is also confirmed by Qadri, who associates other influencing factors such as the nature and hours of duty and interference of politicians.[194] These factors also affect the interrogation process, which takes a back-bench approach, among other duties of a police officer. As observed above, police officers demonstrate that they can improve interrogation skills by avoiding duties such as "providing security, during festivals, at temples, and to the politicians."[195]

Authors like Alexander assign tolerance to corruption as one of the reasons why this practice still exists.[196] This tolerance is from the public in general, and a practice both inside the police and in associating government departments. Tummala has also associated the existence of corruption in India with the society's attitude towards corruption. It is further noted that no amount of "legal restrictions" can assist in combating corruption as the society is "lenient" and "tolerant."[197] While many measures for curbing corruption are taken by legislation, the lack of political will restricts it from being put into practice. It is this consistent trend of corruption both within the police organisation and in the governmental bodies that makes implementation of these police reforms almost impractical. It is this tolerance by the public that also prevents a unified public outcry for immediate police reforms. The other form of corruption exists when the public can avoid interrogation by bribing police officers.[198] This is discussed at length later in this chapter.

Despite this being a controversial issue, most police officers admitted to the existence of corruption in the police department and this alone stands in the way of the implementation of reforms. Eleven out of 15 police personnel interviewed confirmed the presence of corruption and that it stood in the way of reform implementation. Among the others who completely deny the presence of corruption attribute this to the efforts of a particular senior member.[199] Clearly, the presence of corruption has an impact on the police's accountability and transparency.

2.9 Rule of law

A fully functional police organisation is a good sign of an autonomous department working under the rule of law in a democracy. As observed, the substantive law relating to policing has been codified in the IPC and the procedural law is codified in the CrPC. Thus, procedure must be followed in the strictest manner but due to constraints it cannot be done, allowing the police officer the use of discretion. As observed above, this issue can be a sensitive matter while addressing contempt of court on failure to abide by the guidelines. Since an investigation is the initial point of any proceeding, it is at this point that utmost care and due diligence needs to be observed. There have always been questions about the credibility and reliability of an effective police investigation system. Along with the presence of corruption in the system, political interference can hinder the efficiency of the rule of law. Eminent authors like Bayley who have carried out extensive research in the early 1980s on police interrogation point out that the unexpected stress on the police is due to the increased political interference into policing.[200] Indian authors like Verma also write that the politicisation of the police across the country is the root cause for many failings in the process of police interrogation.[201] It is highlighted here that there is a difference of nearly four decades between these studies and no action has been taken regarding eliminating political interference from policing. The Supreme Court mentions that this situation regarding political interference still continues to hinder the effectiveness of the police investigation.[202] With the concerns relating to the consequences of the non-compliance of these duties, the questions of police training, accountability and transparency need to be addressed.

2.10 Police accountability and transparency

The growing rate of corruption has in the past and continues to affect police accountability as raised by the Supreme Court.[203] The police are alleged to lack accountability owing to the absence of an effective monitoring and regulating agency. The practice of investigations into police misconduct being conducted by police agencies themselves does not ensure transparency. As mentioned by Belur, there is scope for a great deal of manipulation regarding evidence before this police agency.[204] Even if the recommendation of the Supreme Court of setting up of the Police Complaints Authority is implemented, the presence of retired police officers does not guarantee transparency. It is this lack of an independent investigating agency that makes it easier for the police not to be held accountable for their actions. The police force as a whole and the individual police officers must be held accountable for their actions during investigation and need constant monitoring.

The NHRC is a public body created to protect and promote the human rights of individuals and was established in 1993. The NHRC may enquire on its own initiative or on a petition presented by a complainant whose human rights have been violated by an actor of the state. The NHRC may be pursuant to the receipt of a complaint or after enquiry, order the state concerned to initiate proceedings or may approach the High Court or the Supreme Court to imitate legal proceedings. While setting up of the NHRC was a step towards improving police accountability, in practice this commission lacks efficiency.[205] An independent commission relies on the government for other financial and manpower requirements.[206] This jeopardises independence due to governmental control and as observed above, this invites political interference. State Human Rights Commissions were also set up under the directions of the court in Prakash Singh's case. But the state commissions were also criticised for their lack of effective action. It has been observed that only a few states have implemented this system, and even those who have suffered from the perils of inefficient functioning, lack of political will and lack of funding.[207] An elaborate analysis of the NHRC and state commissions is carried out in the last chapter.

Further, two separate measures need to be dealt with regarding investigative accountability. Firstly, there needs to be an independent authority that can both regulate the police investigations and conduct enquiry in case of misconduct. Secondly, measures need to be taken to assure the general public that the process of investigation is transparent. The Supreme Court has in the case of *Prakash Singh* made an effort to address the first issue by ordering the states to set up a Police Complaints Authority and the National and State Human Rights Commissions.[208] Victims of police misconduct will have remedies under public law or criminal law and are liable for compensation.[209] However, in the absence of clear legislation clarifying the amount of compensation in cases of police misconduct, this provision is far from practical. In practice, this would result in lengthy proceedings before the State Human Rights Commission. The practicality of state and national commissions is questionable for ensuring police accountability. This has a direct impact on the public perception of the police and may affect the police-public interaction during investigation and, inter alia, the fairness of an interrogation.

2.11 Public perception of the police

With police accountability being taken so lightly, it is no surprise that the public perception of the police is that of distrust. It is a common practice for police officers to file false criminal cases and carry out arrests at the behest of powerful political figures or other forms of corruption.[210] This creates a sort of fear in the minds of the public to approach the police either to complain or to provide information.

In the case where a suspect is summoned by the police, the continuous instances of custodial violence legitimise this fear of the public. In the absence of any mechanism to ensure public protection from police misconduct during interrogation, public perception of both fear and distrust is legitimate. In a certain way, this allows the police to continue using force and other unlawful means of interrogation. While lessons have been taken from foreign jurisdiction about police reforms from time to time, no reforms have been efficiently enforced.

It is concluded here that the police interrogation has suffered not only because of political interference and corruption but also because of the lack of a proper legislative enactment. The guidelines provided in the case of *D K Basu* have been subject to the state police organisation's interpretation entirely. Clearly, these guidelines have not been implemented by the state police organisation giving various reasons. A national legislation may ensure implementation of these proposed reforms and also transparent and consistent application of the interrogation process. While the Model Police Act was a good recommendation by the courts, its implementation was to be carried out by the state police organisation. There is also very little evidence of safeguarding the suspect's rights during interrogation, as no positive duty is placed on the police. Comparative studies may provide a starting point towards finding a solution to this problem of application of police reform.

2.12 Comparing India with England and Wales

In England and Wales, police interrogation[211] has undergone a variety of changes since Sir Robert Peel enacted the New Police Act in 1829,[212] which has been influenced by various enactments and reforms. These changes have been influenced by high-profile cases of miscarriage of justice,[213] legislative enactments,[214] large-scale empirical studies on police interviewing[215] and formalised training compendiums.[216] Police interrogation thus defied the sole purpose of "obtaining a confession."[217] In England and Wales, police interrogation is carried out where the police officer aims to gain further information about a crime reported or suspected. Police interview is governed by a strict framework of rules and guidance and legislation. This is after careful regard to the rules of interviewing elaborately contained in the Police and Criminal Evidence Act, 1984 (PACE). PACE was enacted to protect both the suspect and the police. One of the main problems which existed before the enactment of PACE was irregularities with the legislative compliance.[218] This situation may be compared with the present police interrogation provisions in India to ascertain the similarities and differences. Since the major changes brought about in the field of police interview were after the enactment of PACE, it is important to study the position of police interviews before PACE came into effect.

2.12.1 Pre-PACE

Before the introduction of PACE, police powers were governed by the Judges' Rule, which was a set of guidelines formulated by judges of the King's Bench Division in 1912.[219] The interrogations were conducted in private settings shared only by police officers and the suspect. This obviously meant that the custodial activity was shielded from external scrutiny.[220] In the absence of this scrutiny, the interrogation would be admissible in evidence, making it unassailable regardless of any unfair means used by the police officer. The suspect was also in this era of pre-PACE that allowed giving a written statement to the police. However, in a study conducted by Softley, it was evident that none of the suspects actually wrote down their own statements.[221] It was being brought to the attention of both the public and the government by way of soaring rates of recorded crimes that the police were meeting with limited success in fighting crime. Contributing factors such as growing unemployment and economic tensions gave rise to social unrest and serious riots.[222] Authors such as Wilding describe the police service during the pre-PACE era: "to lack professionalism," "testosterone driven" and were fuelled with frustration against the suspect favouring criminal justice system.[223] The absence of a mechanism to ensure checks and balances to limit abuses made the process in urgent need for police reform. Misuse of police process included keeping the suspect in custody for longer than required and without safeguards.[224] This is a common phenomenon under the present Indian police interrogation system, where a lack of safeguards allows police officers to prolong the custody of the suspect.[225]

This misuse was being overlooked by their supervisors, who also allegedly believed that the criminal justice system was suspect favouring. Public confidence in policing was weakening with the rise in the cases of miscarriage of justice.[226] Similar lack of action and supervision over misuse of police power has been observed under the Indian police system. Similar views of alleging the system to be suspect favouring by following safeguards were demonstrated by an Indian interviewee.[227]

Coulthard has observed that prior to PACE, police interviews were recorded by the interviewing officer after the actual interview and this was based on memory.[228] Needless to mention, this process was likely to lead to inaccuracies and distortions despite the intent of the police officer recording the interview. It would be evident later that this flaw was sought to be rectified by PACE by way of introduction of tape-recording the interview. Academics criticised the system of separation of the "charges" and the "refused charges" custody records.[229] Until the late 1980s, majority of the prosecutions' cases at magistrate's courts were presented by police officers. This role of police officers acting as prosecutors stopped and prosecution became the role of the Crown Prosecution Services (CPS). From these actions of police officers, the legislators felt the need to put certain safeguards in place, thereby making police officers more accountable. This led to the forming of various commissions in order to recommend various police investigative reforms required. When compared to the Indian system of policing, there are certain similarities in the process during this pre-PACE era. It is observed that this lack of coherent legislation for recording the investigation is similar to the present Indian investigation system.

2.12.2 Paving a way for PACE

Police interviewing had always been a subject of discussion and seemed in need of reforms since the late 1970s.[230] The urgency for the reforms was felt after the 11th Report of the Criminal Law Revision Committee.[231] However, the recommendation of drawing adverse inference from the silence of the suspect in police stations caused it to remain submerged. As a result of this flaw, the House of Commons rejected all the recommendations made by this committee.[232]

In a few years, other major reports were made by committees such as the Thompson Committee on Criminal Procedure in Scotland working on all aspects of criminal justice. The Royal Commission on Criminal Procedure (RCCP) was set up under the leadership of Philips to make recommendations on the pretrial criminal procedure in England and Wales. The RCCP report was submitted in January 1981. This commission was set up as a response to criminal procedure reforms resulting in various miscarriages of justice. The Philips Royal Commission consulted various commissions and prepared an elaborate report on all aspects of criminal justice.[233] The commission was set up after the enquiry of Fisher into the famous *Confait* case.[234] It was determined in this enquiry that there were systematic problems with police interrogation, which could not be confined to a review of a single case. This case highlighted two major drawbacks: lack of regulation in police stations, and the perils of falsely obtained confessions. This commission reflected in its central message that "the need for fundamental balance" between prosecution and defence starts at the policing stage. This formed the basis of the Police and Criminal Evidence Bill, which was encouraged by the House of Commons at the time. The RCCP considered the three main principles while drafting the investigative powers of the police: fairness, openness and workability.[235] While due consideration to these provisions was given, the use of force under certain circumstances was justified and this allegedly reflected in the PACE provisions.[236] However, in May 1983, political inference resulted in abandonment of the first Bill during the "Thatcher era" when she called for a general election. After major changes being made to this Bill along with other drafts and the Home Office being very keen on listening and responding to suggestions, this Bill was ready for enactment. The work of all the commissions on the impact of police interrogation reflecting on PACE was commended by various authors. As commented by Baldwin, "the idea of police interviewing is, or is becoming neutral or objective search for truth cannot be sustained."[237] As Brown reports:

> [PACE] is the direct outcome of the Royal Commission on Criminal Procedure's recommendations for systematic reform in the investigative process. The provisions of the Act are designed to match up to principles of fairness (for both police and suspect), openness, and workability. Overall, they are intended to strike a balance between the public interest in solving crime and the rights and liberties of suspects.[238]

Authors like Brown also point out, "PACE is the direct outcome of the Royal Commission on Criminal Procedure's recommendations for systematic reform in the investigative process."[239] While the recommendations of these reports were extensive and in-depth, it was given leverage while enacting the PACE. It is fair to say that similar recommendations were made by the Indian commissions, but they have not been considered in similar lights as the English commissions. Clearly, the Indian commission reports lacked an in-depth analysis of police reforms when compared to the English commission reports. Unlike the English reports, most Indian reports fail to recommend measures for making police interrogation more rights based. The need for urgent legislative enactments was highlighted in the PACE bill in the wake of various cases of miscarriage of justice.[240] Despite Supreme Court of India jurisprudence highlighting the need for police reform, very little is done towards legislating police reforms.[241]

2.12.3 Post-PACE

The PACE received Royal Ascent in 1984 but came into effect around January 1986. The delay was caused by the Miners' Strike from March 1984 to March 1985, during which the police were dedicating most of their time to resolve issues and otherwise engaged in the enquiry.[242] Following the emphasis on the reform needed in police interviewing and the enactment of PACE, due leverage was given to elements of "ethical interviewing."[243] The lack thereof in police interviews also helped in determining what acceptable police behaviour was and what was not. PACE had been in effect for nearly six years, when the Runciman Royal Commission questioned in detail the basic structure of the act. As a result, many amendments were made to the Act resulting in the implementation of the codes of practices. This commission suggested that in case the objectives are not met by the investigating police officers, further training needs to be given and they must be properly supervised.[244] This commission also reported in one of its findings that police officers often made assumptions about the guilt of the suspect, which affected the interrogation process. Reformative measures suggested by this commission resulted in the formation of a new code of practice titled "Principles of Investigative Interviewing."[245]

The Phillips Commission, which laid down the foundation of PACE, emphasised that the Act should reflect an adversarial system. The enactment of PACE introduced a regulatory framework that brought clarity to the methods of investigation, the rights of a detainee and the appropriate measures for breach of duties. PACE brought a sense of assurance that investigation will be carried out with integrity and objectivity, which was very crucial to public confidence in policing.

Wilding rightly points out that the introduction of PACE was a cultural shock to many police officers to the way in which investigation had developed.[246] The clear regulatory framework that contained what was and was not acceptable in an investigation was perceived as a threat to police officers. It is natural for police officers to react with resistance; however, this did not have an impact on the enactment of PACE. This reflects the current resistance of the Indian Police towards the implementation of police reforms and the Model Police Act. The difference between the two systems is that the reforms were implemented despite police resistance. It is also assumed that among other reasons, PACE reforms were successful as they were done at a national level. When compared to the Indian reforms, it is observed that they delegated all the responsibility to the state police.[247] This may be the reason why police reforms have failed to be implemented in India, along with the lack of a national legislation. Interrogation under PACE now included safeguards such as giving a caution informing the suspect of their rights and tape-recording of the interview at the time of the arrest. Any non-compliance with the specific provisions of PACE by the police officer invited strict disciplinary action and exclusion of evidence.[248] The latter part is discussed at length in Chapter 4. The PEACE (Preparation and Planning, Engage and Explain, Account, Clarify and Challenge) model was developed on the basis of developing rapport, explaining the allegation and the seriousness of the offence, emphasising the importance of honesty and truth gathering and respecting the suspect's version of the events.[249] All of these factors are analysed in this section.

2.12.4 Arrest

Arrests in England and Wales are carried out by the police in two ways: with an arrest warrant, and without a warrant. Arrests may be carried out by a warrant issued by the Magistrate and usually for offences such as non-payment of fines or answer bail conditions.[250] These are covered under Section 1 of the Magistrates' Courts Act, 1980, and are similar to the provisions of a Magistrate's Order under the Indian system.[251] The arrests which do not require a warrant are contained under Section 24 of PACE. The most common among these are the powers to stop and search, following which the police officer is allowed to carry out an arrest for further interrogation. A lawful arrest requires two elements: a person's suspected involvement in an offence, and reasonable grounds to believe a person's arrest is necessary.[252] The police officer exercising these powers to arrest without a warrant is expected to use "reasonable suspicion."[253] If questioned, the police officer has to prove that he had reasonable ground for suspecting the commission of an offence and allowing for a prompt and effective investigation.[254] Failure to prove the necessity of arrest on the basis of reasonable suspicion can result in an arrest being deemed unlawful.[255] This section reflects the provisions of cognisable offences under the Indian system, requiring a record in the FIR. Quinton et al. in an empirical study found considerable variation in the level of suspicion that individual officers considered necessary to be used in the cases of stop and search.[256] They add that it is usual to find the grounds of arrest beyond the threshold of reasonable suspicion.

PACE codifies the powers to arrest and also empowers police officers to detain a suspect in order to preserve evidence relating to an offence.[257] A maximum period of 24 hours is acceptable in cases relating to detention without a charge. The codes of practices determine how the actual questioning should take place. This is discussed later in this chapter.

2.12.5 Interview and interrogation

These two terms are often used interchangeably in England and Wales depending on the audience it is being addressed. There is however a lot of academic discussion and analysis on differentiating the two terms. An interview is "non-accusatory" in character as described by Inbau et al., even if the investigator has doubts about the involvement of the suspect in the suspected crime.[258] This attitude even assists the investigator in maintaining a "rapport" with the suspect, leading to further stages of interrogation. Another characteristic of an interview is its purpose should be to gather information.[259] The investigator's attitude and behaviour are expected to change with the behaviour of the suspect as the interview progresses. This is probably why interviews are free-flowing and unstructured. Interrogations, on the other hand, are characterised as primarily accusatory in nature.[260] This is evident when an interrogator begins by stating "There is no doubt you were involved in this crime." This more or less makes the suspect realise that he is in an accusatory position. Another interesting feature pointed out by Inbau et al. is that the purpose of an interrogation is to learn the truth.[261] This distinctively separates an interview from an interrogation. An interrogation is carried out in a controlled environment in order to avoid any disturbance and maintain privacy. It is interpreted here for the sake of argument that a police station may be a controlled environment. It is argued by Inbau et al. that there is not much difference between the two terms, but it clarifies which techniques need to be adopted by the interrogators. It is suggested here that being aware of this distinction, the use of the word interview appears in the English context and is more open to a fact-finding process of investigation.

2.13 How is a police interrogation conducted?

Code of Practice C defines interview as the questioning of a person regarding their involvement or suspected involvement in a criminal offence.[262] The suspect is brought to the police station on a suspected charge by a police officer; thereafter the custody officer is in charge of the suspect. The custody officer also determines if the continued detention of the suspect is justified.[263] The arresting officer and the interviewing custody officer are different individuals under PACE ensuring transparency in the investigating proceedings. On arrival at the police station, the suspect has the right to have someone informed about his arrest, right to legal assistance and the right to consult the codes of practices. All this information is provided to the suspect by a caution at the time of his arrest.

2.13.1 Caution as a police duty

A verbal caution is given to the suspect at the time of the arrest and at the initiation of an interrogation.[264] With the introduction of the Criminal Justice and Public Order Act, 1994 (CJPO), a caution included the right to silence and its implications. The wordings of the caution which are given verbally are very clear and precise and inform the suspect about three main things: the arrest, right to silence and the right to legal assistance.[265] The courts have also emphasised the importance of the police officer providing the suspect with this verbal caution.[266] The police officer is also expected to make sure that the suspect understands the caution; this may entail repeating the caution a few times. The caution is also repeated at the police station before the commencement of the interrogation and before the beginning of each stage of interrogation.

However, the comprehensibility of the caution for a lay man has been questioned by authors such as Cotterill.[267] Cotterill argues that the problem is more fundamental than factors limiting to cross-culture and cross-language barrier. An understanding of the caution is most important as it affects the use of right to silence by the suspect. Various studies show that police officers fail to make sure that the detainee or suspect has understood or even administered the caution.[268] Authors therefore argue that in cases where the suspects do not understand their rights, they may still give unreliable statements, falsely incriminating themselves.[269] This may have an impact on a selected "intellectually disadvantaged" group of individuals who might fall in this category. On the other hand, the "old hands" representing regular offenders might know all the aspects of the system, trying to take advantage of this. Comprehensibility was tested by asking police officers to explain the caution and very few of them could accurately explain this.[270] However, it may be argued that the issue of comprehensibility was common in the late 1990s. There have been no issues with the comprehensibility of a caution lately. This is owing to the lack of any studies, previous or recent. However, authors suggest ameliorating the caution for a better understanding among the general public after extensive empirical studies.[271] Despite these shortcomings, this practice of providing a verbal caution acts as a positive duty on the police officer to inform the suspect of his fundamental rights. In the absence of a similar positive duty on the Indian police officer, the suspect remains unaware of his fundamental rights.

2.13.2 Duties of a custody officer

The custody officer has wide powers and an elaborate set of duties under PACE. It is the duty of the custody officer to inform the suspect of his rights and he must do so "clearly."[272] The custody officer is in charge of carrying out risk assessment for all the detainees. In case the custody officer has enough evidence, either a charge decision is made or in the absence of this the suspect must be released.[273] All entries must be made in the custody record. The custody officer considers the grounds for detention, granting of bail and authorising or refusing bail. Failure to observe any of the following procedural rules amounts to a breach of law and the officer may face disciplinary action under PACE Code C. This may also result in inadmissibility of evidence of any admission or confession made during the interview.[274]

The main duties also include the right to have someone informed, medical advice, fitness to be interviewed and interpretation.

2.13.2.1 Right to have someone informed

A person detained in custody has the right to have a friend or a relative informed of his arrest if he so requests.[275] The provisions are specific, and conferring of this right is subject to the condition that allowing the suspect to do so does not tamper or alter any evidence relevant to the investigation.[276] This right can be delayed up to a maximum of 36 hours if the suspect has been detained in connection to an indictable offence, if a superior officer authorises the delay or if the suspect has not been charged yet.[277] This "sufficient evidence to charge" is subject to practical interpretation of the custody officer. Academics write that they may detain the suspect further even if they have sufficient evidence to prospect conviction.[278] The codes of practices provide that in case a nominated person cannot be contacted, up to two other persons can be tried. The custody officer can allow any further calls to be made at his discretion. All of this information is recorded in the custody records and thus exists in the form of written records. This procedure reflects the provisions of Section 50(1) of the CrPC in India, which makes it an obligation on the police.[279] The Indian courts have acknowledged the non-compliance of this practice of having someone informed of the suspect's arrest.[280] The system of recording any delay in contacting a friend ensures compliance with the PACE provisions under the English system.

2.13.2.2 Right to medical advice

Code C of PACE allows for the detained person to have proper medical attention in case they have suffered an injury or if they have a physical or a mental condition. This is a part of the risk assessment mentioned above. This provision also looks into the possibility of assessing a vulnerable suspect, including a minor or a suspect suffering from mental health. This Code also makes clear provisions for the availability of medical attention in case the suspect requests it and if he is in need for it. This procedure is also similar to the provisions of Sections 53 and 54 of the CrPC under the Indian legislation. Its implementation however varies in practice and this concern is raised by the courts on various occasions.[281]

2.13.2.3 Fitness to be interviewed

PACE Code of Practice C elaborately mentions the provisions under which a suspect may be considered fit to be interviewed. This made it a matter of consideration for the custody officer to decide if the interrogation would cause physical or mental harm to the suspect. In addition to the provision mentioned above about the consultation by a medical practitioner, the "functional ability" of the suspect was also supposed to be considered.[282] This code of practice also provides for the supervision by an appropriate adult during the interrogation and if a specialist opinion is required. If a healthcare professional carries out a risk assessment and provides the custody officer with the outcome, this shall form a part of the custody record. The custody officer decides after considering this report whether the interview should be allowed to proceed or otherwise. Such a provision does not presently exist under the Indian legislation, but a provision ensuring the physical well-being of the suspect may be highly beneficial.

2.13.2.4 Interpretation

The PACE Code provides that proper arrangements should be made by the chief police officers for a qualified interpreter for deaf people and people who cannot understand English.[283] The code has been accommodating in providing that the suspect cannot be interrogated in the absence of an interpreter.[284] The Indian legislation is under dire need of such a provision for a mandated interpretation owing to the diversity of the Indian population. The lack of such sophisticated yet basic provisions needs recognition under the Indian legislation. The PACE Code also mentions that an interpreter shall be called when the suspect cannot speak to a solicitor.[285] While the code makes provisions for an interpreter at the time of interrogation, it is silent on informing the suspect of his rights before the interview commences. This issue is also argued by authors after carrying out extensive empirical research in four jurisdictions in Europe.[286] The Law Society has provided guidelines for solicitors on the use of interpreters and sign language.[287] The Law Society has additionally suggested that the solicitors should establish whether the suspect has a particular language problem or a speech or hearing impediment, particularly in the legal language.[288] However, the continuous effort made by way of codes of practices along with the Law Society towards a fair interrogation is appreciated.

2.13.3 Non-compliance

The provisions of the code make sure that police officers do not abuse their power and ensure the faith of the public in the criminal justice system. PACE and codes of practice must be referred by the police officer while interviewing a suspect. Failure to comply with these codes of practice and the code results in certain evidentiary exclusions. There are two exclusionary evidence rules in relation to non-compliance: exclusion of confession obtained unlawfully and the judges' discretionary power to exclude any evidence affecting the fairness of a proceeding.[289]

In case a police officer fails to caution the suspect, it would still amount to an "interview," but any evidence contained in the interview is rendered inadmissible in the criminal proceedings.[290] In *R v. Bryce*, the court held that the failure to provide a caution before the commencement of each interview would render the evidence obtained in the interview inadmissible.[291] Any other non-compliance with the police duties or misconduct was looked into by various commissions immediately after the inception of PACE. The legislative provisions for failure to provide a caution are clear and cast a duty of failure on the police officer. Any non-compliance is regulated by an independent body. It is evident that the English legislation and jurisprudence emphasise the importance of a caution being the medium to inform the suspect of his rights before any police interview. Other issues relating to non-compliance include exclusion of evidence or confession, which are discussed at length in Chapters 3 and 4.

2.14 Independent Police Complaints Commission (IPCC)

Initially, a majority of complaints against police officers were investigated through internal investigation, in line with the Home Office Guidance. The Police Complaints Authority was set up in 1984 to oversee investigation of police complaints. This authority was subjected to criticism owing to the lack of credibility and the high standard of proof required for the investigation. This provision reflects the current internal investigation system in the Indian Police. The IPCC then replaced the Police Complaints Authority in the UK in 2004. The police investigation culture has always been at the heart of the discussion surrounding *quis custodient ipsos custodies*.[292] The reforms of police complaints procedure were subjected to the "is almost always preceded by some observable crisis of public legitimacy in the police."[293] The enquiry into the Brixton riots in 1981 and the Stephen Lawrence case in 1999 led to the establishment of an independent institution. Initially a model was prepared by the Scarman Inquiry board, suggesting a dual model approach to the police complaints system accommodating the complaints procedure for a lay person. The first one was an independent investigation of the police, and the second provided lay supervision for serious complaints. However, after receiving criticisms from the McPherson report on the earlier suggested model, the Police Complaints Authority commenced work on the formation of an independent board.

Following this, the government carried out a consultation on a new complaints system, which resulted in the Police Reforms Act, 2002. This Act created the IPCC and this commission has been active in England and Wales since 2004.[294] This non-departmental public body has been funded by the Home Office and has been looking into disciplinary issues concerning police officers. The police must refer complaints of death or serious injury to the IPCC. The police officer is at discretion to report other matters to the IPCC that he may deem fit.[295] The IPCC has national and regional offices. The IPCC not only takes punitive action against the wrong doers but also aims to solve the underlying problem that led to the cause of the complaint.[296]

This makes the IPCC accountable to the public for any complaints they have against the process of police interrogation or even against the police officer. The IPCC have also been referred to as the gatekeepers of the criminal justice system, especially with the wide array of powers and responsibilities they possess.[297] A complaints process for police misconduct therefore acknowledges and guarantees public confidence in the police.[298] Any negative impact on the complaints procedure and system by the public therefore affects the accountability mechanism of the police interrogation system.

The IPCC consists of a chair and a commissioner, who form its governing body and looks into the policy formation. Police officers have a duty to cooperate with the IPCC's investigation and are obliged to provide access to documents and other materials. The involvement of the community has been effective in restricting the use of coercive police powers.[299] This involvement by the community ensures external and internal involvement, which aims to reduce oversight if not totally avoid it. In a recent report presented by the government, the issue of corruption among the police, which was not a priority for the public concern, was sought as an important issue for reform.[300] The NHRC and SHRCs under the Indian legislation try to reflect the spirit of the IPCC, they are far from comparison in practice. It is fair to say that the inception of the IPCC and its functioning were relatively fast and consistent. If compared to the NHRC and SHRCs, there has been little success with the demonstration of complaints management. It has been nearly two decades and yet very few cases have been brought before the NHRC and SHRCs.

2.14.1 Criticisms

Despite a relatively stable growth in the complaints-monitoring system, various issues have been raised about the IPCC's investigation not living up to the accountability and transparency elements originally criticised by the McPherson report. The presence of a police officer in the investigation and the absence of a skilled civilian investigation staff pose a risk to the IPCC's ability to be held accountable to the public.[301] Many recommendations have been made to remove the ex-police officer from the investigation panel in order to ensure transparency in the complaints procedure.[302] The lack of resources for not looking into all the public complaints deeming it impractical is also criticised.[303] Since the IPCC was created with a view to restoring public faith and confidence in the police, its actions have been under close scrutiny. When compared with the systems in Scotland and Northern Ireland, the models used by England and Wales are criticised for having the least public involvement.[304] A latest study also showed the continual lack of involvement of the public even in the policymaking regarding the functioning of the IPCC.[305] However, lessons are being drawn from the independence of the complaints system in Northern Ireland, which is completely independent of the police.[306] Authors have opined that amongst other complaints systems in neighbouring jurisdictions, the system of Northern Ireland can serve as an ideal example. It is pointed out that the relevance of public faith and confidence in the complaints system highlights the importance of police accountability in the investigation system. Despite these criticisms, continuous development made by comparative learning has enhanced the performance of IPCC in England and Wales.[307] This effort by the government and the legislative bodies to improve can be demonstrated by their continuous effort to look for a better model. While the IPCC is subject to criticism of lacking public involvement in policymaking, public participation is a lot more when compared to the Indian NHRC and SHRCs. In the latter, there is no public involvement as demonstrated by the absence of the members of the public at the complaints proceedings.[308] The NHRC and the SHRC lack transparency as their decisions against police officers are not made available to the public.[309] The existence of other provisions ensuring safeguards was then made available in England and Wales.

Due to the above-mentioned drawbacks and anger and mistrust over lack of investigation, the IPCC was replaced by the Independent Office of Police Conduct (IOPC) around 2018. However, the IOPC was alleged to only have replaced the old 'commission structure' and was headed by Director General supported by deputies.

2.15 Tape-recording of the interviews

PACE Code E para 3 makes it mandatory for the interview of the persons cautioned under Code C Section 10 in respect of any indictable offence to be audio recorded. The suspect if charged is also entitled to a recorded copy of the investigation.[310] In the early 1980s, the use of resources such as tape recorders posed a concern owing to the expenditure.[311] This was further highlighted when the tape recorders had been in use for a few years but yet police interrogation was criticised for being unfair.[312] The record of police interrogation is adduced in evidence by the prosecution in England and Wales. Along with maintaining up-to-date police records at the police station, the provision of tape recording provides checks and balances of the interrogation process. For this purpose, the prospects of a fair trial depend on recording the interrogation accurately. Tape recording of the investigation also ensures that the suspect has been cautioned by the police officer before the interview. It is observed by authors that reliance was placed on tape recording of the interviews in order to determine the credibility of the confession given to police officers.[313]

However, even after the enactment of PACE, miscarriages of justice involving police behaviour continued. As a result, a review of police interviewing procedures was carried out.[314] Initial concerns amongst authors about police training for the use of tape recorders was soon justified by the provision of extensive training amongst police officers.[315] Authors like Baldwin have stated that "the introduction of an effective system of tape recording is proving to be the single most important reform of the criminal justice system in this country since the 1980s."[316] Tape recording of the police interview ensured discontinuation of practices such as officers commencing the interview at the back of the police cars as observed in a few cases in Birmingham.[317] The mandated use of tape recording of interviews has resulted in a drop in the number of coercive and manipulative interrogations in Britain.[318] One of the major advantages of tape-recording interviews was the possibility of academic analysis for continual development. Studies carried out at regular intervals also help suggest further areas of improvement. There was initial police scepticism about the use and value of tape recording of interviews.[319] It is evident that the extensive usage of tape recording has reduced the burden of note taking on the investigating police officers. It is highlighted here that the provision of taped interviews has more advantages despite various shortcomings. A provision of this nature may assist in providing data for academic analysis and feedback for continual police development. Despite various Indian commissions recommending taped police interviews, it has not reflected in any legislation. Even the jurisprudence recognition such a provision has received in India has been by way of a High Court decision, which is not binding on all the states.[320] In the absence of any other measures ensuring an effective monitoring system, it is suggested that a national legislation in India may be enforced.

2.15.1 Drawbacks

Baldwin carried out a review of 400 video recordings and 200 audio recordings and concluded that the general competence of the interviewers was low. Many shortcomings were highlighted in this study, such as struggling to build a rapport with the suspect, adopting a confession-seeking approach and trying to persuade the suspect to adopt the interviewer's version of events.[321] In another study which reviewed 118 taped interrogations, it was found that the interviewing approach was confrontational and confession-seeking.[322] Latest studies have shown that many police officers despite being trained in conducting interviews would disregard most of the principles.[323] This continuous disregard is due to the human error factor, which seems to be dealt with by continuously revising the provisions of training under the various PACE Codes of Practices. The existence of other linguistic boundaries was also highlighted, which resulted in the provision of continuous and updated police training. Such a system of continual police training may assist the Indian police if tape recording of the interviews is legislated.

2.16 Police training

Police training in England and Wales has been under academic and legislative scrutiny for a long time. Academic empirical survey has provided data showing the gap in the practices and suggesting reforms in police training.

After conducting extensive empirical research, authors like Gudjonsson have stated that police investigators received no formal training until 1992.[324] Until 1992, the investigators were only interested in obtaining a confession and used all methods to obtain one. When PACE came into effect, it assisted the police training for ethical interviewing by way of guidance and notes.

2.16.1 PEACE

A new approach called the PEACE was developed through the collaboration of lawyers, police officers and psychologists. PEACE was a model of interviewing which reflected open-mindedness and an effort to gather information. This was also an attempt to move away from the cases of miscarriage of justice in the past, which had tarnished the police repute. The acronym PEACE highlights five distinct stages in the interview process:

> (P) Planning—stresses the importance of planning an interview prior to its commencement so that clear aims and objectives of the interview are established, topics of interest are identified, questions designed and issues such as interview location, timing and recording procedure are considered; (E) Engage and explain—involves explaining to the witness what the purpose of the interview is, what they should expect and how the interview will proceed; (A) Account—refers to the manner in which an account or version of events is elicited from the witness, this depends upon the purpose of the interview and different methods will be discussed below; (C) Closure—stresses the importance of bringing the interview to a comfortable conclusion whilst maintaining rapport with a witness and avoiding negative emotional reactions such as anger or anxiety; (E) Evaluate—reminds the interviewer to evaluate the product of their interview and their performance to identify other informational needs.[325]

The PEACE model stresses development and maintenance of rapport throughout any interview. Authors mention that this rapport encourages the suspect to divulge information on the basis of trust towards the interviewer, thereby reducing the risk of unreliable information.[326] The principles of PEACE are related to fairness and open-mindedness, and expect the interviewer to avoid the assumption of guilt and to seek the truth.[327] The PEACE model is now "ubiquitous" in England and Wales.[328] PEACE models also excluded any confusion created by PACE of what the police officer ought to and ought not to do. In 2011, a study was conducted with the aim to determine the efficiency of PEACE-trained officers. The authors concluded that the officers' interviewing skills improved after being PEACE trained. Persistent issues of the impact of the officers' social and communication skills will continue to impact the interrogation.

Gudjonsson concludes that PEACE brought about a marked reduction in the manipulative practices in the police interrogation.[329] However, if under pressure "to get a result" in high-profile cases, these officers will deploy full arsenal of tactics, paying no regard to the training they receive.[330] While this is a fact, it is worth mentioning here that the magnitude of high-profile cases is very limited and any use of techniques outside of training causes little harm. Total elimination of the use of techniques outside of training is non-practical. Authors like Griffiths and Milne also criticised PEACE saying it could not adopt a "one size fits all" attitude.[331] These authors also argue that serious crime needs specific training and the PEACE model would cause limitations in effective interviewing. Some authors also suggest that the use of PEACE and other communication methods are useless if an interview is not lawful.[332] These instances again are limited in number and frequency. This implies that the PEACE model can be used as an additional method along with the provisions of PACE. Despite these shortcomings, the police training for interviewing has undergone major changes and is still evolving with necessary changes with the needs of time. A PEACE model may provide elaborate training to police officers for interviewing in India. Considering the present police training lacking any specific training for interviewing, such a model may assist in providing a detailed interviewing approach for officers in India. Not only should the PEACE model be implemented, but it must also be constantly updated and reviewed by the Indian police officers.

2.16.2 Legitimate questioning

With all the information provided about interrogation, it is also important that the questions put to the suspects are legitimate and the time frame of the interview is reasonable. In *Murray v. UK*, the European Court of Human Rights (ECtHR) defined the purpose of questioning as "to further the criminal investigation by way of confirming or dispelling the concrete suspicion grounding the arrest."[333] This direction was specific to the openness of the police interrogation. The incorporation of this judgement has been expanded in the Code of Practice C in para 11. 6.

The ambit of legitimate questioning also involves the legitimate duration of the questioning under this code. As mentioned above, the longest duration the suspect can be detained and questioned without a charge is 36 hours.[334] The efforts made through PACE and Code of Practice C for legitimising the interrogation are updated and are also subject to constant amendments. However, the determination of legitimacy of the questions is a subjective area for the police officer and is open to interpretation. It is fair to highlight that the awareness of legitimate questioning in England and Wales aims at increasing police accountability. A fair amount of what constitutes legitimacy during an interview is given to police officers during training. The Indian police officers do not receive even the basic interrogation training; expecting them to ascertain what constitutes legitimacy in the absence of such training is highly unlikely.

2.17 Rule of law

Justice Bingham describes the rule of law as the cornerstone of a democratic society.[335] This also includes the state's ability to balance power while constitutionalising law and order. Police officers represent a powerful organisation and are accountable to the public and carry out necessary duties while using adequate amount of authority. The proportionality factor is also associated with the rule of law and a lot depends on the use of power by the police. The interrogatory process reflects the effectiveness of the rule of law. Any dereliction of the interrogatory duty results in the miscarriage of proceeding, including affecting court proceedings. It is also essential for the effectiveness of the rule of law that laws and judgements are not only enacted but also implemented in practice. Governance of police in England and Wales was formalised by the Royal Commission in 1962. It was based on the partnership between the local government and central government with the shared accountability of chief constables. This was referred to as the tripartite model of policing and responsibilities were shared between the Home Office, Local Police Authority and the Chief Constable of the force. Despite being a part of the investigative process, arrest and detention requires strict regulation as it causes an infringement of civil liberties. Like most of the powers contained in PACE, investigative powers are regulated by both external and internal mechanisms.

As Fuller writes, the basic prerequisites to the existence of an effective legal system are the "morality of duty" and the "inner morality of law."[336] Most of the provisions of PACE fulfil the elements of eight requirements of the rule of law by Fuller.[337] According to the characteristics of the rule of law by Fuller, the provisions of PACE are clear, widely promulgated, general and congruent. Law is "the enterprise of subjecting human conduct to the governance of rules."[338] When analysed the provisions of providing updated investigating training to police officers, having an independent authority (IPCC) conduct enquiry into cases of police misconduct reflect Fuller's provisions.

In order to attain objectivity in a democratic society, the balance between the rule of law recognising human rights and the deterrent criminal effectiveness could be maximised. This concept is also a reflection of Packer's due process and crime control methods.[339] Obtaining this balance is practically impossible and classifying a system into either of these categories is also difficult. However, when police officers violate the rule of law, they cause more harm for whatever reason they might consider necessary.[340] It is common amongst police officers to believe that adhering too closely to the rule of law can result in the criminal going unpunished.[341] However, with constant updating of the police procedures and legislation governing interviews, the police aim at adhering to the rule of law.

2.18 Police culture

Police interrogation relies a great deal on the police officers' representation of crime and criminals. Police officers in England and Wales have always been criticised for racial profiling of suspects. In 1981, Lord Scarman in his report pointed out that "Britain is an institutionally racist society."[342] However, at the time Lord Scarman did not see the problem with the gravity associated with racism. He placed reliance on the issue of racism relating to policymaking pursued by an institution. This ambiguity left by Lord Scarman was attempted to be rectified by the Macpherson Committee overseeing the Stephen Lawrence case. The case of Stephen Lawrence has been called the most important case in recent times depicting racial stereotypes in the police system in England and Wales. Macpherson extended racism from institutional racism to an elaborate extension of persons being targeted by police officers.[343] While the issue of racism is not particularly highlighted as an issue by the Indian police, it exists nonetheless. However, in the absence of important safeguards, training and legislation, the issue of racism is not considered of the same magnitude as it is considered in England and Wales.

Police culture impacts the behaviour of officers, and this is manifested in strong crime control norms. Police culture also has a dominant impact on the police officer's actions.[344] Individual mannerisms related to policing, as described by Culhane et al., can be divided into three categories: authoritarianism, legal authoritarianism and social deviance.[345] Police officers tend to be high on authoritarianism, and their job requires them to be assertive and dominant.[346] The supporters of legal authoritarianism are in favour of violating civil liberties in the interest of punishing social deviants.[347] It is further added that any person who does not ascribe to this social hierarchy can be punished. Therefore, in essence, this authoritarianism has a direct impact on police officers and their actions condoned in the name of authority.

2.19 Police accountability and transparency

The criminal justice system in England and Wales has been relying on the principles of accountability in terms of both continuous improvement measures and punitive measures. In order to make police more accountable and secure legitimacy, an authority must be able to bring the police to be answerable to their roles and responsibilities. The tripartite system mentioned above and the duties of the police authorities together are put in place to facilitate transparency and a higher degree of accountability. Despite this clear notion, authors believe that there is very little public access and involvement in the process where the public can also influence policing.[348] The introduction of PACE has rightly been referred to as being relevant among other legislations introduced in the twenty-first century due to the constant review and update of many provisions of PACE.[349] The constant criticism has assisted in the development of PACE and its working towards making police officers more accountable for their actions. PACE provided wider powers to police officers, expecting a higher level of accountability mechanisms. The Police and Magistrates' Court Act, 1994, is said to have made the police independent of the local government. This independence has proved to make the police more accountable. Police officers in India lack this independence from the government resulting in a low level of accountability. The IPCC has aimed at restoring public faith in the police and making it easy for the public to make a complaint against a police officer for misconduct, further adding to the police accountability. When compared with the accountability of the Indian police officers, there is a lack of legislation and a process to make police officers accountable for their actions. The NHRC, an equivalent of the IPCC, takes few measures to ensure that the police are held accountable. This is demonstrated by many authors who have complained about the lack of action taken by the NHRC on complaints against police officers.[350] The NHRC and SHRCs also lack the specific authority required to hold police officers accountable. With so many issues surrounding the body regulating police accountability, it is difficult to ascertain the actions of the Indian police officers.

The use of discretion by police officers in matters relating to arrest and investigation often reflect both the accountability and the transparency of the working of the police. The use of discretion can be "structured" and "confined" through rules and can be easily "checked" through mechanisms of accountability.[351] This practice can be easily supported by the use of IPCC for overseeing the interrogation and the use of tape recorders at the police stations. The use of discretion can be further managed if the rules exist and are precise.[352] In these circumstances, the rules are implemented by PACE, the codes of practice and case laws and are precise in directing the amount of discretion to be used by police officers. It is also evident that rules are not the sole dominant factors influencing the use of discretion. It is also difficult to confine the usage of discretion merely by putting relevant rules in place. As explained by Black, it is not always that non-conformity to a rule will be treated as non-compliance.[353] Gaining compliance to the correct usage of discretion is a matter decided by statutes and enforced by officials. Authors like Williamsons have stated that interrogations in England and Wales are less confrontational and more transparent.[354] This can be affirmed as the inference drawn from the PACE procedures make the police interrogation process transparent considering the safeguards put in place. Police accountability can be reformed further by having more consultative groups and increasing the monitoring of the officers. It is observed that the Indian police officers have wide legislative powers for using their discretion to arrest and investigate. However, this power is neither regulated nor supervised. In the absence of any authority challenging the use of discretion by the police, it is easy for police officers in India to violate these powers of discretion.

2.19.1 Public perception

Public perception of the police is essential whether the public have to face them as suspects, witnesses or complainants. Good policing requires public confidence and as observed, this also interrelates with police accountability. In order for the police organisation to be called a fair and a just authority, it has to adjust with and treat the citizens with fairness and dignity. It therefore comes as no surprise that only when the public trust the police and its system will they assist them in any matter. Alternatively, it is also in the interest of the police to try and be fair, just and transparent if they want to succeed in carrying out their functions. People are easily convinced that the police do not abide by the law and misuse their power.[355] Yet, as Bayley describes, even in countries with high regard for human rights, the police are regularly accused of being involved with unjustified stops and searches.[356] It is not difficult for the public to view this as an abuse of power, being aware of the pressure on police officers to meet performance-based deadlines. However, just as the public need to be made aware of these peer pressures on the police officer, the officers also need to be made aware of the cost of violating the rule of law.

Obtaining public trust in the police is paramount considering the inter-reliability between themselves: the extent to which the public trusts the police associate's judgements about effectiveness, engagement with community values and fairness when dealing with people.[357] Generally, the public when placing trust may place the trust on the police as an institution and as individuals collectively. Thus, the accountability measures which prove the effectiveness of the police ease the process of the public placing trust in the system and the individual officers. The tape recording of the proceedings may assist the public in placing trust in the police organisation. In the absence of such safeguards under the police interrogation system in India, there is a constant distrust and lack of faith in police officers. The general public in India are also less likely to approach police officers to provide information while being interviewed.

2.19.2 Police legitimacy

Reiner discusses the process of legitimating the police in England and Wales rested partially in the successful communication of the police competence.[358] Legitimacy is defined as "fundamental property of legal institutions, the right to govern, and the recognition by the governed of that right."[359] The regular notion of the public owning the police in England and Wales is often supported by the prominence and assurance of the police in political and social life.[360] Good policing is also associated with legitimacy on the basis of public consent and not public repression.[361] Therefore, police officers who are ineffective in protecting the public, illegitimate or unfair, are easy to lose public confidence.[362] "Trust and legitimacy are social facts."[363] Police officers are therefore required to demonstrate legitimacy in order to secure public cooperation voluntarily. In the absence of this voluntary public cooperation, police officers are compelled to be even more oppressive.[364] The other most important feature of legitimacy is the Weberian concept of "justification."[365] This is read along with the concept of people's judgement about legitimacy of an institution based on an assessment of the congruence between its goals, practices and behaviour.[366] This reliance on justification also prevents the police to be taken as an unquestioned authority. In the present context, the IPCC keeps a check on the justification of the use of authority by police officers. A study on the police-community relationship has deduced that the police can enhance police legitimacy by improving the way they treat citizens.[367] Bradford et al. also describe the two potential sources of legitimacy: the relationship of the public with the police as an organisation, and the police process and style.[368] Contributing factors such as following procedural justice and fairness might assist but are not exhaustive. Each encounter between a police officer and a member of the public is "a teachable moment," and each event counts in teaching both the participants.[369] This insists on the continual development of the police by way of training in order to prove its legitimacy to the general public. Despite the continual effort to maintain a good police-public relationship, there are gaps in the process, which are usually attributed to corruption.

2.20 Corruption

Many studies have found that corruption exists in England and Wales amongst the small minority of police staff.[370] It is a fact that corruption is an obstacle in incorporating reforms to make the police more rights based and accountable and transparent. Newburn in his research evidence concludes that it is impossible to define the characteristics of corruption.[371] One interesting fact Newburn mentions is that corruption is "pervasive and not bounded by rank."[372] Therefore, trying to change the regulation of policing in order to make it more ethical became a post-war reform theme. However, reports have suggested that ethical policing is not the answer to curbing corruption.[373] The development of policing has been affected by corrupt cases of misconduct and malpractice and suppression of evidence. High-profile cases which came to light from time to time also affected public consciousness.[374] As a response to reform police corruption, the main focus was on regulating police behaviour. This resulted in the introduction of legislation such as PACE, setting up of anti-corruption units and setting up of the professional standards departments.[375] This was followed by many enquiries among the lower levels of police officers uncovering systematic corruption and exposed bigger problems such as police culture and police management.[376]

Many of the personal problems of police officers were also brought to the attention of the higher officials and a risk assessment was set in place to remedy this.[377] This was considered a major contributing factor to the performance of police officers and affected public trust and confidence. This continuous presence of corruption in the police also has a negative impact on police legitimacy, which fails to secure public confidence and cooperation. An inference can therefore be drawn that the presence of high levels of corruption can impact all the above factors. The mention of the level of corruption rather than absence of corruption is taken for its practical application. All the systems in the world point to the fact that eradicating corruption completely from the police organisation is a myth. The continuous improvement with PACE and the aimed transparent approach taken by the IPCC towards curbing corruption is witnessed by the public.[378] Thus, obliterating individual and departmental corruption starts with periodical reforms of police activities, making them more accountable and increasing transparency through the investigative actions taken by the IPCC. Greater emphasis on morale, professional standards and respect for authority within the police organisation may act as contributing factors to curb corruption.[379] While measures are being taken for curbing corruption, it is also essential that there is an absence of bureaucracy from the police organisation in order for the process to be transparent. While the presence of corruption exists in both the comparative countries, it is the magnitude of corruption in India that causes bigger problems. Corrupt practices also prevent the implementation of police reforms and safeguards for the suspect. The overall presence of corruption is witnessed among both police officers and the general public, which has a negative impact on the entire criminal justice process.

2.20.1 Reducing bureaucracy

With the inception of PACE, many police powers have been widened with the aim to reduce bureaucratic interference. Bureaucracy can be an advantage when the official has "mastered the skill of bureaucracy."[380] In order to ensure transparent policing, more effort has been made to make policing democratic and removing bureaucracy. To run an effective and efficient police service, some amount of bureaucracy is needed; however, extra layers of bureaucracy are created for meeting the present demand. As Flanagan mentioned, bureaucracy is like cholesterol; there is both good and bad.[381] However, extreme bureaucracy resulted in overemphasis on the requirement to record compared to the quality of investigation.[382] Many reports such as the Taylor Review in 2004 have suggested recommendations to reduce bureaucracy, and more recommendations are still being made. This resulted in the establishment of the Police Advisory Board for England and Wales for hearing disciplinary procedures against police complaints. As a result, the hearings were akin to criminal court hearings aiming to reduce the bureaucratic hold on the police complaints hearings. This was followed by various other reviews held at regular intervals in order to further remove bureaucracy from policing. It can be inferred that the efforts are continuously made by various committees to reduce bureaucracy.

2.21 Analysis of comparison

There are quite a few differences and similarities while comparing India and England and Wales with reference to the provisions of police interrogation. In both these countries, the police acts have been under constant scrutiny and therefore subjected to periodical reforms. While the Government of India seems to be reluctant in reforming the police acts, the Supreme Court has been more proactive in jurisprudential reforms.[383] However, case law provides guidance and this lacks certain authority that needs to be filled in by legislative provisions. The fact that police interrogation reforms suggested by the Supreme Court guidelines have not been implemented demonstrates this lack of authority. It is further pointed out that the present scenario in India with regard to police interrogation is similar to the pre-PACE era in England and Wales. The recommendations of the Law Commission Reports in England and Wales have been followed while enacting the PACE, in contrast to the Indian criminal justice system which has been reluctant to follow the recommendations of the Law Commission Reports. Despite various Law Commission Reports over the period of three decades recommending the same issues, none have been given effect into legislation. One could claim only two reasons for the non-implementation of these recommendations by the Indian criminal justice system. These are lack of political will and bureaucracy. Legislative enactments like PACE may assist in providing guidelines for interrogation of a suspect and these are not the same as Supreme Court guidelines.

McConville found that in the absence of a clear definition of concepts such as reasonable suspicion, the police officer resort to informal working rules.[384] In India, alongside the lack of clear grounds justifying the ambit of police interrogation techniques, the use of disproportionate power is unaccountable. This is similar to the use of reasonable suspicion in cases of stop and search cases in England and Wales.

The elaborate provisions of training related to police interrogation, providing the suspect with the basic human rights that would assist in rectifying certain practices at the time of interrogation. The lack of training among the Indian Police Officers is a contributing factor to the way they treat suspects at the time of interrogation. The training that police officers receive in India is a one-off thing; this is a two-year training period before they qualify. There are no updated trainings at regular intervals in India to ensure a fair interrogation by the police officer. As most of police officers interviewed also emphasise the need for better training, certain legislative reforms related to training need to be implemented. As evident from the enactment of PACE and the associated codes of practices, which have provided better training to police officers, these could be used as a basis for improvement for interview techniques and training. An effective police training model based on PEACE and its attributes may be adopted by the Indian police in order to improve the interrogation process, making it more rights based. The emphasis on the structure of the interview and the actual legitimacy of the questions being asked form the basis of the training in England and Wales. This may also be incorporated in the police training. The police in India need training, educating them of the suspects' rights and safeguards. This could help both the suspect and the police officer. The provision of an interpreter at the time of police interrogation should also be incorporated in a multicultural country like India. This is both practical and effective as observed in the comparator jurisdiction.

The importance of supervision and record keeping are emphasised and can be implemented in the Indian Police system. This is displayed by the lack of recording the FIR and station diary entries in India. Damaska emphasised the importance of these features, further mentioning the importance of written records that would assist when analysed in supervision sessions.[385] The lack of providing the suspect with a copy of the notification of the charge and any account of the police-suspect exchange may also be a result of this. Both these provisions ensure transparency and legitimacy, which can be achieved through effective and periodical training.

Tape recording of the interrogation process may also be used as an example for making the police interrogation in India effective and transparent. This assists in monitoring the role of the police officer and ensuring the fair treatment of the suspect. Although the recent Bombay High Court judgement suggests the installation of CCTV at the police stations, it has not been implemented. A nationwide approach should be taken to provide for tape recording of the interrogation in India. This is a necessary safeguard which should also be mandated by national and uniform legislature.

Having stringent legislation for non-compliance to policing duties, which might be punitive in nature have shown to work in England and Wales.[386] The previous system of internal investigation was replaced with the IPCC after severe criticism. While it is agreed that the formation of the IPCC took nearly two decades after the formation of PACE, the performance of the IPCC compensated for the time lapse. Despite various criticisms, the IPCC has been effective in monitoring the behaviour of police officers. It has also been accessible and approachable for the public to make complaints against police officers. Despite the delays in reaching towards a decision, the IPCC has been accountable to the public, providing them with a written copy of the outcome of their complaints. On the contrary, in India, police complaints are still being internally investigated. The public do not receive a copy of the outcome of their complaint. The importance of having an independent body investigating police complaints and overseeing the police interrogation process is further highlighted after analysing (above) the role played by the IPCC. The role of the NHRC is not effective as a police complaints body and is not accessible to the general public.

One can acknowledge that no legal system can be perfect.[387] However, as Endicott argues, these rule of law factors are ideals to aspire to, even if they cannot be attained.[388] If the police do not adhere to the rule of law in a country it, inter alia, affects the criminal justice system. Since police officers are at the stage of initial public contact, their behaviour displays the effectiveness of the rule of law. In order to confer legitimacy on the police, it is essential to justify the powers conferred on them. In England and Wales where the powers of the police are wider, they are endowed with a greater responsibility towards the public and there is a method in place for monitoring that power. As described above, the two main sources of legitimacy—people's relationship with the police as an organisation, and the policing styles—help in identifying the workability of the police system. When observed in both these countries, it is apparent that the relationship of the public with the police in England and Wales is a lot more transparent than its counterparts in India. With the introduction of PACE, the public faith in the police organisation has increased in England and Wales. Many additional factors such as lack of accountability and corruption also affect the legitimacy and the following of the rule of law by the police.

Police accountability is an essential part of the deliverance of the rule of law and proving police legitimacy. If police officers are not held accountable for their actions, then the public faith in the police organisation will easily dwindle. In the case of England and Wales, police officers are held accountable as a result of the safeguards such as the use of tape-recorded interrogations and records. As observed, the IPCC also plays an important role in holding police officers accountable. Not only do the penal provisions specified under PACE assure accountability, but they are also seen effectively applied in practice. In India, police accountability is a legislative "mention" in the form of punitive provisions, but they are not seen applied in practice. In the absence of an independent authority to hold police officers accountable, police officers are not held accountable for any of their actions.

Police culture in both these countries is a subjective matter and varies from one police officer to another. The impact of training has little effect on the authoritarian culture amongst police officers in both the countries. But with the imposition of the above-mentioned safeguards, which are in place under the PACE provisions in England and Wales, they are accountable and procedural. Authoritarianism among police officers in India is paramount and unaccounted for. This along with corruption both inside the police force and in the government failing to incorporate the urgently needed reforms abets the unaccounted authoritarian culture of the police.

This research takes both a narrow and a broad approach to corruption. A narrow approach is taken in the context of the corrupt conduct associated with the police officer. And a wider approach is taken in the political sense of corruption in the government organisation, which prevents from reforms being incorporated to improve policing. Authors like Sherman and Newburn make the most practical observation about corruption. They state that "corruption is found in virtually all countries, in all forces and at every level of the organisation at some time."[389] However, in addition to this observation, it may be added that the magnitude of corruption in every system and at every stage is the reason why the police reforms in India have not been incorporated. The English legal system also benefits from minimum bureaucratic accountability and interference from the police organisation. To add to this, further attempts are being made to reduce this interference in England and Wales further. It is concluded here that the police interrogation system in England and Wales may be taken as a precedent for the above-mentioned reasons.

2.22 Conclusion

In the light of the above observation and the comparison between the two systems, it is fair to conclude that due to a number of factors the Indian police system is in dire need of reform. The areas that need urgent attention are filing of the FIR, police training, transparency, independent investigation body, provision of interpreter and tape recording of interrogation. While most of these issues are addressed by the Supreme Court case laws, it has not been imposed till date. The lack of authority and consistency may be the reasons for the non-implementation. It is suggested that a national legislation clarifying the provisions of a police interrogation may assist in resolving this issue. Methods for educating the suspect of their rights via a police caution prior to the arrest of a suspect may also be adopted. While the English system of police interrogation has certain drawbacks, it may assist in providing a working model. Since the present situation in India is similar to the pre-PACE era in England and Wales, a legislature similar to PACE may be adopted to fill in the gaps. It is suggested here that it is because of the gaps in the legislature and the implementation of jurisprudence in India that a suspect may be deprived of his fundamental rights. In the absence of a taped interrogation, the only other way to ascertain the protection of the suspect's fundamental rights is by the presence of a lawyer during police interrogation. It is therefore essential to study the position of the right to legal assistance and its impact on police interrogation.

Notes

1 This acronym has been used throughout the book in a manner that is commonly used in the Indian context and by Indian academics and the Indian courts.
2 E Stokes, *The English Utilitarians and India*, OUP, 1959, 224; T Metcalf, *Imperial Connections: India in the Indian Ocean Arena, 1860–1920*, University of California Press, 2007.
3 Ibid.
4 B Uma Devi, *Arrest, Detention, and Criminal Justice System: A Study in the Context of the Constitution of India*, OUP, 2012.

5 Article 246 of the Constitution of India, 1960—subject matter of laws made by Parliament and by the Legislatures of States:

(1) Notwithstanding anything in clauses (2) and (3), Parliament has exclusive power to make laws with respect to any of the matters enumerated in List I in the Seventh Schedule (in this Constitution referred to as the Union List).
(2) Notwithstanding anything in clause (3), Parliament, and, subject to clause (1), the Legislature of any State also, have power to make laws with respect to any of the matters enumerated in List III in the Seventh Schedule (in this Constitution referred to as the Concurrent List).
(3) Parliament has power to make laws with respect to any matter for any part of the territory of India not included (in a State), notwithstanding that such matter is a matter enumerated in the State List.

6 The word "cognizable is spelled throughout this book using the American spelling because it is used as it appears in the CrPC. It is meant to be understood to have the same meaning as 'cognizable.'
7 Section 2(c) of the CrPC.
8 Section 156(3) CrPC.
9 Section 157(1) of the CrPC.
10 Article 227 of the Constitution of India: Power of superintendence over all courts by the High Court

(1) Every High Court shall have superintendence over all courts and tribunals throughout the territories interrelation to which it exercises jurisdiction.
(2) Without prejudice to the generality of the foregoing provisions, the High Court may
    (a) call for returns from such courts;
    (b) make and issue general rules and prescribe forms for regulating the practice and proceedings of such courts; and
    (c) prescribe forms in which books, entries, and accounts shall be kept by the officers of any such courts.
(3) The High Court may also settle tables of fees to be allowed to the sheriff and all clerks and officers of such courts and to attorneys, advocates and pleaders practising therein: Provided that any rules made, forms prescribed or tables settled under clause (2) or clause (3) shall not be inconsistent with the provision of any law for the time being in force, and shall require the previous approval of the Governor.
(4) Nothing in this article shall be deemed to confer on a High Court powers of superintendence over any court or tribunal constituted by or under any law relating to the Armed Forces

11 *Vinod Kumar Sethi v. The State of Punjab*, AIR 1982 P & H 372 (FB).
12 As discussed above under Section 154 of the CrPC.
13 As understood to refer to the record under Section 154(1) of the CrPC.
14 Section 154 of the CrPC: Information in cognizable cases

1. Every information relating to the commission of a cognizable offence, if given orally to an officer in charge of a police station, shall be reduced to writing by him or under his direction, and be read over to the informant; and every such information, whether given in writing or reduced to writing as aforesaid, shall be signed by the person giving it, and the substance thereof shall be entered in a book to be kept by such officer in such form as the State Government may prescribe in this behalf. Provided that if the information is given by the woman against whom an offence under section 326A, section 326B, section 354, section 354A, section 354B,

section 354C, section 354D, section 376, section 376A, section 376B, section 376C, 376D, section 376E or section 509 of the Indian Penal Code is alleged to have been committed or attempted, then such information shall be recorded, by a woman police officer or any woman officer; **Provided further** that—

1. in the event that the person against whom an offence under section 354, section 354A, section 354B, section 354C, section 354D, section 376, section 376A, section 376B, section 376C, section 376D, section 376E or section 509 of the Indian Penal Code is alleged to have been committed or attempted, is temporarily or permanently mentally or physically disabled, then such information shall be recorded by a police officer, at the residence of the person seeking to report such offence or at a convenient place of such person's choice, in the presence of an interpreter or a special educator, as the case may be;
2. the recording of such information shall be video graphed;
3. the police officer shall get the statement of the person recorded by a Judicial Magistrate under clause (a) of sub-section (5A) of section 164 as soon as possible.

2. A copy of the information as recorded under Sub-Section (1) shall be given forthwith, free of cost, to the informant.
3. Any person, aggrieved by a refusal on the part of an officer in charge of a police station to record the information referred to in Sub-Section (1) may send the substance of such information, in writing and by post, to the Superintendent of Police concerned who, if satisfied that such information discloses the commission of a cognizable offence, shall either investigate the case himself or direct an investigation to be made by any police officer subordinate to him, in the manner provided by this Code, and such officer shall have all the powers of an officer in charge of the police station in relation to that offence.

15 *Court on Its Own Motion v. The State* (2010) 175 DLT 110 (DB).
16 *Jitender Kumar v. State of Haryana* (2012) 6 SCC 204.
17 The police officer may deny registering an FIR in circumstances mandated by the Supreme Court of India or a High Court of any state.
18 Canada: Immigration and Refugee Board of Canada, *India: First Information Reports (FIRs), including procedures and time frames followed by police to inform complainants that an investigation will not be conducted*, 22 March 2011, IND103687.E, available at http://www.refworld.org/docid/50b48d9d2.html, accessed 16 March 2015.
19 Section 154(3) of the CrPC; 2007(8) SCC 226.
20 Only the following participants confirmed providing the suspect with an FIR; Interview Transcript PO3, 4, 5, 7, and 9.
21 The National Police Commission, Government of India, Fourth Report, June 1980, 1.
22 *Mabarak Ali Ahmed v. State of Bombay*, AIR 1957 SC 857.
23 Interview Transcript PO5.
24 N Shah and M Ganguly, *Broken Systems: Dysfunction, Abuse, and Impunity in the Indian Police*, Human Rights Watch, New York Publication, 2009.
25 NHRC, Manual on Human Rights for Police Officers, 2011, available at www.nhrc.nic.in/.../Manual_On_Human_Rights_for_Police_Officers.pdf, last accessed on 14 November 2015.
26 Ibid.
27 Ibid.

28 In response to a Right to Information request, the Office of Senior Superintendent of Police, Lucknow, stated that police failed to register FIRs for 30,356 complaints in 2006 and 26, 303 complaints in 2007. *Times of India*, "Police still reluctant to register FIRs," 26 July 2008.
29 S K Chaturvedi, 'Good Governance: Police and Human Rights' in Sweta Mishra et al. (eds), *Public Governance and Decentralisation*, New Delhi: Mittal Publications, 2003, 358.
30 *Broken System: Dysfunction, Abuse and Impunity in the Indian Police*, 2009, Human Rights Watch Report, available at http://www.hrw.org/sites/default/files/reports/india0809web.pdf, accessed on 24 January 2013.
31 Human Rights Watch interview with Dr. U.N.B. Rao, consultant for Delhi police, Delhi, December 3, 2008.
32 *Mohindro v. The State of Punjab*, 2001 Crim LJ 2587.
33 Ibid.
34 J Vadackumchery, *Indian Police and Miscarriage of Justice*, APH Publishing House, 1997, 29.
35 Ibid, 31.
36 See generally 152nd Law Commission Report, 177th Law Commission Report.
37 *D K Basu v. State of West Bengal* (1997) 1 SCC 216.
38 Ibid.
39 *Abhay Nath Dubey v. State of Delhi*, 2002 (2) Chand Cri 354(Delhi).
40 Delhi Police Manual, available at http://www.delhipolice.nic.in/home/rti/rti.aspx, last accessed on 12 September 2015.
41 Use of discretion under Section 157(b) of the CrPC.
42 N R Madhava Menon, 'Towards Making Criminal Justice Human Rights-Friendly: Policy Choices and Institutional Strategies' in C Raj Kumar and K Chockalingam (eds), *Human Rights, Justice and Constitutional Empowerment*, New Delhi: Oxford University Press, 2007, 420–436.
43 Interview Transcript PO5.
44 *State of Haryana v. Ch Bhajan Lal* AIR 1992 SC 604.
45 *B S Sundaresh v. State of Karnataka* 2012 (3) PLJR (SC) 258.
46 Human Rights Watch 2009, 9; *The Hindu* 31 December 2009; *Hindustan Times* 30 December 2009; The Press Trust of India 5 January 2010; Professor 3 March 2011.
47 See generally, *State of Haryana v. Ch. Bhajan Lal*, AIR 1992 SC 604; *Ramesh Kumari v. State of UP*, 2006(1) Crimes 230 (SC); *Lalan Choudhary v. State of Bihar*, 2007(1) BBCJ 205; *Lalita Kumari v. State of UP*, AIR 2014 SC 186 (F.B.).
48 K Mathur, 'Social Deviance and Marginal Crime in Police Organisations: How to Control the Police?' September 1994, in compilation of the lectures delivered at XXVI All India Police Science Congress, Hyderabad, 42.
49 Ibid, 42.
50 Section 155 of the CrPC:

(1) When information is given to an officer in charge of a police station of the commission within the limits of such station of a non-cognizable offence, he shall enter or cause to be entered the substance of the information in a book to be kept by such officer in such form as the State Government may prescribe in this behalf, and refer, the informant to the Magistrate.
(2) No police officer shall investigate a non-cognizable case without the order of a Magistrate having power to try such case or commit the case for trial.
(3) Any police officer receiving such order may exercise the same powers in respect of the investigation (except the power to arrest without warrant) as an officer in charge of a police station may exercise in a cognizable case.

(4) Where a case relates to two or more offences of which at least one is cognizable, the case shall be deemed to be a cognizable case, notwithstanding that the other offences are non-cognizable.

51 Section 156 (2) of the CrPC.
52 *Ramesh Kumari v. State of UP*, 2006(1) Crimes 230 (SC); *Lalan Choudhary v. State of Bihar*; 2007 (1) BBCJ 205.
53 *Mohammed Yousuf v. Afaq Jahan* 2006 CRI LJ 788.
54 Section 202(1) in The Code of Criminal Procedure, 1973.

(1) Any Magistrate, on receipt of a complaint of an offence of which he is authorised to take cognizance or which has been made over to him under Section 192, may, if he thinks fit, postpone the issue of process against the accused, and either inquire into the case himself or direct an investigation to be made by a police officer or by such other person as he thinks fit, for the purpose of deciding whether or not there is sufficient ground for proceeding: Provided that no such direction for investigation shall be made,
(a) where it appears to the Magistrate that the offence complained of is triable exclusively by the Court of Session; or
(b) where the complaint has not been made by a Court, unless the complainant and the witnesses present (if any) have been examined on oath under Section 200.

55 *Anil K Khandelwal v. Maksud Saiyed* 2006 CRI LJ 3180.
56 Ibid.
57 *Brij Lal Bhar v. State of UP*, 2006 CRI LJ 3334.
58 *Sukhveer Singh v. State of UP*, 2006 CRI LJ 4816.
59 CrPC (Amendment) Act 2005 (25 of 2005).
60 This list is not exhaustive but an inclusive list of duties set out for the police under various provisions of the CrPC.
61 *Malimath Committee Report: Committee on Reforms of Criminal Justice System,* Government of India, 2003, mha.nic.in/pdfs/criminal_justice_system.pdf, recommendation no. 28–30.
62 A Mehra, *Police, State and Society: Perspectives from India and France*, Dorling Kindersley (India) Pvt Ltd., 2011, 210.
63 *Amnesty International, India: Report of the Malimath Committee on Reforms of the Criminal Justice System: Some Observations*, 19 September 2003, ASA 20/025/2003, available at http://www.unhcr.org/refworld/docid/3f914cba4.html
64 Section 1 of the Code of Criminal Procedure, 1973.
65 Article 19 of the Constitution of India: "Protection of certain rights regarding freedom of speech etc.

(1) All citizens shall have the right
(a) to freedom of speech and expression;
(b) to assemble peaceably and without arms;
(c) to form associations or unions;
(d) to move freely throughout the territory of India; and
(e) to reside and settle in any part of the territory of India."

66 *State of Haryana v. Dinesh Kumar* AIR 2008 SC 1083.
67 *Niranjan Singh v. Prabhakar* AIR 1980 SC 785.
68 Article 22 of the Constitution of India, 1960.
69 These duties include the amendments made by the Code of Criminal Procedure (Amendment) Act, 2008.
70 *H N Rishbud and Inder Singh v. The State of Delhi*, 1995 (1) SCR 1150.

71 Interview Transcript PO 14.
72 *Joginder Kumar v. The State of UP* 1994 AIR 1349, para 21 of the judgement.
73 *D K Basu v. State of West Bengal* (1997) 1 SCC 216.
74 *D K Basu v. State of West Bengal* (1997) 1 SCC 216, para 35.
75 This provision was under Section 173(4) of the Code of Criminal Procedure, 1898.
76 *K Veeraswami v. Union of India*, 1991 3 SCC 655.
77 The cases under the provision of Section 173(4) of the Code of Criminal Procedure, 1898.
78 **Section 50 of the CrPC: Person arrested to be informed of grounds of arrest and of right to bail.**

(1) Every police officer or other person arresting any person without warrant shall forthwith communicate to him full particulars of the offence for which he is arrested or other grounds for such arrest.
(2) Where a police officer arrests without warrant any person other than a person accused of a non-bailable offence, he shall inform the person arrested that he is entitled to be released on bail and that he may arrange for sureties on his behalf.

79 The 152nd Law Commission Report, 1994.
80 *Vikram v. The State* 1996 Crim LJ 1536.
81 Interview Transcript PO 13.
82 *Gauri Shankar v. State of Bihar*, AIR 1972 SC 711.
83 Each state has a different language. Each police department in every state implements this rule in their state guidelines to be followed by all officers.
84 **Section 50A of the Criminal Procedure Code: obligation of person making arrest to inform about the arrest, etc., to a nominated person**

1. Every police officer or other person making any arrest under this Code shall forthwith give the information regarding such arrest and place where the arrested person is being held to any of his friends; relatives or such other persons as may be disclosed or nominated by the arrested person for the purpose of giving such information.
2. The police officer shall inform the arrested person of his rights under subsection (1) as soon as he is brought to the police station.
3. An entry of the fact as to who has been informed of the arrest of such person shall be made in a book to be kept in the police station in such form as may be prescribed on this behalf by the State Government.
4. It shall be the duty of the Magistrate before whom such arrested person is produced, to satisfy himself that the requirements of Sub-Section (2) and Sub-Section (3) have been complied with in respect of such arrested person.

85 *D K Basu v. State of West Bengal*, AIR 1997 SC 610.
86 *Joginder Kumar v. State of UP* AIR 1994 SC 467, proposition (e).
87 For a state-wise ratio of illiteracy, please refer to http://censusindia.gov.in/Census_And_You/literacy_and_level_of_education.aspx, accessed on 29 March 2015.
88 See generally; *Joginder Kumar v. State of UP* AIR 1994 SC 467, *D K Basu v. State of West Bengal*, AIR 1997 SC 610, *Madhu Limaye v. The State of Maharashtra*, AIR 1978 47.
89 Interview Transcript PO3.
90 The provisions as mentioned above are contained under Section 53, 53A and 54 of the CrPC, respectively.
91 *D K Basu v. State of West Bengal*, AIR 1997 SC 610, para 39.8.
92 Interview Transcript 3, 4, 9, and 12.

93 Interview Transcript 14.
94 Article 22(2) of the Constitution of India 1949:

> Every person who is arrested and detained in custody shall be produced before the nearest magistrate within a period of twenty-four hours of such arrest excluding the time necessary for the journey from the place of arrest to the court of the magistrate and no such person shall be detained in custody beyond the said period without the authority of a magistrate.

95 Article 22(2) of the Constitution of India 1949:

> Every person who is arrested and detained in custody shall be produced before the nearest magistrate within a period of twenty-four hours of such arrest excluding the time necessary for the journey from the place of arrest to the court of the magistrate and no such person shall be detained in custody beyond the said period without the authority of a magistrate.

96 B Uma Devi, *Arrest, Detention, and Criminal Justice System: A Study in the Context of the Constitution of India*, OUP, 2012, 64.
97 Ibid.
98 The term production of the person arrested is used throughout the CrPC and the Constitution of India with the intention of physically bringing the suspect before a magistrate.
99 Section 56 in the Code of Criminal Procedure, 1973:

> Person arrested to be taken before Magistrate or officer in charge of police station. A police officer making an arrest without warrant shall, without unnecessary delay and subject to the provisions herein contained as to bail, take or send the person arrested before a Magistrate having jurisdiction in the case, or before the officer in charge of a police station.

100 152nd Law Commission Report on Custodial Crimes, 1994.
101 B Uma Devi, *Arrest, Detention, and Criminal Justice System: A Study in the Context of the Constitution of India*, OUP, 2012, 58.
102 152nd Law Commission Report on Custodial Crimes, 1994, p. 94.
103 Interview Transcript PO7.
104 Section 217 of the Indian Penal Code

> Public servant disobeying direction of law with intent to save person from punishment or property from forfeiture—Whoever, being a public servant, knowingly disobeys any direction of the law as to the way in which he is to conduct himself as such public servant, intending thereby to save, or knowing it to be likely that he will thereby save, any person from legal punishment, or subject him to a less punishment than that to which he is liable, or with intent to save, or knowing that he is likely thereby to save, any property from forfeiture or any charge to which it is liable by law, shall be punished with imprisonment of either description for a term which may extend to two years, or with fine, or with both.

105 *Joginder Kumar v. State of UP* AIR 1994 SC 467.
106 *D K Basu v. State of West Bengal* (1997) 1 SCC 216.
107 *Arnesh Kumar v. State of Bihar & Anr*, Criminal Appeal No. 1277 of 2014 on 2 July, 2014.
108 As reported by the *Times of India*, 'Businessmen held "improperly": Court sees red, available at http://timesofindia.indiatimes.com/city/mumbai/Businessmen

-held-improperly-court-sees-red/articleshow/45862067.cms, accessed on 24th March 2015.

109 See generally; Bombay Police Act, 1951, Karnataka Police Act, 1963 and Delhi Police Act, 1978.

110 *Malimath Committee Report: Committee on Reforms of Criminal Justice System,* Government of India, 2003, mha.nic.in/pdfs/criminal_justice_system.pdf, accessed on 12 February 2013.

111 Human Rights Watch interview with Srikumar, Director General of Police in 2008, Bangalore, 9 December 2008.

112 Interview Transcript PO12.

113 See generally; NHRC, *Manual on Human Rights for Police Officers*, 2011, available at www.nhrc.nic.in/.../Manual_on_Human_Rights_for_Police_Officers.pdf, last accessed on 14 November 2015.

114 *State of Gujarat v. Kishanbhai*, 2014 Indlaw SC 11, para 20.

115 Interview Transcript PO8.

116 Professional Policing, National Human Rights Commission, available at http://nhrc.nic.in/Documents/Publications/ProfessionalPolicing.pdf, last accessed on 2 March 2015.

117 *State of Delhi v. Ashok Kumar Jain*, 2014 Indlaw DEL 707.

118 Ibid, para 9–11.

119 J Vadackumchery, *Indian Police and Miscarriage of Justice*, APH Publishing House, 1997.

120 Human Rights Watch interview, details withheld, Uttar Pradesh, January 8, 2009.

121 *State of Gujarat v. Kishanbhai* case, as reported in 2014 Indlaw SC 11, paragraph 18.

122 Interview Transcript PO 13.

123 Human Rights Watch interview, details withheld, Uttar Pradesh, January 8, 2009, 32.

124 Ibid.

125 As highlighted by the courts in the case of *State of Gujarat v. Kishanbhai* case, as reported in 2014 Indlaw SC 11.

126 Ibid, para 20.

127 These issues generally include rape, dowry death and sexual harassment.

128 A Verma and S Gavirneni, 'Measuring Police Efficiency in India: An Application of Data Envelopment Analysis' (2006) 29 *Policing: An International Journal of Police Strategies & Management* 125–145 doi: 10.1108/13639510610648520, accessed on: 18 March 2015.

129 Police (Rupees 46,390.26 crore), in 2014, available at indiabudget.nic.in/ub2014-15/eb/npe.pdf, accessed on 2 April 2015.

130 See generally; *S. R. Subramanian and Others v. Union of India and Others*, 2013; Indlaw SC 722; AIR 2014 SC 263.

131 Interview Transcript PO1.

132 Interview Transcript PO4.

133 Interview Transcript PO6.

134 Interview Transcript PO7.

135 Interview Transcript PO5.

136 Interview Transcript PO3.

137 This was mentioned in the first report produced by the Ribeiro Committee in 1979.

138 Commonwealth Human Rights Initiative Analysis of the Ribeiro Commission, available at http://www.humanrightsinitiative.org/index.php?option=com_content&view=article&catid=91%3Ashiva&id=753%3Asummary-of-ribeiro-committees-recommendations&Itemid=100, 1998-1999, accessed on 12 March 2015.

139 Ibid.
140 Ibid.
141 The Padmanabhaiah Committee on Police Reforms Report, Human Rights Initiative, available at http://www.humanrightsinitiative.org/index.php?option=com_content&view=article&catid=91%3Ashiva&id=687%3Apolice-india-padmanabhai-committee&Itemid=100, accessed on 12 May 2015, para 5.6.2.
142 J Umrishankar, *A Sisyphean Saga, Functional Review of the Indian Police: A Step towards Good Governance*, Ameya Inspiring Books, India, 2009, 64.
143 Interview Transcript PO14.
144 *Malimath Committee Report: Committee on Reforms of Criminal Justice System,* Government of India, 2003, mha.nic.in/pdfs/criminal_justice_system.pdf, accessed on 12 February 2013, para 2.19.4.
145 Ibid, para 2.7.9.
146 Ibid, para 7.12.
147 Ibid, para 7.9.6.
148 Soli Sorabji Committee Report on Model Police Act, Chapter XI, available at http://www.humanrightsinitiative.org/index.php?option=com_content&view=article&catid=35%3Apolice-reforms&id=600%3Athe-police-act-drafting-committee&Itemid=98, accessed on 2 April 2015.
149 Soli Sorabji Committee Report on Model Police Act, Chapter XI, available at http://www.humanrightsinitiative.org/index.php?option=com_content&view=article&catid=35%3Apolice-reforms&id=600%3Athe-police-act-drafting-committee&Itemid=98, accessed on 2 April 2015.
150 J Umrishankar, *A Sisyphean Saga, Functional Review of the Indian Police: A Step towards Good Governance*, Ameya Inspiring Books, India, 2009, 64.
151 Ibid.
152 Ibid, 63.
153 U Baxi, *The Malimath Committee on Reforms of Criminal Justice System: Premises, Politics and Implications for Human Rights,* mentioned in A Mehra and R Levy, *The Police, the State, & Society: Perspectives from India and France*, Pearson Publication, India, 2011.
154 Commonwealth Human Rights Initiative Analysis of the Sorabji Commission, available at http://www.humanrightsinitiative.org/index.php?option=com_content&view=article&catid=35%3Apolice-reforms&id=600%3Athe-police-act-drafting-committee&Itemid=98, accessed on 2 April 2015.
155 J Belur, N. Tilley, D Osrin, N Daruwalla, M Kumar, and V Tiwari, 'Police Investigations: Discretion Denied yet Undeniably Exercised' (2014) *Policing and Society: An International Journal of Research and Policy*, available at doi: 10.1080/10439463.2013.878343, viewed on 12 March 2015.
156 J Umrishankar, *A Sisyphean Saga, Functional Review of the Indian Police: A Step towards Good Governance*, Ameya Inspiring Books, India, 2009, 63.
157 Commonwealth Human Rights Initiative Analysis of the Sorabji Commission, available at http://www.humanrightsinitiative.org/index.php?option=com_content&view=article&catid=35%3Apolice-reforms&id=600%3Athe-police-act-drafting-committee&Itemid=98, accessed on 2 April 2015.
158 P Alexander, 'Governance, Policing, and Human Rights', in *Policing India in the New Millennium* 337, 2002, 100.
159 A Verma, *The New Khakhi: The Evolving Nature of Policing in India (Advances in Police Theories and Practice)*, CRC Press, Taylor and Francis Group, 2012.
160 *Vineet Narayan v. Union of India* 1998(1) SCC 226.
161 Ibid, para 5.5, Summary of recommendations.
162 *Vineet Narayan v. Union of India* 1998(1) SCC 226, Section III, Para 5.
163 The Seven Directives are summarised by Thakur and Sharma, 'Myths and Realities in Police Reforms in India' (2013) *Indian Police Journal*, Table 3:

Supreme Court Directives of 22nd September, 2006 in *Prakash Singh and Others v. Union of India and Others* Directives:

1. Constitute a State Security Commission to (i) ensure that state governments does not exercise unwarranted influence or pressure on the police, (ii) lay down broad policy guidelines, and (iii) evaluate the performance of the state police.
2. Ensure that the Director General of Police is appointed through a merit-based, transparent process and enjoys a minimum tenure of two years.
3. Ensure that other police officers on operational duties (including Superintendents of Police in-charge of a district and Station House Officers in-charge of a police station) also have a minimum tenure of two years, 20 April-June, 2013.
4. Set up a Police Establishment Board, which will decide all transfers, postings, promotions and other service-related matters of police officers of and below the rank of Deputy Superintendent of Police and make recommendations on postings and transfers of officers above the rank of Deputy Superintendent of police.
5. Set up a National Security Commission at the union level to prepare a panel for selection and placement of Chiefs of the Central Police Organizations (CPO), who should also be given a minimum tenure of two years.
6. Set up independent Police Complaints Authorities at the state and district levels to look into public complaints against police officers in cases of serious misconduct, including custodial death, grievous hurt or rape in police custody.
7. Separate the investigation and law and order functions of the police

164 *Prakash Singh v. Union of India* Writ Petition (civil) 310 of 1996.
165 Special Provisions under Article 38 of the Constitution of India promote the Directives Principles of State Policy.
166 Commonwealth Human Rights Initiative (2007), Police Reform, Debates in India, New Delhi, April.
167 The term Union is used to refer to the nation. India is a Union of States. This term is used in the Constitution of India, Part 1, Schedule 1.
168 Commonwealth Human Rights Initiative (2007), Police Reform, Debates in India, New Delhi, April, 42–46.
169 Ibid.
170 Interview Transcript PO3.
171 The Committee did not have the time to visit all the states in the country, as a result of which the Committee visited four main states: Maharashtra (west), Uttar Pradesh (north), Karnataka (south) and West Bengal (east).
172 *Prakash Singh v. Union of India* Writ Petition (civil) 310 of 1996.
173 Commonwealth Human Rights Initiative (2007), Police Reform, Debates in India, New Delhi, April.
174 Commonwealth Human Rights Initiative, Police Complaints Authority in India: A Rapid Study, 2011, available at http://www.humanrightsinitiative.org/index.php?option=com_content&view=article&id=182&Itemid=511, accessed on 20 March 2015.
175 As observed above, many states seek time to implement these, while others have complained against the directives calling them unpractical. Many other states are yet to be accounted for. A full study is ongoing on this topic.
176 Inferred from the Interview Transcript PO1.
177 Interview Transcripts of PO1, PO2, PO6, PO7, PO10 and PO13.
178 Interview Transcript PO7.
179 Interview Transcript PO4.

180 *Leonard Valdaris v. The Officer in Charge* Writ Petition no. 2110 of 2014.
181 Ibid, para 4; and L Hempel and E Topfer, 'Urban Eye: Final Report to the European Commission' 5th Framework Programme, Berlin: Technical University of Berlin, (2004), available at: http://www.urbaneye.net/results/ue_wp15.pdf, accessed on 2 February 2015.
182 Ibid, para 9.
183 Interview Transcript PO3.
184 Interview Transcript PO5 and PO8.
185 P Scott, *The Jewel in the Crown*, New York: William Morrow Publications, 1966, 140.
186 Ibid, 131.
187 Ibid, 203.
188 S Karthikeyan, 'Foreword' in A Reddy's (ed.), *Dimensions of Crime and Corruption in India*, New Delhi: Serial Publication, 2005, vi.
189 D Bailey, *Police and Political Development in India,* New Jersey: Princeton University Press, 1969, 280.
190 Ibid, 283.
191 For information on corruption, see TI-India (TII), see Transparency International India, http://www.transparencyindia.org/, accessed on 12 March 2015.
192 CHRI, Police Complaints Authority in India: A Rapid Study, available at http://www.humanrightsinitiative.org/index.php?option=com_content&view=article&id=182&Itemid=511, 2012.
193 L Palmier, *The Control of Bureaucratic Corruption: Case Studies in Asia*, New Delhi: Allied Publishers, 1985, 272.
194 S Afzal Qadri, 'Police Corruption: An Analysis' (1994) 22(1) *Indian Journal of Criminology* 5–8.
195 Interview Transcript PO1 and PO3.
196 P Alexander, 'Governance, Policing, and Human Rights', in *Policing India in the New Millennium* 337, ed., 2002, 103.
197 K Tummala, 'Corruption in India: Control Measures and Consequences', 2002, 10(2) *Asian Journal of Political Science* 43–69, 64.
198 N Shah and M Ganguly, *Broken Systems: Dysfunction, Abuse, and Impunity in the Indian Police*, Human Rights Watch, New York Publication, 2009.
199 Interview Transcript PO5.
200 D Bayle, *The Police and Political Development in India*, Princeton: Princeton University Press, 1969.
201 A Verma, 'Politicization of the Police in India: Where Lies the Blame?' (2000) XLVII(4) *Indian Police Journal* 19–37.
202 *State of Delhi v. Ashok Kumar Jain*, 2014 Indlaw DEL 707.
203 *Prakash Singh v. Union of India* Writ Petition (civil) 310 of 1996.
204 J Belur, 'Police Shootings: Perceived Culture of Approval' in N Unnithan (ed.), *Crime and Justice in India*, OUP, 2012, 220.
205 This was set up under the Protection of Human Rights Act, 1993. This commission was set up at a national level under the same act.
206 Sections 11 and 12 of the Protection of Human Rights Act, 1993.
207 CHRI, Police Complaints Authority in India: A Rapid Study, available at http://www.humanrightsinitiative.org/index.php?option=com_content&view=article&id=182&Itemid=511, 2012
208 *Prakash Singh v. Union of India* Writ Petition (civil) 310 of 1996.
209 Under the Model Police Act, enforced by way of the State Police Commission.
210 National Police Commission "Third Report," para. 22.24, quoted in the Law Commission of India, "177th Report on Law Relating to Arrest," 50.
211 The term interview appears in the Police and Criminal Evidence Act but has been used interchangeably with interrogation.

212 See generally; http://www.nationalarchives.gov.uk/education/candp/preventio n/g08/g08cs2.html and http://content.met.police.uk/Article/The-Metropolitan -Police-how-it-all-began/1400015336362/1400015336362.
213 The Birmingham Six, The Guildford Four, The Cardiff Three, to name but a few of these cases.
214 Brought about by the enactment of the Police and Criminal Evidence Act, 1984.
215 Empirical studies carried out by S Moston, G Stephenson, and T Williamson, 'The Effects of Case Characteristics on Suspect Behaviour during Police Questioning' (1992) 32 *British Journal of Criminology* 33; and J Baldwin, 'Police Interview Techniques: Establishing Truth or Proof?' (1993) 33(3) *British Journal of Criminology* 325–352.
216 Introduction of the Planning & Preparation, Engage & Explain, Account, Closure, and Evaluation, acronym for the PEACE model.
217 S Kassin and G Gudjonsson, 'The Psychology of Confessions: A Review of the Literature and Issues' (2004) 5 *Psychological Science in the Public Interest* 33–67.
218 A Ashworth and M Redmayne, *The Criminal Process*, 3rd edn, OUP, 2004, 3; L Campbell, A Ashworth, and M Redmayne, *The Criminal Process*, 5th edn, 2019.
219 A Sanders and R Young, *Criminal Justice*, OUP, 2007.
220 C Phillips, *Royal Commission on Criminal Procedure, the Investigation and Prosecution of Criminal Offences in England and Wales*; The Law and Procedure 1981, para 4.2.
221 P Softley et al., *Police Interrogation: An Observational Study in Four Police Stations*, Home Office Research Study No. 61, April 1980, available at http://library.npia.police.uk/docs/hors/hors61.pdf
222 This was observed in areas such as Birmingham, Handsworth, Brixton and Notting Hill during the period of 1970–1985.
223 B Wilding, in E Cape and R Young, *Regulating Policing, the Police and Criminal Evidence Act 1984: Past, Present and Future*, Hart Publishing, 2008, 124; A Choo, *Evidence*, 5th edn, OUP, 2018.
224 Ibid, 125.
225 V Sithannan, *Police Investigation: Powers, Tactics, and Techniques*, Chennai: Jeywin Publication, 2013.
226 The Birmingham Six, The Guildford Four, The Cardiff Three, to name but a few of these cases.
227 Interview Transcript PO2.
228 M Coulthard, 'Suppressed Dialogue in a Confession Statement' in M Coulthard, J Cotterill, and F Rock (eds), *Dialogue Analysis VII: Working with Dialogue*, Tübingen: Max Niemeyer Verlag, 2000, 417–424.
229 E Cape and R Young, *Regulating Policing: The Police and Criminal Evidence Act 1984 Past, Present and Future*, Hart Publishing, 2008, 93.
230 M Zander, 'PACE (The Police and Criminal Evidence Act, 1984): Past, Present, and Future' 2011 LSE Legal Studies Working Paper 1–14; A Choo, *Evidence*, 5th edn, OUP, 2018.
231 Criminal Law Revision Committee, *Evidence (General)*, Cmnd 4991 (1972).
232 M Zander, 'The CLRC Evidence Report: A Survey of Reactions' (7 October 1974) *Law Society's Gazette*.
233 Royal Commission on Criminal Procedure, Report Cmnd 8092 (1981).
234 Report of an inquiry by the Hon. Sir Henry Fisher into the circumstances leading to trial of three persons accused of causing the death of Maxwell Confait and the fire at 27 Doggett Road, London, 1977.
235 Royal Commission on Criminal Procedure, Report Cmnd 8092 (1981), 20.
236 PACE Section 24.
237 J Baldwin, 'Police Interview Techniques: Establishing Truth or Proof?' (1993) 33(3) *British Journal of Criminology* 325–352.

238 D Brown, *PACE: 10 Years On: A Review of the Research*, library.npia.police.uk/docs/hors/hors155.pdf
239 Ibid.
240 The Birmingham Six, The Guildford Four, The Cardiff Three, to name but a few of these cases.
241 The only legislation is the Model Police Act, which is still not implemented even after nine years of the judgement where the recommendation was made.
242 M Zander, 'PACE (The Police and Criminal Evidence Act, 1984): Past, Present, and Future' 2011 LSE Legal Studies Working Paper 1–14.
243 K Roberts, 'Police Interviewing of Criminal Suspects: A Historical Perspective' (2012) *Internet Journal of Criminology*, available at http://www.internetjournalofcriminology.com/, accessed on 14 April 2015.
244 The Runciman Committee Report, available at https://www.gov.uk/government/uploads/system/uploads/.../2263.pdf.
The National Police Commission, Government of India, Fourth Report, June 1991, accessed on 9 March 2014.
245 RCCP, *Report of the Royal Commission on Criminal Justice*, London: HMSO, 1993.
246 B Wilding, in E Cape and R Young, *Regulating Policing: The Police and Criminal Evidence Act 1984: Past, Present and Future*, Hart Publishing, 2008, 126.
247 The Seven-Point Directive by the Supreme Court in *Prakash Singh v. Union of India,* Writ Petition (civil) 310 of 1996.
248 A Choo, *Evidence*, 5th edn, OUP, 2018.
249 C Meissner, A Redlich, S Bhatt, and S Brandon, 'Interview and Interrogation Methods and Their Effects on True and False Confessions' (2012–2013) *Campbell Systematic Reviews*, Campbell Collaboration.
250 Section 1 of the Magistrate's Court Act, 1980.
251 Non-cognizable offences under Section 2 (1) of the CrPC.
252 Section 24 of PACE.
253 There is no clear definition as to what constitutes reasonable suspicion, but there is an elaborate mention of this provision under Section 2 of PACE Codes of Practice A.
254 *Hayes v. CC Merseyside Police* (2011) EWCA Civ 911.
255 *Richardson v. CC West Midlands Police* (2011) EWHC 773.
256 Quinton et al., Police Research Paper Series 2000.
257 Section 37(2) of PACE.
258 F Inbau, J Reid, and J Buckley, *Criminal Interrogation and Confessions*, 5th edn, Jones and Bartlett Publishers, 2011.
259 Ibid.
260 Ibid.
261 Ibid.
262 Code of Practice C, para 11.
263 Section 34 of PACE.
264 Code of Practice G, para 3.
265 Code of Practice G, para 3.5. Originally contained in PACE Code C Section 10. The wordings are as follows:

> "You do not have to say anything. But it may harm your defence if you do not mention when questioned something which you later rely on in Court. Anything you do say may be given in evidence."
> Where the use of the Welsh Language is appropriate, a constable may provide the caution directly in Welsh in the following terms:

"Does dim rhaid i chi ddweud dim byd. Ond gall niweidio eich amddiffyniad os na fyddwch chi'n sôn, wrth gael eich holi, am rywbeth y byddwch chi'n dibynnu arno nes ymlaen yn y Llys. Gall unrhyw beth yr ydych yn ei ddweud gael ei roi fel tystiolaeth."

266 *R v. Fulling* 1987 2 All E R 65; *R v. Bryce* 1992 4 All E R 567.
267 J Cotterill, *Language and Power in Court: A Linguistic Analysis of the O J Simpson Trial*, Basingstoke: Palgrave Macmillan, 2003.
268 S Fenner, G Gudjonsson, and I Claire, 'Understanding of the Current Police Caution (England and Wales) among Suspects in Police Detention' (2002) 12 *Journal of Community & Applied Social Psychology* 83–93.
269 Ibid, 85.
270 I Clare, G Gudjonsson, and P Harari, 'Understanding of the Current Police Caution (England and Wales)' (1998) 8 *Journal of Community & Applied Social Psychology* 323–329.
271 S Kassin and G Gudjonsson, 'The Psychology of Confessions: A Review of the Literature and Issues' (2004) 5 *Psychological Science in the Public Interest* 33–67.
272 Code of Practice 3.1.
273 Section 37(7) of PACE.
274 Sections 76 and 78 of PACE.
275 Section 56 PACE.
276 Section 56(5) of PACE.
277 Section 56(2)(3) of PACE.
278 E Cape, Z Namoradze, R Smith, and T Spronken, *Effective Criminal Defence in Europe*, Antwerp: Intersentia, 2007.
279 *Joginder Kumar v. State of UP* AIR 1994 SC 467.
280 *D K Basu v. State of West Bengal* (1997) 1 SCC 216.
281 Ibid, *Prakash Singh v. Union of India* (2009) 17 SCC 329.
282 Codes of Practice C, Annex G, Part 4.
283 Code of Practice C, para 13.1.
284 Code of Practice C, para 13.5.
285 Code of Practice C, para 13.9.
286 J Blackstock, E Cape, J Hodgson, A Ogordova, and T Spronken, *Inside Police Custody: An Empirical Account of Suspects' Rights in Four Jurisdictions*, Intersentia, 2014, 147.
287 The Law Society 2011, available at http://www.lawsociety.org.uk/support-services/advice/practice-notes/interpreters-in-criminal-cases/.
288 Law Society, Use of Interpreters in Criminal Cases, 2012, available at http://www.lawsociety.org.uk/support-services/advice/practice-notes/interpreters-in-criminal-cases/, accessed on 12 April 2014.
289 Under the provision of Section 76 and 78 of PACE.
290 Code of Practice C.
291 *R v. Bryce* 1992 4 All E R 567.
292 Translated to mean 'Who will keep watch over the guardians?' In this case, the reference is made to the police officers as the guardians of the public safety and custody.
293 A Goldsmith, 'New Directions in Police Complaints Procedures: Some Conceptual and Comparative Departures' (1988) 11(1) *Police Studies* 60–71.
294 See generally; www.ipcc.gov.uk
295 As mentioned in the statutory guidance provided by the IPCC. For further details. please see www.ipcc.gov.uk.
296 Commissioner Davies' Key decision speech, available at http://www.ipcc.gov.uk/news/ipcc-publishes-commissioner-tom-davies-key-decisions-lynette-white.

297 M Seneviratne, 'Policing the Police in the United Kingdom' (2004) 14(4) *Policing and Society: An International Journal of Research and Policy* 329–347.
298 A Goldsmith, 'New Directions in Police Complaints Procedures: Some Conceptual and Comparative Departures' (1988) 11(1) *Police Studies* 60–71.
299 A Goldsmith, 'Necessary But Not Sufficient: The Role of Public Complaints Procedures in Police Accountability' in C Stenning (ed.), *Accountability for Criminal Justice*, Toronto: University of Toronto Press, 1995, 110–134.
300 Corruption in the police services in England and Wales: Second Report—A Report Based on the IPCC's Experience from 2008 to 2011, May 2012, London, available at http://www.official-documents.gov.uk/, last accessed on 15 May 2016.
301 M Seneviratne, 'Policing the Police in the United Kingdom' (2004) 14(4) *Policing and Society: An International Journal of Research and Policy* 329–347.
302 T May, H Warburton, and I Hearnden, 'Appellants', Complainants', and Police Officers' Satisfaction with the Independent Police Complaints Commission' The Institute of Criminal Policy Research, available at www.nao.org.uk/wp-content/uploads/2008/11/ipcc.pdf, accessed on 22 April 2015.
303 K Reid, 'Current Developments in Police Accountability' (2002) 66(2) *Journal of Criminal Law* 172–195.
304 M Seneviratne, 'Policing the Police in the United Kingdom' (2004) 14(4) *Policing and Society: An International Journal of Research and Policy* 329–347.
305 F Millen and M Stephens, 'Policing and Accountability: The Working of Police Authorities' (2011) 21(3) *Policing and Society: An International Journal of Research and Policy* 265–283.
306 The Police Ombudsman of Northern Ireland (PONI) system in Northern Ireland.
307 Review of IPCC's involvement in relation to cases involving death, available at https://www.ipcc.gov.uk/page/review-ipccs-work-relation-cases-involving-death, accessed on 18 April 2015.
308 NHRC, *Manual on Human Rights for Police Officers*, 2011, available at www.nhrc.nic.in/.../Manual_On_Human_Rights_for_Police_Officers.pdf, last accessed on 14 November 2015.
309 Ibid.
310 Code of Practice E and F.
311 S Jones, 'The Police and Criminal Evidence Act, 1984' (Nov 1985) 48 *The Modern Law Review* 679–693.
312 J Baldwin, 'Police Interview Techniques: Establishing Truth or Proof?' (1993) 33(3) *British Journal of Criminology* 325–352.
313 Ibid.
314 Ibid.
315 Ibid.
316 J Baldwin, 'Police Interviews on Tape' (1990) 11 *New Law Journal* 662, 663.
317 T Kaye, 'Unsafe and Unsatisfactory? Report of the Independent Inquiry into the Working Practices of West Midlands Police Serious Crime Squad, London, Civil Liberties Trust 1991', available at https://www.ncjrs.gov/App/Publications/abstract.aspx?ID=134391, accessed on 13 April 2015.
318 M Hartwig, P Granhag, and A Vrij, 'Police Interrogation from a Social Psychology Perspective', 2005, 15 *Policing and Society* 379–399.
319 T Williamson, 'Strategic Changes in Police Interrogation; An Examination of Police and Suspect Behaviour in the Metropolitan Police in Order to Determine the Effects of New Legislation, Technology, and Organisational Policies' unpublished thesis, University of Kent, Faculty of Social Sciences.
320 *Leonard Valdaris v. The Officer in Charge* Writ Petition no. 2110 of 2014.

321 J Baldwin, 'Police Interview Techniques: Establishing Truth or Proof?' (1993) 33(3) *British Journal of Criminology* 325–352.
322 S Moston and T Engelberg, 'Police Questioning Techniques in Tape Recorded Interviews with Criminal Suspects' (1993) 3 *Policing and Society* 223–237.
323 V Kemp, '"No Time for a Solicitor": Implications for Delays on the Take-Up of Legal Advice' (2013) 3 *Criminal Law Review* 184–202; J Blackstock, E Cape, J Hodgson, A Ogordova, and T Spronken, *Inside Police Custody: An Empirical Account of Suspects' Rights in Four Jurisdictions*, Intersentia, 2014, 374.
324 G Gudjonsson, *The Psychology of Interrogation and Confessions: A Handbook*, Chichester: Wiley, 2003.
325 R Milne and R Bull, 'Interviewing by the Police' in D Carson and R Bull (eds), *Handbook of Psychology in Legal Contexts*, Chichester: Wiley, 2003.
326 E Shepherd, A Mortimer, V Turner, and J Watson, 'Spaced Cognitive Interviewing: Facilitating Therapeutic and Forensic Narration of Trauma Memories' (1999) 5 *Psychology, Crime & Law* 117–143.
327 A Shawyer, R Milne, and R Bull, 'Investigative Interviewing in the UK' in T Williamson, B Milne, and S P Savage (eds), *International Developments in Investigative Interviewing*, Cullompton: Willan, 2009.
328 ACPO, 'National Investigative Strategy' NPIA, Briefing Paper, HMSO, 2009.
329 G Gudjonsson, *The Psychology of Interrogation and Confessions: A Handbook*, Chichester: Wiley, 2003, 55.
330 Ibid.
331 A Griffiths and B Milne, 'Will It All End in Tiers? Recent Developments in Police Interviews with Suspects in Britain' in T Williamson (ed.), *Investigative Interviewing: Rights, Research, Regulation*, Cullompton: Willan, 2006.
332 C Clarke, R Milne, and R Bull, 'Interviewing Suspects of Crime: The Impact of PEACE Training, Supervision and the Presence of a Legal Advisor' (2011) 8 *Journal of Investigative Psychology and Offender Profiling* 149–162.
333 *Murray v. DPP* 1993 Cr. APP. REP. 151, para 55.
334 PACE Code of Practice C.
335 T Bingham, *The Rule of Law*, Penguin Publication, 2010.
336 C Murphy, 'Lon Fuller and the Moral Value of the Rule of Law' (2005) 24 *Law and Philosophy* 239–262.
337 Ibid.
338 L Fuller, *Morality of Law*, revised edition, New Haven: Yale University Press, 1969.
339 H Packer, *The Limits of the Criminal Sanction* by Herbert L. Packer, Stanford University Press, 1968.
340 D Bayley, 'Law Enforcement and the Rule of Law: Is There a Tradeoff?' (November 2002) 2(1) *Criminology and Public Policy* 133–154.
341 R Crawshaw, *Police and Human Rights: A Manual for Teachers, Resource Persons, and Participants in Human Rights Programme*, Martinus Nijhoff Publishers, 1999.
342 Scarman, *The Brixton Disorders 10–12 April 1981*. Cmnd 8427. London: Her Majesty's Stationary Office, 1981.
343 L Macpherson, *The Stephen Lawrence Inquiry*. Cm 4262-I. London: The Stationary Office, 1999.
344 D Carlson, *When Cultures Clash: Strategies for Strengthening Police-Community Relations*, 2nd edn, Upper Saddle River: Pearson/Prentice Hall, 2005.
345 S Culhane, H Hosch, and C Heck, 'Interrogation Technique Endorsement by Current Law Enforcement, Future Law Enforcement, and Laypersons' (2008) 11(3) *Police Quarterly* 366–386.

346 D Narby, B Cutler, and G Morgan, 'A Met-Analysis of the Association between Authoritarianism and Jurors' Perceptions of Defendant Culpability' (1993) 78 *Journal of Applied Psychology* 34–42.
347 Ibid.
348 F Millen and M Stephens, 'Policing and Accountability: The Working of Police Authorities' (2011) 21(3) *Policing and Society: An International Journal of Research and Policy* 265–283.
349 This is with reference to the introduction of the Police Reform Act 2002.
350 K Balagopal, 'Terrorism of the Police Kind' (July-August 2007) 6(4) *Combat Law*.
351 K Davis, *Discretionary Justice*, Baton Rouge: Louisiana State University Press, 1969.
352 J Black, 'Managing Discretion' (2001) Published as ARLC Conference Papers: Penalties: Policy, Principles and Practice in Government Regulation, available at http://www.lse.ac.uk/collections/law/staff/julia-black.htm, accessed on 20 January 2015.
353 J Black, 'Managing Discretion' (2001) Published as ARLC Conference Papers: Penalties: Policy, Principles and Practice in Government Regulation, available at http://www.lse.ac.uk/collections/law/staff/julia-black.htm, accessed on 20 January 2015.
354 T Williamsons, *Investigative Interviewing: Rights, Research, Regulation*, Devon: Willlan Publishing, 2006.
355 D Bayley, 'Law Enforcement and the Rule of Law: Is There a Tradeoff?' (November 2002) 2(1) *Criminology and Public Policy* 133–154.
356 Ibid.
357 J Jackson, B Bradford, B Stanko, and K Hohl, *Just Authority, Trust in the Police in England and Wales*, Routledge Press, 2013.
358 R Reiner, *The Politics of the Police*, 3rd edn, Oxford University Press, 2000.
359 J Jackson, B Bradford, M Hough, J Kuha, R Stares, S Widdop, et al., 'Developing European Indicators of Trust in Justice' (2011) 8(4) *European Journal of Criminology* 267–285.
360 J Jackson, B Bradford, B Stanko, and K Hohl, *Just Authority, Trust in the Police in England and Wales*, Routledge Press, 2013.
361 K Murphy, L Hinds, and J Fleming, 'Encouraging Public Cooperation and Support for Police' (June 2008) 18(2) *Policing and Society* 136–155.
362 D Bayley, *Changing the Guard, Developing Democratic Police Abroad*, OUP, 2006; K Murphy, L Hinds, and J Fleming, 'Encouraging Public Cooperation and Support for Police' (June 2008) 18(2) *Policing and Society* 136–155.
363 J Jackson, B Bradford, B Stanko, and K Hohl, *Just Authority, Trust in the Police in England and Wales*, Routledge Press, 2013.
364 T Tyler, 'Legitimacy and Criminal Justice: The Benefits of Self-Regulation' (2009) 7 *Ohio State Journal of Criminal Law* 307–359.
365 M Weber, *Economy and Society*, Volume 2, Berkley: University of California Press, 1978.
366 D Beetham, *The Legitimation of Power*, London: Macmillan, 1991.
367 J Jackson, B Bradford, B Stanko, and K Hohl, *Just Authority, Trust in the Police in England and Wales*, Routledge Press, 2013.
368 Ibid.
369 T Tyler, 'Trust and Legitimacy: Policing in the USA and Europe' (2011) 8 *European Journal of Criminology* 254–256.
370 J Miller, 'Police Corruption in England and Wales: An Assessment of the Current Evidence, Home Office online report, 11/03, available at http://www.belui.ru/Doc/Mejdunar/Angl/33.pdf, accessed on 20 April 2015.

371 T Newburn, *Understanding and Preventing Police Corruption: Lessons from the Literature*, Police Research Series paper 110, London: Home Office, 1999.
372 Ibid.
373 Ibid.
374 Cases such as The Birmingham Six, Guildford Four, Cardiff Three.
375 Corruption in the police services in England and Wales: Second Report—a report based on the IPCC's experience from 2008 to 2011, May 2012, London, available at http://www.official-documents.gov.uk/, last accessed on 15 May 2016.
376 Ibid.
377 Many problems, such as accepting bribe in the form of gifts, use of credit cards and police officers having a second or more jobs, were highlighted in the report mentioned above.
378 Independent Police Complaints Commission, *Corruption in the Police Service in England and Wales: First Report,* London: IPCC, 2011.
379 M Punch, 'Police Corruption and Its Prevention' (2000) 8(3) *European Journal on Criminal Policy and Research.*
380 M Damaska, 'Structures of Authority and Comparative Criminal Procedure' (1975) Faculty Scholarship Series, Paper 1590, 486.
381 J Berry, 'Reducing Bureaucracy in Policing' Final Report, October 2010, available at https://www.gov.uk/government/uploads/system/uploads/attachment_data/file/117162/reduce-bureaucracy-police.pdf.
382 Ibid.
383 As evidenced from the judgements from *D K Basu v. State of West Bengal* (1997) 1 SCC 216 till *Prakash Singh v. Union of India* (2009) 17 SCC 329.
384 M McConville, A Sanders, and R Leng, *The Case for the Prosecution,* London, Routledge, 1991.
385 M Damaska, 'Structures of Authority and Comparative Criminal Procedure' (1975) Faculty Scholarship Series, Paper 1590, 485.
386 This is with reference to the work of the IPCC.
387 L Fuller, *Morality of Law*, revised edition, New Haven: Yale University Press, 1969.
388 T Endicott, 'The Impossibility of the Rule of Law' (1999) 19 *Oxford Journal of Legal Studies* 1.
389 L Sherman, *Controlling Police Corruption: The Effects of Reform Policies*, Summary Report, Washington: US Department of Justice, 1978; T Newburn, *Understanding and Preventing Police Corruption: Lessons from the Literature*, Police Research Series Paper 110. London: Home Office, 1999.

3 The way forward

Enhancing the right to custodial legal assistance

3.1 Introduction

As demonstrated in Chapter 2, police interrogation in India requires urgent reforms in order to make police officers more accountable. In the absence of other safeguards such as tape recording of the police interrogation, it is essential to analyse the presence of a lawyer and its impact on the interrogation. The purpose of this chapter is to identify the scope and nature of the right to custodial legal assistance as an important part of the right to fair trial. This chapter looks into the legislative provisions, scholarship and jurisprudence pertaining to the right to legal counsel in India focusing on the provisions of Article 22 of the Indian Constitution and relevant provisions under the CrPC. It also examines the efforts made by various law commissions in analysing the implementation of this right. It asks whether the right to counsel as guaranteed under the Constitution of India is applied in practice. The consequences of violation of the provisions of Article 22 by the police and various courts are also studied. Similar provisions surrounding the right to legal assistance and its journey over the period of time with the assistance of law commission are also examined. An analysis of the impact of the presence of a lawyer on other rights such as the right to silence and the right against self-incrimination also helps in determining the importance of the right to legal assistance. By undertaking a comparative study with similar provisions on the right to legal assistance under PACE in England and Wales, this study asks whether legislative reform in relation to the right to legal assistance is required in India. A discussion of the provisions of the right to legal assistance in India will be followed by an analysis of similar provisions in England and Wales, which offer an interesting comparative vista when examining India's need to reform custodial interrogatory practices.

3.2 Indian context for the right to legal assistance

The effectiveness of a country's criminal justice system depends on achieving a balance between crime control and due process.[1] This can be achieved

DOI: 10.4324/9781003213024-3

by ensuring a transition from police interrogation to trial while maintaining consistent protection of procedural safeguards. Lawmakers, police officers, lawyers and judges play their roles within the wider procedural framework determined by the antithesis between due process and crime control.[2] The presence of a solicitor during any police interrogation is aligned with the due process polar in Packer's model and ensures respect of the right to fair trial and adherence to norms and wider jurisprudence set by the ECtHR.[3]

As observed previously, in India, an investigation starts when the arrest is made by the police officer and it is mandatory for the police officer to note down the details of the crime in the FIR.[4] The police officer in charge is also by law obliged to give a copy of this to the arrestee and retain one for the police station's records, but this practice is not followed in practice.[5] The Constitution of India protects fundamental rights such as the right to legal advice and provides the arrestee with the right to informing his relatives.[6] Despite these safeguards mentioned in the legislation and jurisprudence, they are not enforced in practice.[7] In the absence of a lawyer at the time of investigation, it is difficult to ensure that the suspect receives the basic fundamental rights. The right to legal assistance is a fundamental right guaranteed under the Indian Constitution as enshrined under Chapter III, specifically under Article 22.[8] Section 303 of the Code of Criminal Procedure also mentions that any person accused of an offence before a criminal court or against whom proceedings are instituted under this code may be defended by a pleader of his choice.[9] While the Constitution of India and the CrPC enshrine the right to legal assistance in a criminal trial, it does not extend to pretrial interrogation. This chapter will examine what efforts has the Supreme Court made in reinforcing this right and if they are implemented. It will be argued that although the Constitution of India, the CrPC and various Supreme Court judgements place the right emphasis on the right to counsel in order to ensure due process, the right is not applied in practice.

3.2.1 Constitutional provisions

The Constitution of India is the unique work undertaken by Dr Ambedkar, in order to ensure the protection of fundamental rights in India.[10] Dr Ambedkar, who is known as the father of the Indian Constitution, very meticulously studied and incorporated the provisions pertaining to fundamental rights from the Bill of Rights in the American Constitution.[11] The right to legal representation is protected by Article 22 of the Constitution of India. Though the article is very obscure and was originally thought to apply to the trial phase only, the Supreme Court has over the years attempted to extend the right to counsel to cover both the pretrial custodial period and the trial period.

3.2.2 Right to be presented before a Magistrate

As observed in the previous chapter, it is mandatory for the accused to be presented before a Magistrate within 24 hours of the arrest; hereafter the right to a counsel is a fundamental right.[12] There has been a considerable amount of literature on this subject of mandating the presence of a lawyer at the trial stage.[13] It is argued here that while this is an important stage at which the right to legal assistance is given due leverage, the mandatory presence of a legal counsel at the custodial stage is equally important. The duty for the police to present the suspect before a magistrate seems to be in line with the right to a lawyer at the police station. It is no doubt the duty of the Magistrate to ensure the well-being of the suspect, but it does not replace the role a solicitor can play at the custodial interrogation. Law commissions and reports have asked whether the period of detention can be modified in a manner to suit the system more efficiently.[14] Ideally this would include the period of custodial legal assistance. No doubt this provision ensures the well-being of the suspect, but a period of up to 24 hours is long enough for the suspect to require legal assistance, and this chapter emphasises the respect of this right.

3.2.3 *International obligations and the right to custodial legal assistance*

Universal human rights standards such as those applying at the police station are not effectively implemented in Asia, particularly in India. Indian courts have tried to give effect to provisions of the UDHR and the ECHR, in providing the accused with fair trial rights, but it is questionable whether these rights are applied in practice.[15] Article 14(3)(d) of the International Convention on Civil and Political Rights (ICCPR) refers to the provision of free legal aid. India has ratified this convention. However, the extent of international obligation is limited to legal aid only and there is no specific provision for custodial legal assistance.[16]

3.2.4 *Institutional interpretation*

The efforts of the Supreme Court of India to extend the right of having a lawyer present at the time of interrogation have been initiated in the early colonial era.[17] Most of the Supreme Court judgements give an impression of clarifying legal assistance during police interrogation. In 1926, regarding *Llewelyn Evans*, the Bombay High Court held that the accused should be

> Not only at liberty to be defended at the time of judicial proceedings but also that he should have reasonable opportunity, if in custody, of getting into communication with his lawyer.[18]

In 1932, it was also held in the case of *AmolakRam v. Emperor* that a person arrested merely on suspicion is also entitled to having access to legal counsel when in police custody.[19] There are two distinct parts to the right to consult and be defended by a legal practitioner: right to consultation when the accused is in custody and defence at the time of trial. In 1951, it was held by the Supreme Court that the choice of consulting and being represented by a legal practitioner of one's choice, though a right constitutionally guaranteed, is really not an absolute right in terms of practice.[20] This sudden change in interpretation is unexplained and unexplored by the legal fraternity and academics alike. In 1965, in the case of *State of Punjab v. Surinder Singh*, the Court found that there is no hard and universal application that no questioning or interrogation can ever be made by police of an accused unless his counsel is called.[21] In 1951, in the case of *Janardhan Reddy v. State of Hyderabad*,[22] the Supreme Court held that "It cannot be laid down as a rule of law that in every capital case where the accused is unrepresented, the trial should be held to be vitiated." Here too the court seemed to restrict the right to legal assistance at the trial stage and no specific mention of the right to legal assistance at police station was made.

3.2.5 Use of foreign case law as precedent

In 1978, in the case of *Nandini Satpathy v. P L Dani*, the accused was interrogated on a number of charges of corruption. During custodial interrogation, the suspect refused to give the answers to many questions and also refused to sign her statement. This use of silence was challenged by police officers who argued that the use of silence was unjustified. This raised the question of unsolicited use of silence during police interrogation, which further raised the importance of having a lawyer present during police interrogation. The court took precedence of the famous *Miranda v. Arizona* case from the United States for pretrial safeguards for the suspect.[23] Justice Krishna Iyer observed that the right to legal counsel also extends the embargo to the police investigation stage.[24] This would ensure the protection of the suspect's right against self-incrimination, as mentioned under Article 20(3) in the Constitution of India. The Court further observed the principle of *"nemo tenetur sceipsum tenetur,"* which translates "no one is bound to accuse himself."[25] The court emphasised that it was in the interest of justice and fundamental to the rule of law. The service of a lawyer should be made available to a suspect even at "near-custodial stage."[26] However, the Court failed to provide any further clarification as to the ambit of near custodial interrogation and whether it extends to police station custodial interrogation. This inability of the court to define "near custodial interrogation" has left its interpretation open to police officers and academics. The court raised two important queries drawing from the conclusions of the Miranda case: is the person interrogated, "accused of any offence" and is he being compelled to be a witness against himself?[27] The court also took the wider construction of the IPC to cover not only the accusations already registered in police stations but those which are likely to be the basis for exposing a person to a criminal charge, Article 20(3). It was finally held that the right to counsel extends to all suspects formally accused and in *praesenti* not in future. The Supreme Court held that the accused shall have the right to have a lawyer present at the time of the interrogation.[28] The Supreme Court has recently affirmed the importance of the right to legal assistance in the case of *Ajmal Amir Kasab v. State of Maharashtra*, also making reference to seminal judgements such as *Salduz v. Turkey* and relevant judgements from other jurisdictions.[29]

Although this was the first attempt at addressing the right to legal assistance at the custodial interrogation stage by the Supreme Court, there are several loopholes in the judgement. Firstly, the wording implies that the suspect should be allowed to meet his counsel, which pushes the burden on the suspect to ask for a counsel. Secondly, while the counsel is allowed to be present, this is not for the entire period of investigation. This is far from practice, as pointed out by the law commission that even if such a rule was introduced in India, the police wouldn't inform the suspect of his right to counsel.[30] This will be discussed at length later in this chapter. And in the event that the police officer informs the suspect of such a right and notes it in the diary, its credence will always be doubted. The Supreme Court of India acknowledged the rivalry between the societal interest in crime detection and the constitutional rights of an accused person.[31] However, there were no measures suggested to overcome this rivalry. An important provision of custodial legal assistance suggested by Supreme Court jurisprudence would be effective immediately. However, in practice, this was not implemented. It is suggested here that complete disregard to this Supreme Court jurisprudence did not have any impact on police officers.

3.2.6 Recognition of legal assistance

After almost a decade, in 1983, the court recognised the opportunity to consult counsel in the case of *Sheela Barse v. State of Maharashtra*.[32] It was expressly held that

> Whenever a person is arrested and taken to the police lock up, intimation of the fact of such arrest must immediately be given to the nearest legal aid committee so that immediate steps can be taken for the purpose of providing legal assistance to the arrested person at State cost. It is necessary to protect the accused from torture and ill-treatment or oppression and harassment at the hands of his custodian.[33]

This case pioneered in highlighting the importance of legal assistance as soon as an intimation of arrest was made to the suspect. This case also introduced the concept of legal aid and the state's responsibility of providing legal aid; this will be discussed at length later. While this case highlighted the importance of legal assistance to the arrested person, greater emphasis was given to "intimation of arrest of the suspect." This raises the issue of whether the right to legal assistance arises after intimation of arrest or immediately upon arrest. It certainly is not a straightforward interpretation that the right to counsel arises soon after arrest. If the suspect is called at the police station only for questioning and is not under arrest, this does not fit in the ambit of this fundamental guarantee.[34] These issues were also highlighted by critics who urged the need for further clarification in depth.[35]

3.2.7 *Custodial legal assistance*

In 1997, the seminal judgement of *D K Basu v. State of West Bengal* saw the first specific mention of provision of custodial legal assistance and other procedural safeguards. The Supreme Court handed down 11 procedural changes to be followed by the police department for arrest and detention.[36] The Supreme Court observed that custodial torture is a naked violation of human dignity. It was also highlighted that the situation is aggravated when violence occurs within the four walls of a police station by those who are supposed to protect citizens.[37] The court accepted that the police have a difficult task in light of the deteriorating law and order situation, political turmoil, student unrest and terrorist and underworld activities.[38] They observed that the police have a legitimate right to arrest a criminal and to interrogate her/him without the use of torture or third degree measures. Actions of the State must be right, just and fair; torture for extracting any kind of confession would neither be right nor just or fair. This judgement may be referred to as containing the most exhaustive list of guidelines for protecting a suspect at the police station.[39] These precious rights guaranteed under Article 21 cannot be denied to convicts, under-trials or other prisoners in custody except for a procedure established by law. These guidelines were to be enforced in all the police stations throughout India within a reasonable time. Further enforcement guidelines were also laid down by the Supreme Court.[40] This judgement like the previous judgements relied upon the case of *Miranda v. Arizona* taking essential guidelines for providing legal assistance at the time of police interrogation.[41] These guidelines are based on the provisions of CrPC and are very much a part of regulations in police manuals and rule books. The Supreme Court has said that failure to comply with these guidelines not only renders the officer liable for punishment through departmental action but also amounts to contempt of court.[42]

The case *of D K Basu* has been quoted on many occasions by eminent jurists, academics and constitutional advocates to highlight the importance of legal assistance. Fortman commended that *D K Basu*'s case was a demonstration of independence and creativity exercised by the Supreme Court in fashioning procedural protection for detainees.[43] However, despite this attempt by the court to lay down clear guidelines, there are technical loopholes which are not addressed by the Court in this judgement. The judgement is silent as to whether the right to legal assistance extends if an arrest is made without a warrant. If the police officer picks up a suspect on routine questioning, which is a common practice in India, this will not be called an interrogation, and hence the police officer would not be required to follow this guideline.[44] However, this may turn into an interrogation if the police officer determines that the information he received from the suspect is credible and requires further action. The judgement mentions that the right to legal assistance cannot be denied to prisoners in custody; however, the court failed to clarify "police custody" or "judicial custody." This is mainly because the right to legal assistance is legislatively clear at the judicial custody stage. The courts have since interpreted this to include both police and judicial custody.[45] Although these guidelines were to be made enforceable within a reasonable time, no actions were taken thereafter to ensure its compliance.

In 2011, in the case of *Anant Brahmachari v. Union of India & Others*, the High Court of New Delhi held that the arrestee has the right to meet his lawyer during interrogation.[46] In this case, the arrestee who was not even a suspect was interrogated by the police in the absence of a lawyer. The court held the right to legal assistance was a fundamental right and should apply to the suspect at all stages of interrogation. The court arrived at this conclusion after interpreting the rights mentioned in the *D K Basu* judgement. This decision was a mere repetition of the previous decisions, almost reiterating similar provisions for custodial legal assistance. Most High Courts however interpret this right in different ways and have held dissenting views from that of the Supreme Court.[47] As a result, there has been an inconsistency in the interpretation of the application of the right to custodial legal assistance. This has never been challenged either by academics or by any other subordinate courts.

3.2.8 Difference between custody and arrest

It is essential to discuss the difference between these two provisions as jurisprudential interpretation of the right to legal assistance varies from "custodial stage"[48] to "arrestee."[49] The legislative provisions under the CrPC do not define or distinguish custody and arrest. Even in the latest judgement of 2014, the courts have interpreted the definition of custody drawn from the Oxford Dictionary and the Black's Law Dictionary.[50] Section 46 of the CrPC explains how an arrest is made, and Sections 438, 439, 442, 451 CrPC, Section 45 of Customs Act and Sections 26 and 27 of Evidence Act mention custody.[51] In *Paramhansa Jadab v. The State*, the court held that "police custody" for the purpose of Section 26 of the Indian Evidence Act does not commence only when the accused is formally arrested but would commence from the moment when his movements are restricted and he is kept under police surveillance.[52] This would imply that custody and arrest may be used interchangeably and the right to legal assistance would apply at both instances. However, this lack of a proper definition in legislation has left a wide area of interpretation and this task is entrusted with the courts. This makes it difficult to interpret whether the fundamental right to legal assistance applies at the custodial stage or at the time of arrest. This is a glaring example of a practice where the laws are constantly changing and hence lack consistency.[53] It may be noted here that most of the pre-independence and near post-independence judgements are clearer on the right to legal assistance than the recent ones. However, neither was incorporated in practice or existing legislation previously nor have any efforts been made to do so lately.

3.2.9 No follow-up

Despite these Supreme Court guidelines and jurisprudence on the right to legal assistance, no follow-up steps were taken either to ensure its compliance. This issue was also raised by international human rights bodies arguing that the right to legal assistance fails to meet international standards.[54]

3.2.10 Need for legislation

The Supreme Court jurisprudence has time and again emphasised the importance of the presence of a lawyer at the police station. However, failing to define the precise terms, "from the time the suspect is brought to the police station" instead of from the time the suspect is in police custody, will provide a solution. This may be due to the lack of specifying if the right to legal assistance begins from the time of arrest and if this constitutes police custody. This loophole caused by the ambiguity in mentioning the instance from which the right to legal assistance begins is, arguably, one of the reasons for the non-implementation of this right. The maxim *expressio unius est exclusion alterious* (express mention of one thing excludes others) has been called a valuable servant but a dangerous master.[55] In the present circumstances, the courts realise the setback caused by not expressly mentioning when the right begins to apply.

Another hindrance that might stand in the way of strict application of the guidelines delivered in the *D K Basu* judgement is the lack of authority. Expecting police officers to strictly follow case law guidelines alone has proved to be inefficient. It is an assumption that this inconsistent interpretation of the Supreme Court and the lack of legal assistance in legislation is because of the evidentiary provisions. This is discussed at length in the next chapter. Evidence obtained as a result of the lack of safeguards provided by the suspect usually result in delays at the trial. A vital feature such as police interrogation marks the beginning of a trial and hence needs to have equality in arms applied even at this stage. I emphasise the need to implement this right legislatively because the Supreme Court guidelines do not have an authoritative impact either on the police or on the public. Academics have failed to acknowledge this as a hindrance to the implementation of the right to legal assistance. On a national level, this issue was raised by the Justice Malimath Committee Report, which looked mainly at criminal justice reforms.[56] This committee report also mentions that the shortcomings of the evidentiary legislation have stood in the way of implementing the right to legal assistance at the police station.[57]

3.3 Justice Malimath Committee Report

Owing to a lot of pressure from many international organisations on the subject of human rights neglect by Indian authorities, a Committee was set up for reform of the Criminal Justice system headed by Justice (Retd) V. S. Malimath. The committee submitted its report in 2003.[58] It was for the first time in 150 years of Indian legal history that such wide-ranging reforms were proposed. The salient features of this report were reforms to criminal justice system mainly pertaining to laws of arrest and rights of the accused. This report was unique in highlighting the importance of suspects' rights, more particularly the right to legal assistance. The Committee sought to expedite the criminal process as it considered that "the criminal justice is virtually collapsing under its own weight as it is slow, inefficient, and ineffective."[59] Three main areas of recommendations pertaining to right to legal assistance were discussed: rights of the accused, duty of police officers and increase in the powers of the Magistrate. At a normative level, this report was located midway between the crime control and the due process system aiming to achieve a balance between the two contrasting positions. Hence, an increase in the investigative powers of the police and a simultaneous increase in adequate safeguards of the suspect were suggested.[60] This report reiterated many safeguards delivered by the Supreme Court in earlier judgements such as in the case of *D K Basu v. State of Bengal*.[61] The presence of a lawyer at the time of interrogation would assist in ensuring a fair interrogatory process and minimise the use of torture and violence.[62] This report recommended that the police follow the set of guidelines set out in *D K Basu*'s case. Various organisations such as Amnesty International expressed concern over non-implementation in practice.[63] This Commission placed particular emphasis on international concerns on the issue of the right to legal assistance.

The review on the Malimath Committee Report pointed out that the recommendations of this committee were just a reiteration of the guidelines given in the case of *D K Basu*.[64] This confirmed that no action was taken since 1998 to implement this right to counsel. The Malimath Committee Report also criticised the lack of consequences for non-implementation of this right. This report suggested changes to be made in the legislation regarding the right to legal assistance but provided no detailed research on various factors surrounding this right. It is pointed out that this report contributed little towards solving the problem of the lack of implementing the right to custodial legal assistance. It is quite obvious that mere jurisprudence is unable to enforce such important right such as the right to legal assistance. I argue here that despite the detailed consideration given to this right in this report, academics have criticised this report for being insensitive towards human rights issues.[65]

Following this, the Law Commission in its report in 2007 continued to emphasise the importance of extending the right to legal assistance to cover the period when the suspect is not charged.[66] The above report also tried addressing the issue of the impact of making the choice between adversarial and inquisitorial systems on the effectiveness of a criminal justice system.[67] It was suggested that a change in the procedural system might encourage extension of suspects' right to legal assistance at the police station and make it a more rights-based system.[68]

3.3.1 *Inquisitorial versus adversarial*

The Malimath Committee considered a change of orientation for the criminal justice system of India. The criminal justice system followed in India is an adversarial system of common law inherited from British colonial rulers. The accused is presumed innocent until proven guilty beyond reasonable doubt. The burden of proof is on the prosecution, who brings the case before the judge. The judge merely plays the role of an umpire to see whether the prosecution has been able to prove the case beyond reasonable doubt. The adversarial system does not impose a positive duty on the judge and therefore the judge plays a passive role. The Malimath Committee suggested that a shift from adversarial to inquisitorial procedure would fill the gaps leading to an efficient criminal justice system.[69] The "quest for truth" should be at the centre of a criminal justice system, as an instrument to assign wider investigative powers to the magistrate and the judge. Suggesting a paradigm shift from a due process to a crime control method was aimed to counter the lack of efficiency in the Indian criminal justice system. The rationale behind this recommendation was that giving wider investigative powers to the courts would lead to higher conviction rates. It will thus imply that a higher conviction rate would reflect the success of investigations carried out by police officers. The report provides no clarification of this theory of a higher rate of conviction. The recommendation mentioned "punishing the guilty and protecting the innocent," with no mention of protecting the accused.

Inquisitorial systems followed in countries such as Belgium did not for a long time acknowledge the right to custodial legal assistance.[70] In Belgium, the reason for denial of the right to legal assistance was feared to have a negative impact, which changed after a seminal judgement of *Salduz v. Turkey*.[71] Similar systems were being followed by countries such as France, Scotland and the Netherlands.[72] Such a shift to an inquisitorial system also carries with it an increase in the competences and powers of the court to order further investigation on its own motion. However, lessons may be taken from such inquisitorial systems, which have recently adopted the practice of the right to legal assistance. The Indian legislators must be prepared for a court-controlled system along with requisite safeguards. This makes it incumbent on the part of the magistrate to shed light on all pertinent facts of conviction. This concept can easily be challenged on the fact that no further burden should be put on the already burdened courts.[73]

Although the report was ambitious in suggesting that the change in the system would ensure an effective judicial system, it was criticised for weakening the safeguards for those in detention.[74] The committee's recommendation of placing more investigative responsibilities with the courts seemed highly impractical.[75] The report was also criticised for being less rights-based system and more punitive in effect. However, there were certain areas of the recommendations that could be adopted even if they required further work. For instance, although the right to custodial legal assistance was suggested, no details were provided as to the role of the lawyer.[76] The report merely referred to the *D K Basu* case and the guidelines set out by the Supreme Court for the provision of custodial legal assistance. While many academics referred to the recommendations of this report, no further work was undertaken either by the government or by law commissions. This report was also criticised for being repetitive and not being able to provide any concrete reforms.[77] This committee highlighted the further need for legal aid.

3.4 Legal aid

The courts recognised the importance of custodial legal assistance and with it surfaced the issue of the provision of legal aid. In many cases, the accused could not afford legal assistance owing to financial difficulties and/or lack of awareness. The Constitution of India under Article 39(A) guarantees equal justice and the right to legal aid.[78] Jurisprudential interpretation of the awareness of the right to legal aid has been clear for a long time. The need for legal aid at the preliminary stage was highlighted in the case of *Sheela Barse v. Union of India*,[79] also previously mentioned by the Supreme Court in the case of *Nandini Satpathy v. Dani*[80] and *Khatri v. State of Bihar*.[81] As early as 1981, the Supreme Court in the case of *Khatri v. State of Bihar* held that it was a constitutional obligation that the suspect be provided with free legal services not only at the trial stage but also when he is produced before the Magistrate.[82] The jeopardy to his personal liberty arises as soon as the person is arrested and produced before the Magistrate, where he applies for bail in order to resist remand to police custody or jail. The Court further emphasised that it is at this stage that the accused needs competent legal advice and representation and no procedure can be said to be reasonable, fair and just, which denies legal advice and representation to him at this stage.[83] It is a constitutional mandate that the right to legal aid must come into existence immediately when a person is deprived of his liberty.[84] Not providing legal aid at this stage leads to the vitiation of the whole process resulting into miscarriage of justice and violation of human rights of personal liberty.[85] This will also be against the principles of natural justice. The courts interpreted that the right to legal assistance and legal aid were interconnected. Thus, the right to counsel by way of legal aid begins when a person is being interrogated and continues through pretrial stages to trial and into appeal since it is an essential ingredient of reasonable, fair and just procedure. It would be prudent for the police officer to allow a lawyer where the accused wants to have one at the time of interrogation, if he wants to escape the censure that the interrogation is carried on in secrecy by "physical and psychic torture."[86] The Supreme Court of India in its verdict stated that the right to legal aid is a fundamental right and must be observed by courts throughout India.[87] Additionally, the Supreme Court has in a range of cases noted the continuing use of torture by police officers, which makes the right to legal aid even more necessary.[88]

3.4.1 Constitutional provision and legal aid

Providing legal assistance by way of legal aid to those who cannot afford to pay privately for legal assistance falls within the interpretative ambit of Article 22 of the Constitution.[89] However, Article 22 of the Constitution provides fundamental rights encompassing fair trial, but it does not guarantee provision of a lawyer by the state. As early as in *Janardhan Reddi v. State of Hyderabad*, the Supreme Court of India held that "the right to be defended by a legal practitioner of his choice" could only mean a right of the accused to have the opportunity to engage a lawyer and does not guarantee an absolute right to be supplied with a lawyer by the State.[90] Thus, there is a provision for a mere "opportunity" to consult a legal practitioner under the provisions of legal aid. This judgement failed to specify the availability of legal aid and the details of its provision.

3.4.2 Provision of legal aid in-trial

It is argued in this section that the importance of providing legal aid has been restricted to the in-trial process. The absence of any legislation or jurisprudence specifying the ambit of the provision of legal aid to extend to the custodial interrogation makes it difficult for interpretation. In the latest Supreme Court judgements on the right to legal assistance, the right is limited to the in-trial process and before the Magistrate.[91] If the Supreme Court expressed the impracticality of providing legal aid, it is considered solely a state responsibility.[92] The court expressed that voluntary agencies and social action groups must assist the state programme in providing legal aid. This in turn flows from the obligation cast under Article 39(A) of the Constitution of India. Article 39(A) is a result of the constitutional amendment and was added in "Chapter IV—Directives Principles of the State Policy." These directives are not enforceable by law but reinstate the obligation of the state described in Articles 14 and 21 of the Indian Constitution.

Over the past years, there has been significant progress in this area. The Legal Services Authorities Act, 1987, provides for free legal services to the Scheduled Castes, Scheduled Tribes, women and children without any qualification regarding their financial status, persons with disabilities, victims of human trafficking, persons with an annual income less than Rs. 9000 (approximately £90) or such other higher amount as may be prescribed, amongst others.[93] The Supreme Court of India has followed the suggestions offered by various international organisations in offering legal aid. While this economic definition of persons who qualify for legal aid gives an arbitrary figure of household income, it does not emphasise the importance of legal aid at the police station. Although the concept of free legal aid was recognised by the court as a fundamental right under Article 21 of the Constitution of India, the scope and the ambit of its application was not made clear. This failure to clarify that the ambit of free legal aid extends to the custodial legal assistance stage results in the non-implementation of the constitutional right. But over a period of time, the concept of legal aid has undergone significant changes.

3.4.3 Latest development in legal aid

In the case of *Ajmal Kasab v. State of Maharashtra*, the Supreme Court of India held that it is the duty and obligation of every Magistrate before whom a person accused of committing a cognisable offence is first produced to make him fully aware that it is his right to consult and be defended by a legal practitioner.[94] In case he has no means to engage a lawyer of his choice, one would be provided at the expense of the State.[95] It is most explicit that efforts for providing legal aid are being made almost mandatory by the Apex Court; however, these take effect at the trial stage and not at the stage of interrogation at the police station. Secondly, although efforts are being made for the provision of legal aid, the application seems to be very selective on the basis of household income. This selective application of law is criticised as it leaves space for the police officer to use his discretion to determine who is poor and to whom this legal aid should be afforded. In the absence of clear and precise legislation, the duty to interpret the application of this law falls upon the interrogating police officer. The court fails to cast a positive duty on the State to provide legal assistance at its expense. This selective application also lacks fundamental principles of universal application. Despite legal developments in legal aid, the implementation of legal aid as a fundamental or statutory right requires vast paraphernalia and huge expenses.

3.4.4 International obligations and legal aid

India has been a signatory to various international conventions such as the UDHR for the protection of human rights and legal aid has been one of the topics.[96] In order to adhere to the international norms, India had aimed at achieving international standards set by the UDHR. Legal aid provides an interesting case study as it has "in practice access to competent counsel often (is) limited, especially for the poor, and the overburdened justice system usually result(s) in major delays in court cases."[97] In the absence of any movement from the legal framework regarding provision of legal aid, *pro bono* work in India is taken up by individual lawyers and NGOs such as Alternate Law Forum, Majlis and Human Rights Law Network. Efforts are also sought from external organisations such as I-Profit, a UK-based online portal connecting lawyers to those in need of legal assistance.[98] This gap should be filled in by the Indian government who may delegate the tasks further to other organisations. But the absence of a legal framework despite jurisprudence in favour of legal aid as early as 1951 is the main reason for effective and coherent legal aid provisions in India.[99] The efforts taken by the Indian lawmakers can hardly be considered satisfactory or in compliance with international standards.[100]

3.4.5 Police attitude towards legal aid

For the purpose of this research, it was deemed necessary to examine police officers' attitude towards the provision of legal aid. Most of the police officers were indifferent to the concept of legal aid at the police station. Only two of them confirmed that there is a systematic approach to legal aid; however, its application in practice is entirely different. One of the police officers commented:

> Yes there is a system in place. The provision is there, a panel of lawyers a legal aid system. But in most of the cases the suspect will not be told about this situation and even if he is told it would be difficult to get hold of a lawyer because of the volume of cases.[101]
>
> Legal aid is provided to those who can't afford. But this is at the Magistrate's court and not in the police station; no one needs legal aid in the police station.[102]

It is clear that police officers are under-informed of the concept of legal aid and its provision at the police station. Police officers should not only be educated on the provisions of legal aid but they should also be trained for notifying the suspect of this right.

3.5 Notification of the right to legal assistance

Another important issue to consider is whether the suspects are notified of their right to legal aid while at the police station. There are no provisions for the notification of the right to legal assistance; and the notification of the right to legal aid is beyond question. This research opines two theories for the lack of notification of the right to legal assistance. Firstly, absence of specific legislative provision for right to legal assistance at the police station stage as opposed to jurisprudence alone. Secondly, it is the absence of any punitive action against the non-implementation of the right to legal assistance that contributes towards this. The first theory has been proved by earlier arguments, which clarify that although jurisprudence has been describing the right to legal assistance as a fundamental right and directed its immediate implementation, this is different in a practical scenario. The second theory is that there are very few regulatory procedures for non-compliance of this duty to arrange for legal assistance at the police station. While the Supreme Court required Magistrate or lower courts to inform the suspect of this right, there is no clarity on the requirement of this at the police station.[103] Mathivanan rightly mentions that it would be a mockery of the criminal justice system if it were left upon the poor and indignant people to have the knowledge of legal aid and ask for it.[104] Better measures need to be incorporated so that there is increased awareness of the availability of legal aid at the police station, and it should be the duty of the police officer to inform suspects of this before commencing investigation.

3.5.1 Lack of punitive measures

It is fundamental for the enforcement of any right in its entirety to ensure that breaches of the right do not go unpunished. In *D K Basu*, Supreme Court has provided guidance on the consequences of breaches of the right to legal assistance.[105] The Supreme Court said that the failure to comply with all 13 directives not only renders a police officer liable for punishment by way of departmental action but also amounts to "contempt of court."[106] Any dereliction of such duty is a failure on the part of the police officer. It is argued here that these provisions are not strict enough to ensure the implementation of the right to legal counsel by the police officer. Vadackumary mentions that even if such a responsibility is endowed upon police officers, it is highly unlikely that they will inform the suspect of such rights.[107] In such circumstances, the lack of strict punitive measures for non-compliance of this right makes its practical implementation almost impossible. It is also argued that such a punitive provision is not sufficient for the breach of such a fundamental right. Owing to the severity of harm caused to the suspect by denying him the right to counsel, an appropriate cause of action ought to be rendering the fruits of the interrogation inadmissible. In the absence of judicial remedies for non-compliance in the form of Supreme Court guidelines, clear legislation on this subject might be able to assist the police officer.

The only remedy against the infringement of any fundamental right is the writ of habeas corpus.[108] No provision in any legislative enactments such as the Code of Criminal Procedure or the Constitution specifically provides any remedy. A writ is not a practical approach towards an infringement such as the denial of custodial legal assistance by the police. In the absence of a positive duty on the police officer ensuring the provision of legal assistance and the lack of a remedy, it is argued that there is no mechanism for enforcing this right to custodial legal assistance.

3.5.2 Constitutional provisions are not sufficient

While the right to legal assistance is mentioned in the Constitution of India, the failure to clarify that this right extends to the custodial interrogation stage highlights the reason for its non-implementation. The lack of clear legislative enactment and the complete reliance on jurisprudence alone are contributing factors for the non-implementation. In 2011, the Supreme Court established the principle of *"Na Vakeel, Na Daleel, Na Appeal"* (No Lawyer, No Hearing, No Appeal).[109] While this is subject to academic interpretation and understanding, it is in practice difficult for police interpretation. Although this stand taken by the Supreme Court is commended to be strong, it was just a precedent case law as no further action was directed to be taken by the court. It is therefore a matter to consider why this fundamental right enshrined in the Constitution and reiterated in the case laws delivered by the courts does not appear in practice.

It is also argued here that the words of the Constitution do not enforce a positive right and merely ensure that the police do not deny suspects' request for legal assistance.[110] The Constitution mentions that "no person shall be denied right to legal counsel," it does not specifically mention the "right to counsel at the police station" as a fundamental right.[111] It is implied here that the suspect is expected to ask for a lawyer and in such a case when he asks, a lawyer shall not be denied to him. Since this is the only solution to the problem of infringement of any right to a fair trial, this deserves legal recognition constitutionally. One cannot help but agree with the eminent jurist Seervai who has said in his *Constitutional Law of India*,[112] "The right to be defended by counsel does not appear to have been stressed, and was clearly not considered in any detail."[113] The eminent jurist further mentions that the right of an accused to be defended by a counsel once the proceedings have been initiated under the Code of Criminal Procedure is a valuable right. In the light of these arguments, it is essential to have a legislative provision mandating the right to custodial legal assistance.

A lawyer's presence plays another important role in ensuring the protection of the suspects' fundamental right against self-incrimination. Lawyers can advise on using two main rights to be exercised during a police interrogation.

3.6 The right to silence and self-incrimination

Two fundamental rights are guaranteed under Article 20(3) of the Constitution of India[114]; the right to silence, and right against self-incrimination. Incorporation of this right in the Constitution was inspired by Article 14 of the International Convention on Civil and Political Rights (ICCPR). As a signatory to the ICCPR, India is obliged to respect Article 14(3)(g), which refers to minimum guarantees and states that everyone has the right not to be compelled to testify against himself or to confess guilt. Similar provisions are also found under Principle 21 of the UN Body of Principles for the Protection of all persons under any form of detention or imprisonment.[115] In order to ensure a fair trial and observing these international obligations, the right to silence has been upheld by many Supreme Court decisions in an effort to reduce abuses of custodial interrogation.[116] In the case of *Nandini Satpathy v. Dani*, J Krishna Iyer held that the right to silence and the right against self-incrimination are fundamental rights for the protection of the suspect in police custody.[117] This section examines the impact of the presence of a legal representative on the right to silence during pretrial detention.

3.6.1 Intimation of the right to silence

Unlike countries such as the United States, France and England and Wales, there is no way of delivering the knowledge of right to silence by way of a caution India. The only other way to inform the suspect and ensure the constitutional guarantee of the right to silence is by ensuring the presence of the lawyer at the police station. In the absence of a positive responsibility on the police officer to inform the suspect of his right to silence, the suspect is expected to know of this right. Owing to the rate of illiteracy in India, where the suspect has no knowledge of his right to legal assistance, assuming that he has the knowledge of his right to silence is unreasonable. The absence of a legal counsel increases the risk of a suspect not exercising their right to silence, as the police officer is not under a duty to inform the suspect of such a right. Thus, two main factors affect the implementation of right to silence: the absence of the legal advisor, and the non-requirement by the police officer to notify the suspect of their right to silence.

In the absence of the lawyer, it automatically falls upon the police officer to notify the suspect of his right to silence. The Supreme Court does not impose any positive right upon the police officer to notify the suspect of the right to silence. In the absence of any form of guidance regarding the notification of the right to silence, it is entirely at the discretion of the accused to answer the questions or remain silent. An eminent lawyer Nariman has opined that the right to silence is not in essence a right but more a privilege.[118] This is contrary to the fact that the right to silence is a fundamental right guaranteed under the Constitution. It was further noted by Nariman that it is the duty of the suspect to cooperate with the police, probably suggesting a tip in the balance moving towards the crime control side. This is a misinterpretation of the right to silence, but this remains unchallenged as there is little awareness of this right.

The Malimath Committee Report has also emphasised that the suspects should not be entitled to right to silence by amending Section 313 of the Code of Criminal Procedure.[119] This has been severely criticised as being in violation of constitutional right. Former Chief Justice Ahmadi favours drawing an adverse inference on the silence of the accused only in relation to matters which are within the special knowledge and not in other cases.[120] Former Chief Justice Ranganath Misra says that requiring the accused to disclose his defence once the prosecution case/charge levelled against him is made known to him will not offend Article 20(3). He, however, says that no adverse inference should be drawn if the accused remains silent. Drawing of adverse inference from the silence of the accused seems to be in contravention of provisions of the Indian Constitution. This is subject to argument and has received mixed reactions from scholars such as Nariman and various committee reports.[121] In the recent case of *DMK K C Palanisamy*, where the defendant was arrested on the allegation of involvement in a land scam, the court held that the right to silence is not an absolute right.[122] The Madras High Court concluded that if an accused is interrogated by the police, he is bound to answer truly all the questions relating to the case and cannot claim absolute silence. However, the suspect is exempt from answering any questions that are likely to incriminate him. While this is just a state delivered judgement and may be taken as precedence by the Madras High Court or any other High Courts, it does not have a nationwide effect. However, it is argued here that this judgement clearly violates the provisions of Article 20(3) of the Constitution of India.

This idea of uprooting this fundamental rule of criminal justice seems far from practical and tends to put the burden of proof on the defence. There is only one rationale of the Malimath Committee that the protection of the accused can be lowered as long as this is accompanied by a guarantee that the accused have a counsel to assist him.[123] If the suspect is advised by the lawyer to exercise his right to silence after consultation and if adverse inference is drawn, this ensures transparency. This will also ensure that the due process of law is followed. This inability to use the right to silence also impacts the right against self-incrimination. It can be suggested here that in the absence of a mandatory requirement of having the police officer provide the suspect with notification of the right to legal counsel, the general public needs to obtain better awareness of the right to legal counsel.

3.7 Awareness of the right to custodial legal assistance

The failure to give effect to the defendant's right to counsel has been attributed, among other things, to a lack of rights awareness among both detainees and judicial officials, combined with high illiteracy rates, as well as judicial corruption.[124] Expecting a suspect to ask for legal assistance during police interrogation is highly unlikely. In the absence of official numbers by way of national or a state survey, this is an open argument. However, it is not very difficult to imagine the extent of ignorance. Uma Devi mentions that no procedure can be "reasonable, just, and fair" when the accused is deprived of legal assistance because of "ignorance" or "indigence."[125] While in custody, pretrial detainees are held in detention facilities under "frequently life-threatening" conditions resulting in approximately 300 custodial deaths per year.[126] Despite these alarming figures, there seems to be no awareness of the suspect's rights during custodial interrogation. Making it a duty for the police officer to notify the suspect of his right to legal counsel seems the only effective legislative solution. However, guidelines relevant to constitutional standards in relation to police interrogation pay little attention to the duty of the police officer to inform the suspect of his right to counsel. When police personnel were interviewed and questioned why there was no awareness for the right to legal assistance, most of them pointed to illiteracy and poverty:

> In India this is not common practice to produce the lawyer in the police station. I know that in US the lawyers are immediately summoned. These lawyers are also ready to provide their services too. Most of the people are so illiterate that they don't even know about this provision or that it is their right.[127]

3.7.1 Do suspects request a lawyer?

The most important issue is whether the suspects are informed or whether they are vigilant enough to ask for a lawyer when arrested. There is no official study conducted on this topic in India either by the government or any independent researcher, which makes it very difficult to support any argument on this topic and very difficult to prove. It comes as a great surprise that a topic of such importance is highly under-researched. This lack of research contributes to the magnitude of importance of the right to custodial legal assistance. It is admitted that any local research conducted by any researcher would only amount to anecdotal research, but a sample survey should exist nonetheless. The prevalent problem of illiteracy in India is one of the main reasons suspects may not ask for a lawyer. As one police officer points out,

> There is so much illiteracy and poverty among the people, they are not aware of rights. Even if they are aware they don't have the social atmosphere where they can open their mouth. Even if they want they cannot hire an advocate, where they are still fighting for their bread and butter, this is a facility, rather a novelty, which is almost impossible to reach them. They cannot open their mouths about their rights either. People would prefer not being in the police station for any reason, let alone for an interrogation and then asking for a lawyer.[128]

It is only an assumption that there are two main, if more, reasons for the suspect denying a lawyer. Firstly, the lawyer might be unnecessary expenditure.

Secondly, the availability of a lawyer being able to attend the police station might be difficult. A full-scale country-wide research conducted in a majority of rural and urban areas would offer helpful data on this topic. In the absence of institutional interpretation and lucid legislature on this topic, the question of whether the suspects ask for legal assistance would determine the efficiency of the right guaranteed under Article 21 of the Constitution.

3.7.2 Police station lawyer

It is questioned here why the concept of "police station lawyer" is so alien or otherwise feared in the criminal justice system in India.[129] There is no system of mandatory legal advice by provision of a police station lawyer.

In the absence of a positive duty cast upon the police officer, it is difficult for the suspect to request a lawyer. It is suggested that like many other countries in the world, a positive responsibility should be cast upon the police officer by way of a caution to inform the suspect of their right to legal assistance.

In the event that the suspects request a lawyer, there are twofold implications with it: either the suspect has to have some form of contacts with the police or he has to bribe the police. This was evident from two different accounts given by police personnel.

> If the accused when arrested has good contacts with the police then he may ask for a lawyer and the police get to decide if they will provide the suspect with a lawyer. The police contact the lawyer and say that if they comply with the investigation process then they will be at an advantage.[130]

While another police personnel observed as follows:

> Sometimes the police will stop all form of communication. If the suspect wants to get out of all this then he can easily give some money to the police and ask for a lawyer. Everyone knows that interrogation means beating, so to avoid this giving money is the best option.[131]

3.8 Police attitude towards legal assistance

This section looks at the provisions covering the police attitude towards the right to legal assistance and its impact on the actual practice. It is also important to analyse when this right begins to apply and if the lawyer can remain present throughout the interview.

3.8.1 Provision in practice

While the law is clear on the police officer "allowing" the suspect to meet his lawyer if he requests to do so, there is no positive obligation on the police officer to inform the suspect of this right. Police officers may in certain cases choose not to inform the suspect of his right to custodial legal assistance. Most of them assume that the suspect has the knowledge of his right to legal assistance because of his previous involvement or encounter with the law. As pointed out by one of the police personnel,

> we don't have to usually tell them about this, most of the suspects have their own lawyer. The habitual criminals have their own lawyer.[132]

When police officers were approached and asked if they inform the suspect of their right to legal assistance, 8 out of 20 police officers said that they did not mention to the suspect that they had a right to legal assistance. Seven police officers said that they informed the suspect of their right to legal assistance and five police officers remained silent on the subject. During the empirical research, one police personnel remarked:

> Yes there is (a duty to inform the suspect of his right to legal assistance). This isn't in the CrPC. But this has been made compulsory by the Supreme Court in one of the cases, that every time they interrogate someone they have to inform them of their right to legal assistance.[133]

Another police officer remarked:

> If they follow the rules then they're supposed to have an earmarked interrogation room. They should have a lawyer present, they can also take him to a room and interrogate him separately without the lawyer if the case so requires. But this is for a short period only. This is what the rules say that the lawyer should be present, but in actual practice what happens is totally different. In most of the cases you will not have a lawyer present.[134]

The other element to be considered is whether police officers would be comfortable with a mandated provision of the presence of a lawyer at the time of police interrogation. When the police personnel were asked this question, the following was the remark that a police officer came up with:

> The ratio of foreign police has accepted the presence of a lawyer is larger than here in India. The police officer doesn't digest that the accused's lawyer is present and advising the accused. This may happen in high profile cases but is not present all the time in all places. This is not a daily practice not even in Mumbai city. Advocates in cities like Mumbai feel lowering their dignity by going to the police station. So you can imagine.[135]

3.8.2 When does the right to legal assistance begin to apply?

It is essential for the right to custodial legal assistance to apply from the time the suspect has been arrested for initial questioning. This is demonstrated after analysing the provisions of the Constitution and Supreme Court jurisprudence.[136] The Supreme Court has recently made reference to the case of *Nandini Satpathy v. Dani*:

> Based on the observations in Nandini Satpathy case it is possible to agree that the constitutional guarantee under Article 22(1) only implies that the suspect in the police custody shall not be denied the right to meet and consult his lawyer even at the stage of interrogation. In other words, if he wishes to have the presence of the lawyer, he shall not be denied that opportunity. Perhaps, Nandini Satpathy does not go so far as Miranda in establishing access to a lawyer at the interrogation stage.[137]

Hence, ideally police officers are required to ask the suspect before the interview if he requires legal assistance. But this is rarely followed and an example was provided by one police personnel:

> *No we do not tell them in the beginning of the interview, we ask them in the end. When we get them in police custody then we ask them whether or not he has a lawyer. We decide from there about the next steps.*[138]

3.8.3 Can the lawyer remain present throughout the interview?

Among various directives which were laid down in the form of these guidelines was Directive number 10, which allowed the arrestee to meet his lawyer during interrogation, though not throughout the interrogation.[139] While this limited presence of a lawyer has been criticised, it has not received the required attention leading to reform. The Law Commission reports highlight this but have failed to pursue any recommendations about this provision.[140] There is blatant ignorance of the importance of custodial legal assistance in the legislation and the implementation of jurisprudence. Very few academics highlight the importance of the lawyer remaining present throughout the interview and protest the present situation.[141] None of the police officers interviewed during the present study showed the importance of the lawyer remaining present throughout the interview. It was noted that the attitude of the police was quite different to the legislative rules. When questioned if police officers would wait till the lawyer arrives to begin the interrogation, the police personnel replied,

> See if the police officer knows that the suspect wants a lawyer, he is afraid that his lawyer will interfere with the investigation and will tell him not to give the information that is required. So obviously he goes ahead with the investigation and actually speeds it up before the arrival of his lawyer.[142]

This practice seems to be a common occurrence throughout the country. In the absence of any mechanism to ensure that the police officer awaits the presence of a lawyer to commence an interrogation, such practices may continue. It is suggested that this ignorance on the part of police officers can be remedied with urgent legislative reformation. It is also essential to consider the view of the lawyers who represent the suspect at the custodial interrogation.

3.9 Attitude of the lawyers

Many lawyers and public prosecutors were approached for the purpose of gathering their views on this topic. They were questioned, if this right is mandated what would the attitude of the lawyers be? Their responses were mainly directed towards the hostile environment of a police station. One of the prosecutors pointed out as below:

> It (The police station) is not exactly the best environment to be in there are lawyers who do just this. There are lawyers who have some form of setting in this. Most of my friends wouldn't like to do this, and it is not a fun job.[143]

Many other defence lawyers pointed out that since they would be present in an advisory capacity, police officers would not appreciate it. This is also one of the reasons why they prevent access of the lawyer to the suspect. This was further emphasised by a defence lawyer:

> The lawyer will tell the victim or suspect not to say a lot of things. They will advise them not to answer too many questions of the police. For eg if I am advising a suspect at the police station then I will advise the suspect to remain quite.[144]

Thus, an effort needs to be made to make the relation between the police and the lawyers more compatible. This can only be achieved by constant practice of having lawyer visits to the police station. In light of the recent developments, the ECtHR may be approached for further legislative developments. The ECtHR has for a long time taken a view that the right to legal assistance arises immediately on arrest. It has recently also decided that this right arises as soon as the person is made aware that he/she is suspected of having committed any criminal offence.[145] Lessons may be taken from such enactments. Specific provisions such as the presence of the lawyer throughout the interrogation and ability to give advice pertaining to the questions being asked on interrogation must be considered. In light of the above ambiguous provision of the right to legal assistance at the custodial interrogation stage, it is suggested that this right be mandated legislatively.

I have argued in this section that there is no *specific* provision under the Constitution about the right to custodial legal assistance at the pretrial stage. There is an implied suggestion that the right to pretrial legal assistance be read along with in-trial legal assistance. However, the importance of having a lawyer present at the police station has been highlighted enough to point out that a clear distinction needs to be made about the existence of this right. The courts must also ensure that there is a positive duty on police officers to inform the suspect of their right to legal assistance before commencing their interrogation. There has been very little academic awareness about the right to counsel and its presence in the CrPC. The impact of various questions pertaining to the right to defence at the pretrial stage need to be considered: How would the presence of a lawyer affect the admissibility of confessional evidence in trial? Lessons must be taken from other jurisdictions on this topic.

The Constitution of India and the CrPC are ambiguous while mentioning access to legal assistance but make no express mention of the terms "pretrial right" and "right to custodial legal assistance at police interrogation." The Supreme Court has on numerous occasions made it compulsory for legal assistance to be provided even at pretrial stage; however, this also needs to be introduced in statutory legislation. The Supreme Court judgements alone have been unable to mandate the provision of legal assistance at the custodial stage. The High Court of Madras jurisprudence on this point provides the perfect illustration of existing risks. Furthermore, since this right correlates to the right to silence, it needs to be specifically mentioned in the CrPC. The basic structure of the Constitution cannot be amended, so the right to silence must be incorporated in the CrPC.

It must be added that major contributions by the Malimath Committee have done little to shed light on this topic. Recommendations relating to change from an adversarial to an inquisitorial system resulted in inaccuracies in the studies by law commissions. The Indian judiciary and the legislature attach little importance to the right of legal assistance at the custodial interrogation stage. Even the position on the right to legal assistance at the trial is ambiguous and hence provides no safeguard to the suspect against potential atrocities of ill-treatment. Since police officers do not await the presence of a lawyer before commencing an interrogation, the right to silence and the right against self-incrimination are almost inexistent. Despite the constitutional backing for these rights, they are clearly not seen to be executed in practice. Similar conclusions were also drawn from the opinions of lawyers and police officers interviewed for the present research. It is therefore evident from the empirical research and current literature that this right needs to be incorporated in legislation and cannot rely on jurisprudence alone.

3.10 Comparing India with England and Wales

The criminal justice system in England and Wales has its roots in the adversarial system. Therefore, all the principles surrounding police investigation aim to balance the power of the state and the procedural safeguards provided to the suspect. In the absence of an investigating judge, the police are vested with the prime responsibility of criminal investigation. The Crown Prosecution Services (CPS) makes the decision to charge and prosecute, initially a responsibility bestowed upon police officers. Upon arrest, a suspect is given a caution advising him of his right to lawyer, his right to silence and the consequences of any statement he might make.[146] England and Wales has been way ahead in ensuring procedural safeguards to the suspect as compared to other European countries such as France, Scotland and the Netherlands.[147] The right to access to a lawyer before and during police interrogation has been in existence since the introduction of the Police and Criminal Evidence Act, 1984.[148] Even before the landmark judgement of *Salduz v. Turkey*, which compelled many states in Europe to introduce new legislation to implement the right to legal assistance, England and Wales have been very considerable in providing safeguards to suspects when interrogated by the police. Custodial legal assistance in England and Wales therefore provides a very useful comparative point of reference for the Indian Criminal Justice System, including from the perspective of its interaction with the ECtHR in this. This section analyses legal assistance in England and Wales before the enactment of the Police and Criminal Evidence Act, 1984 (pre-PACE), after the Police and Criminal Evidence Act (post-PACE) and legal aid. This pre-PACE and post-PACE study provides insight of impact of potential reform. This also demonstrates for the Indian Criminal Justice System that reform is possible and also reveals the limitation of reform, if any.

In England and Wales, central reference to the pretrial rights was placed in the Royal Commission on Police Powers and Procedure (1929); the Criminal Law Revision Commission (1972); the Fisher Inquiry (1977); the Working Group on the Right to Silence (1989); and the Royal Commission on Criminal Justice (1993). The common feature that developed over these reports, among other things, was the need to provide the suspects with enhanced rights at the police station.

In England, the suspect who has been arrested has to be informed immediately upon arrest and reminded again on his arrival at the police station that he has a right to legal advice. However, the police may delay calling a legal adviser as requested if the suspect is detained in connection with a serious offence. If the competent police officer reasonably believes that the exercise of this right would lead to interference or to the alerting of other suspects or hinder the recovery of the proceeds of the crime, he may delay the legal assistance.[149] This was not always the case. It was the circumstances that led to the enactment of PACE, which in turn made the provision of legal assistance before commencement of any investigation a legislative requirement.

3.11 Pre-PACE era

This section discusses the important contributions of the Royal Commission on Criminal Procedure (RCCP) that urged the English lawmakers to introduce the enactment of PACE.

3.11.1 Prior to the RCCP

In the pre-PACE era, authors like Devlin believed that the police functioned in the adversarial process as "disinterested and dispassionate inquirers into the objective facts of a case and not merely as seekers of convictions."[150] In practice, however, there were significant abuses of police powers with a typical illustration being keeping detainees in custody without access to legal advice in order to get a desirable confession.[151] There was also blatant ignorance on the part of the supervisors, who turned a blind eye to this practice.[152] As rightly mentioned by Coppen, in the pre-PACE era, each police station had its own Force Orders, which gave them the liberty to investigate for any length of time and without most of the conversation recorded.[153] Ensuring the suspect the right to legal assistance bore very little significance from one police station to another. It was this lack of uniformity in the investigative process which pushed the drafters of the commission to propose considerable legislative reform to safeguard suspects' rights. During the late 1990s, many other cases of miscarriage of justice followed pursuit giving rise to concern about false confessions. This triggered concerns among the public and is also said to be the main concern of the Royal Commission Report. This situation reflects the current practice in Indian police stations where police officers in each state carry out investigations in a manner they please. With each state in India having its own system of investigation, it condones the practice of allowing a police officer to carry out investigation in a manner they choose.

Before PACE came into effect, the preamble to the Judges' Rule laid down the principle that every suspect at any stage of the investigation is allowed to communicate and consult a solicitor.[154] However, as pointed in the article authored by Bottomley et al., very few suspects actually asked to see a solicitor.[155] This was evidenced in the survey where 11% of the adults made this request and a third of these cases were denied by police officers.[156] As observed above, the constitutional provisions in India are similar to the Judges' Rules on this provision of "allowing" the suspect to see a lawyer at any time during the investigation. However, in England and Wales, there were a series of systematic recommendations provided by various commission reports.

The investigation carried out by police officers was far from neutral. It became a one-sided attempt to assemble and "construct" a case for prosecution.[157] It was pointed out by Jackson that the potential of miscarriages of justice was immense, but it was not easy for them to be uncovered.[158] There were certain other factors that impacted the right to legal assistance at the police station. The Royal Commission took this issue into consideration and made it a highlight of their recommendation. Authors have highlighted the issue of miscarriages of justice in various cases even in India.[159] Law commission reports in India have also highlighted this, but as mentioned above they have not been analysed in greater depth.

3.11.2 RCCP and Legal assistance

The RCCP saw access to legal advice at the police station as one of the fundamental tenets in its proposal for regulating police station interrogation. Legal advice at the police station was thought to be a way for "minimising the effects of arrest and custody on the suspect."[160] It was very evident that the Royal Commission was preparing this report with the aim to make English Criminal procedure more rights based. This report suggested various reforms to police investigation and regulation of police powers and formed the base for the PACE. Another instance that triggered the urgency for reform of the right to legal assistance was the continued cases of miscarriage of justice that surfaced over a period of time.

From 1970 to 1990, many cases of wrongful convictions and improper police investigations occurred in cases such as the Birmingham Six, the Guildford Four, the Maguire family and Judith Ward pointing towards miscarriage of justice.[161] In 1993, the Court of Appeal quashed the convictions of three men convicted of murder in the famous "Cardiff-three" case.[162] One of the main pieces of evidence against the accused in the Cardiff-three case was the confession of Stephen Miller. The main reason for setting aside this evidence was because the manner in which the police had interrogated Stephen and the others was, "hostile ... intimidating."[163] The case of Birmingham Six raised further concerns as the conviction of the suspects was quashed after the Court of Appeal had heard their case twice. These issues about miscarriages of justice surfaced and raised further concerns about the effectiveness of pretrial interrogation. It was becoming evident that the absence of a solicitor at the time of the interrogation facilitates police officers to misuse their power and carry out investigations in any manner they please. While there have been similar miscarriages of justice in many cases in India, the courts have failed to acknowledge the importance of custodial legal assistance. The British courts have identified the lacunae caused by the non-provision of custodial legal assistance and have taken measures to remedy it. This has further been remedied by lawmakers in England and Wales by introducing various legislative provisions in PACE reflecting the guidelines provided by the courts. The next step taken in order to address these issues was introducing PACE and setting up of another Royal Commission.

3.12 Introduction of PACE

PACE changed the way in which interviews were conducted, forced the legal representative to play an active role in the police interview than merely advising silence.[164] There was a lot of protest from police officers against the implementation of PACE initially. However, these protests had little effect on the enactment of PACE. Dixon reports that a body of research had concluded that PACE changed criminal investigation shifting it more towards the American model of due process.[165] This made clear reference to the observance of suspects' safeguards at the time of interrogation and in particular the right to legal assistance. PACE became the most important piece of legislation designed to improve the reliability of investigative practices and increase police accountability.[166]

However, a change of the police culture does not happen overnight. Even after PACE there continued to surface cases which highlighted the fundamental flaw of police interrogation. Cases like the Maguire Seven and reversal of sentences in many other cases pushed for the need of another Royal Commission Report in order to find ways to effectively implement PACE.

3.12.1 The Runciman Commission 1993 and legal assistance

The Runciman Commission was set up by the labour government amidst major debate about political differences about some of the provisions of the Bill. This commission was set up when PACE had been in effect for nearly six years.[167] The commission made meticulous reference to the importance of the waiver of the right to legal assistance and suggested that they should be video- or audio-recorded.[168] The recommendations further mention the privilege of the solicitor to review the investigated material recorded by the police prior to the arrival of the solicitor.[169] The Runciman Commission's recommendations also mention balancing the rights of the suspect with the increase in police powers. However, these recommendations were criticised for not being as far-reaching as those of the Philips Commission.[170] The Runciman Commission report was criticised for not recommending any major changes to the criminal justice process.[171] This report also allegedly favoured the interest of the police and prosecution rather than the suspect's rights.[172]

Much later in 1996, in the case of *Murray v. UK*,[173] the European Court of Human Rights held that a right to fair trial under Article 6 of the Convention extended to the investigative stage, guaranteeing the right to legal advice and assistance at the police station. The Runciman Commission had already taken charge of formulating this by way of legal aid offered by police station legal advisers.[174] However, authors such as Cape and Young commented that the committee was afraid to take further action on this front and lacked assertiveness.[175] The Committee was further criticised for acting timidly while concerning itself too much with the political aspect and interference. The essence of mentioning the efforts made by this report is the way in which political indifferences were overcome and the necessary safeguards were implemented. This demonstrates the attitude of the British lawmakers surpasses the political will and achieves the safeguards it aimed to provide to the suspect. This may be the area which can assist the Indian lawmakers to attempt to surpass the political will and ensure suspects' right to legal assistance. The Indian commission's recommendations report also fails to provide an in-depth analysis of the position of legal assistance in the police station. An observation as to the non-implementation of these recommendations may be due to the interference of the political will in implementing laws as observed in the previous chapter.

3.12.2 Post-Runciman report

In 1997, the role of the solicitor was further highlighted by the Court of Appeal, as held in *R v. Argent*, *R v. Imran and Hussain* and *R v. Roble.*[176] The *Court of Appeal* held that if the police disclose little or nothing of the case against the suspect, so that a legal advisor cannot usefully provide advice to their client, then this may be a good reason for the solicitor to advise the suspect to remain silent. Thus, although this may seem to be a premature stage of interrogation, the presence of a solicitor here ensures the beginning of a fair trial. This means that the interviewing or investigating officer must disclose sufficient information to enable the suspect to understand the nature and circumstances of their arrest. Having a solicitor present is most crucial for the suspect. There is no requirement for the police to present a prima facie case or give the defence solicitor a full briefing before questioning the suspect as held in *Imran and Hussain* and in *Farrell.*[177] Prosecutors are then notified of the pre-interview disclosures in order to draw inferences and prepare for the defence at the trial stage. Such a disclosure assists in any inferences drawn from the silence of the accused and at the same time preparing a rebuttal by the defence. The right to silence in England and Wales has never been a purely domestic issue.[178] Authors such as Quirk mention the wider implications of the use of right to silence advised by the solicitor in great detail.[179] This will be dealt with at a later stage in this chapter.

In 2010, the Supreme Court followed the decision made by the ECtHR in the case of *Salduz v. Turkey*[180] and held that absent compelling reasons, denying suspect access to a solicitor whilst he was detained by the police violated his rights as guaranteed under Article 6(1) and Article 6(3)(c) of the ECHR. The decision made in the case of *Cadder v. H M Advocate*[181] overturned the ruling in *Paton v. Ritchie*,[182] *Dickson v. H M Advocate*[183] and *H M Advocate v. Lean*[184] and held that it would breach Article 6 to admit confessions made during detention where a suspect had not been offered legal assistance. Further emphasis was laid on the decision given by the Grand Chamber of ECtHR in *Salduz v. Turkey.*[185] In the *Salduz* case, a Grand Chamber decision of the ECtHR, it was held that "as a rule" suspects should be entitled to legal advice from the point of their detention.[186]

3.12.3 Legislative provisions

Section 58 of PACE provides that a detained person may have access to independent legal advice on request unless delayed: a clear provision stating that a breach of Section 58 may be a ground for exclusion of evidence under Sections 76 and 78. This was reflected in case laws such as *R v. Alladice*, *R v. Mason* and *R v. Walsh*.[187] The standards set by the ECHR are reflected throughout the enactments of PACE concerning legal assistance. Right of access to solicitor has been implied by the commission and the Court in Article 6(3). The ECtHR has rejected the argument that the right to legal representation becomes relevant only at the trial.[188] The initial interrogation is considered the first stage of a trial and rightly here the right to legal assistance is extended at the interrogation stage.

A clear definition of the specific role of the defence lawyer advising at the police station is set out in the PACE, under Code of Practice C, note for guidance 6. This distinctive description was a result of many commission reports that were given due consideration accompanied by judgements elaborated herein.[189]

There are however two major concerns with regard to enacting Article 6 in domestic legislations. The first concerns delay in access to a solicitor in context to Sections 34–37 of Criminal Justice and Public Order (CJPO), 1994, which permits the drawing of adverse inference from a defendant's failure to answer questions. The second area of difficulty is the availability and provisions relating to telephonic consultation. These will be discussed later.

3.12.3.1 ECHR and the right to legal assistance

Article 6 of the ECHR imposes two different types of obligations on the state on the topic of the right to legal assistance:

- A positive obligation to establish a court system which upholds this right—for example, by providing interpreters or legal aid in criminal proceedings.[190]
- A negative obligation not to punish anyone without a fair trial.

It is observed here that a positive obligation is endowed on the states to ensure the provision of legal assistance and legal aid in cases where the suspect cannot afford it. There is also a growing awareness of the provision of interpreters at the time of initial interrogation. Hence, with an ultimate aim to provide a suspect with a fair trial, all jurisdictions must include the latter, which involves more lawyer participation.

In the case of *Salduz v. Turkey*,[191] the applicant challenged that his rights under Article 6 of the ECHR had been violated as he was denied legal assistance while in police custody. The Court held that it was the fundamental right of the applicant to have legal assistance at the time of interrogation. The court further emphasised that there was a need to protect the suspect's right in both adversarial and inquisitorial systems. According to the Court, this is the case when the rules on criminal procedure provide for the possibility that the silence of the accused during police interrogation is used against him at the trial, because such a scheme confronts him already at the beginning of the police interview with a fundamental dilemma which calls for qualified advice by a lawyer.[192] This comprehensive judgement on the topic of the right to legal assistance address issues surrounding safeguards that a suspect must have at the time of custodial interrogation. The interpretations of this judgement have had a major impact on legislations in many jurisdictions in Europe.[193] Countries like Scotland have recently adopted the mandatory system of custodial legal assistance following this judgement.[194]

The emphasis on the right to custodial legal assistance from the initial interrogation was further emphasised in the case of *Dayanan v. Turkey*.[195] The ECtHR held that the requirements of Article 6 had not been met when the suspect was not assisted by a lawyer, irrespective of the fact that he remained silent throughout the interrogation.[196] The court also emphasised that the absence of a lawyer affected the suspect when his statement was taken.[197] In the case of *Demirkaya v. Turkey*, the suspect had been denied legal assistance at the time of initial interrogation but was provided a lawyer during his questioning before the judge. It was therefore held that since the statement was taken by the police, it was essential that the suspect be provided with legal assistance at this stage. This ruled out any confusion about when the suspect's right to legal assistance begins to apply. As observed above, the Indian legislation is criticised for having loopholes because of the lack of specification of such clear terms as laid down by the ECtHR. The facts of this case reflect the current practice in India where the suspect is produced before a Magistrate, during which period the right to legal assistance is confirmed. Clear legislative provision confirming the right to legal assistance may assist in ensuring the practice of custodial legal assistance in India. It is essential to now study the provisions of legal aid in case where a suspect cannot afford legal assistance.

3.12.4 Legal aid at the police station

In England and Wales, the legal aid system was created by the Legal Advice and Assistance Act, 1949, and was a result of the Rushcliffe Committee recommendations.[198] Legal aid includes legal advice from solicitors, police accredited representatives and paralegals. Legal aid is available for suspects at all stages from the time they are arrested and detained at the police station through to the appeal stage. The suspect is usually informed of his right to legal aid before the interrogation begins.[199] The suspect is entitled to free consultation by a "duty-Solicitor," available 24 hours a day and is independent of the police.[200] The duty solicitor scheme is and continues to be operated by the solicitors operated by the Law Society and the Legal Services Commission.[201] When a suspect requests a lawyer, the police contact the Defence Solicitor Call Centre as soon as practicable.[202] If the suspect wishes to appoint his own solicitor and pay for the solicitor, the Defence Solicitor Call Centre would contact the nominated solicitor. In any case, the authentication of the nominated solicitor would be verified by the Defence Solicitor Call Centre. Apart from exceptional cases like arrest under the Terrorism Act, access to the Solicitor may be delayed. If the suspect requests for a duty solicitor, the police officer must wait for the solicitor to arrive in order to commence the interrogation. The suspect cannot be interviewed, or continue to be interviewed until they have received advice, although there are exceptions where (i) delay in access to legal advice has been authorised in accordance with the certain provisions; (ii) it is authorised by a senior officer on the grounds that delay might lead to one or more of the consequences that would permit access to a lawyer to be delayed or that waiting for the lawyer to arrive would cause unreasonable delay to the investigation; (iii) where the nominated solicitor cannot be contacted or will not attend and the suspect refuses advice from a duty solicitor; or (iv) where the suspect changes their mind and confirms this to a senior officer and in writing. These exceptions have been interpreted strictly by the courts, and evidence suggests that formally delaying access to legal advice is rare.[203] However, although inferences from "silence" are not permitted where a suspect is interviewed under (i) and (ii) above, the product of any such interview may be used as evidence at trial.[204] When legal aid is given during the police interview, the indication "presence of legal aid during the police interview" is also used. In England and Wales, legal aid is permitted before and during the police interview. Legal aid at the police station is provided free of cost irrespective of the suspect's income. The provisions of legal aid at the police station are clearly legislated and have been enacted well in accordance to the other provisions of the PACE.

The provisions of legal aid are in compliance with Article 6 of the ECHR and have been further highlighted by the ECtHR in its decisions.[205] The development of domestic institutions which supports and promotes a fair trial in the criminal courts and tribunals in England and Wales is reflected by the legal aid scheme. A recent study also found that there are some other loopholes in the legal system regarding legal aid. While these are surface-level loopholes, which require further work, they are still in compliance with the provisions of Article 6.

However, the high costs that are to be paid to the private solicitors and the covert surveillance of the solicitor-client private consultations are beginning to surface as major setbacks in the provision of legal aid.[206] As a result, over the past few years, there have been many stipulated legal aid cuts and further cuts are anticipated to be imposed soon.[207] Intermittent political interference with the legal cuts has had a heavy impact on the provision of a lawyer at the police station.[208] The main reason for mentioning the provision of legal aid in England and Wales was the effort made in order to facilitate the right to legal assistance irrespective of whether the suspect cannot afford it. This is done to ensure that the suspect uses his right to silence effectively and under the advice of the solicitor as this has adverse implications.

3.12.5 The right to silence and the right against self-incrimination

In England and Wales, under Section 37(2) of PACE, detention without a charge is possible if it is necessary to obtain evidence by questioning the suspect. The suspect is informed of his right to silence at the time of his arrest, when he is being read out the caution. English Criminal Law has pioneered in establishing the principle of presumption of innocence and the burden of proof on the prosecution. This has been aided by the provision of the right to silence. However, under the provisions of the Criminal Justice and Public Order Act, 1994 (CJPO), a court can draw adverse inference from a defendant's silence.[209] While the right to silence is a safeguard provided by the Indian Constitution, it does not have the similar bearing of the right expressed in England and Wales. In the absence of a systematic provision to custodial legal assistance in India, the right to silence applies only to the in-trial process. The provision of right to silence exercised after receiving legal assistance might be introduced in India only after the mandatory provision of legal assistance is ensured.

The EU Directive on the right to legal assistance requires member states to ensure that the suspect has a lawyer present when questioned and inform the suspect of their right to silence until such assistance is provided.[210] This has subsequently been reflected in the cases of *Mader v. Croatia*[211] and *Sebalj v. Croatia.*[212] The ECtHR has also emphasised in the case of *Salduz v. Turkey* that the suspect is vulnerable and

> This particular vulnerability can only be properly compensated by the assistance of a lawyer whose task it is, amongst other things, to help ensure respect for the right of an accused not to incriminate himself.[213]

3.12.5.1 Adverse inference from silence

The drawing of adverse inference from silence has far-reaching implications for the suspect who chooses to remain silent during police interview. The drawing of adverse inferences has received a mixed reaction from academics, police officers and lawyers in England and Wales.[214] While remaining silent protects the suspects right, it also increases the burden on investigating police officer. The ECtHR has no express provision for drawing adverse inference from the silence of the accused. It has held that "is a matter to be determined in the light of all the circumstance of the case."[215] The right to legal assistance has a significant impact on the use of silence or the advice to using silence at the police station. However, the use of the right to silence poses a threat given the present circumstances of drawing of adverse influence at the trial. The lawyer advising on the use of the right to silence has very little information on the case against the suspect. The lawyer must therefore assess and advise appropriately in a short span of time relying on whatever little information is provided by the police and the suspects' encounter.

The CJPO also added that a conviction based solely on the basis of adverse inference would render the trial unfair.[216] It is thus fair to infer that a conviction would not be solely based on the adverse inference drawn from the silence of the suspect. By making this provision, the court has in a way increased the prosecution's powers and investigative powers of the police.[217] The police naturally objected to the right to silence. This is understandable, thinking that almost all of the interviews would be rendered ineffective with the suspect using this right. To counterbalance this, the Royal Commission on Criminal Justice (RCCJ) came up with the provision under Section 34 of the CJPO of drawing adverse inference from the use of silence. This made the evidentiary value of what was said at the time of the police interrogation significant in the court of law. It may be that as a result of this provision, the use of right to silence has actually declined since 1994.[218] However, Cape explains that the failure to answer any questions put by the police officer is unlikely to lead to adverse inference being drawn at the trial.[219] At the same time, ensuring the suspect has legal assistance at this stage, the courts have attempted to balance the distribution of powers and rights. Academics such as Quirk also question the quality of advice given by lawyers, which also includes the use of the right to silence.[220] Drawing of adverse inference from the silence of an accused therefore rests on the advice given by the solicitor. Hence, it may be argued that the presence of a solicitor may not always have a positive impact at the hearing.

The right to silence is not absolute if a prima facie case is established against the accused and when he is in possession of special knowledge. Initial concerns about the suspects' silence to questions being asked before coming to the police station were raised by authors like Ward and Card.[221] However, this was before the presence of solicitor at the custodial legal assistance was formalised.

The courts have questioned the extent to which adverse inference shall be drawn on the use of silence on the advice of the lawyer.[222] In *Condron v. UK*, the courts asserted that appropriate weight should be attached to the legal advice on the use of silence if any inference is to be drawn.[223] This was also asserted by the courts in *R v. Betts and Hall*, further adding that in order to satisfy the requirements of Article 6, it must be demonstrated that the use of silence was pursuant to legal advice.[224] This was however not adopted in the case of *R v. Howell*, where the court held that drawing of adverse inference was not sufficient on the grounds that it was pursuant to legal advice.[225] This inconsistency has often been described as frustrating by authors such as Choo who maintain that drawing of adverse inference pursuant to legal advice alone is insufficient.[226]

Adverse inferences from silence can be used for "corroboration and assurance" at the trial.[227] Along with this, it has been argued by many that this provision is totally in contravention with the right to silence. The practice of drawing adverse inference from silence received criticism from the academics and lawyers but was appreciated by police officers.[228] Those opposing adverse inferences have been assured by vesting the responsibility of the burden of proof on the prosecution. In conclusion, it may be said that while adverse inference comes with a liability, it is not the sole basis for securing a conviction and therefore balance the values of due process and the crime control values upheld by the criminal justice system. This has also prevented the suspects who were guilty from being able to hide behind the veil of the right to silence. If similar safeguards are provided in the Indian criminal justice system and are seen to be implemented, then similar adverse inferences may be drawn. This may act as a trade-off where the suspect may be provided with a right to legal assistance, subject to consequences in order to avoid a dead-end in an interrogation.

3.12.6 Caution

As mentioned earlier, when a person is arrested in England and Wales, a caution must be given to the suspect by the arresting police officer.[229] The caution is a well-worded instrument used to provide the suspect with the right to legal assistance, right to legal aid and right to silence. The police officer after providing the caution must take the suspect to the police station in order to be questioned, with an exception to cases of stop and search.[230] Once at the police station, the custody officer must inform the suspect both orally and in writing of their right to consult a solicitor, the right to have someone informed of their arrest and the right to consult the codes of practice at any time.[231]

Additionally, the suspect must be cautioned at the commencement or re-commencement of every interrogation and be reminded of the above-mentioned rights.[232] This entire procedure ensures transparency of the evidentiary procedure of police interrogation. This is an exceptional way to create awareness and to ensure the notification of these rights to a suspect. The provision of caution is given throughout the country and ensures universality without any exceptions. However, there is no obligation upon the investigative officer to disclose their report or findings to the suspect of their lawyer; they are entitled to no such right.[233] Failure to provide a caution has significant impacts on the evidence obtained during such an investigation. It was held in *R v. Fulling* that a confession provided in an interrogation will be inadmissible in evidence if the suspect has not been cautioned.[234] The Code also provides that no inference shall be drawn from the use of silence if the suspect has not been cautioned prior to an interrogation.[235] It is suggested that provision of a caution may be introduced in India, making it a police officer's duty to read the suspect his rights. In the absence of any other mechanism presently in practice informing the suspect of his right to custodial legal assistance, a caution may notify the suspect of his right. The next section analyses the role of a lawyer at the custodial legal assistance stage in England and Wales.

3.13 The role of lawyer

The code does not lay down specific duties or the length of consultation for the lawyer to be fulfilled at this stage. The lawyer is present throughout the interrogation and intervenes to seek clarification at any time during the investigation. This procedure ensures that the suspect is treated fairly at this stage of interrogation and eliminates any unfair treatment by the police. Thus, ideally in England and Wales, the lawyer is present both at the police station to provide advice and throughout the police interrogation.[236] This action is regulated by the Solicitors Regulation Authority who also oversees the lawyer's visits to the police station. A lawyer signifies a person who is qualified in any particular jurisdiction and registered with a bar association or a law society. As observed previously, there may not be "qualitative" advice given by the solicitor and at times the use of such advice may result in practices such as drawing of adverse inferences from the suspect's silence.[237]

3.13.1 The role of a paralegal

With the increase in the demand for custodial legal assistance, it was a common practice to send the paralegal as the police station advisor to the suspect. A paralegal is a non-lawyer who has the necessary skills and training to carry out some of the functions of a lawyer in working with suspects, defendants and those convicted of criminal offences.[238] Some of the duties of these professionals overlap considerably. It is worth noting that the role of paralegals has increased in advising suspects at the police station, mainly because they are less costly.[239] Cape mentions that since the introduction of PACE, there have been instances where paralegals and unqualified solicitors have been appointed either as duty solicitors or legal aid solicitors.[240] It is argued here that despite the qualification, the advice given by the paralegals did not have an adverse effect. However, with the introduction of the Police Station Advice scheme in England and Wales, the suspects were entitled to state-funded legal advice.[241] This included access to lawyers and paralegals working under the supervision of a lawyer who have a contract with the Legal Services Commission.[242] This scheme was articulated with the provision that the paralegals would receive periodical training for offering advice. This would make sense as the number of paralegals as opposed to Police Station Representatives or Solicitors was significantly high.

Thus, having paralegals and lawyers advice at the early stage rightly reassures public faith and confidence in the criminal justice system and respect for the rule of law.[243] However, this idea of putting too much confidence in paralegals for advising suspects at the police station is questioned by many.[244] This is a crucial stage at which the advice given by a professional lawyer ensures protection of the suspect's fundamental rights. Having an unqualified professional such a paralegal give advice at this stage could interfere with the practice. However, given the present scenario of legal aid cuts, putting more responsibilities on the paralegal might seem like a practical solution.

The role of a lawyer in India at the custodial legal assistance stage is very minimal and underutilised. Unlike the Solicitors Regulation Authority, its equivalent authority, the Bar Council of India, have little participation with the provision of services similar to the police station lawyer. Even the individual approach of the Solicitors in India is that of mere reluctance for advising the suspect during the police station interrogation.[245] This practice is time restrictive and arbitrary in application as only the "rich people who can afford a lawyer get to see one at the police station."[246] Both lawyers and police officers interviewed held similar views about the arbitrary nature of application of this provision.

3.13.2 At what stages of criminal process does right to legal assistance apply?

The stages at which the right to legal assistance applies are further and broadly examined by eminent authors such as Cape following the enactments of PACE and inclusion of international statutes ensuring fair trial.[247] The ground rule laid down in *Salduz v. Turkey* was also followed in the trendsetting case of Cadder in Scotland as early as 2010. As observed by Lord Hope,

> The conclusion that I would draw as to the effect of Salduz is that the contracting states are under a duty to organise their systems in such a way as to ensure that, unless in the particular circumstances of the case there are compelling reasons for restricting the right, a person who is detained has access to advice from a lawyer before he is subjected to police questioning.[248]

Following this, the European Union adopted what Cape calls the "road map" for implementing procedural rights in criminal proceedings, including right to legal assistance. It has been rightly concluded that the right to legal assistance applies to "all" stages of criminal proceedings. The European Committee for the Prevention of Torture had described access to a lawyer for those detained by the police as follows:

> One of the three fundamental safeguards against ill-treatment of the detained persons should apply as from the very outset of deprivation of liberty, regardless of how it may be described under the legal system concerned.[249]

This clear terminology extends the right to legal assistance to persons detained "with or without a charge."[250] As discussed above, the ECtHR has for a long period taken a view that the right to legal assistance arises immediately on arrest. The suspect has the right to waive this right, but this waiver of right needs to be taken in writing by the investigating officer. These provisions are laid down by the ECtHR and incorporated into the English criminal justice system. A statutory framework for these rights provides a clear format, which is understood by the general public and enforced by police officers. Police officers have the duty to inform the suspect of his right to legal assistance and ensure that the interrogation commences only on arrival of the lawyer. When compared with the judgement of the Indian courts, they confirm that the lawyer may advise the suspect but cannot remain present throughout the interview.[251] This provision needs to be amended in order to comply with the standards laid down by international bodies such as the ECHR. The provisions of Article 6 of the ECHR and its jurisprudence may be read along with the provisions of the English courts and legislation in order to ensure that the interrogation leads to a fair trial. Apart from the presence of lawyer, other safeguards such as tape recording of the interrogation are analysed in the next section.

3.14 Tape recording and legal assistance

PACE Code E advises that “Tape recording of interviews shall be carried out openly to instil confidence in its reliability as an impartial and accurate record of the interview.” Thus, the entire investigation involving the tape-recording process must be carried out in full view of the interviewee, beginning with the unwrapping of the audio tapes and their loading into the recorder.[252] PACE Code C describes in detail the guidelines to be followed by the investigating police officer for recording the interview. Any breach of the code will be considered by the Court and can have impact on the admissibility of evidence. As evidenced in the case of *R v. Absolam* and *R v. Delaney*, any breach in recording the interrogation may be evidence of oppression or contention of unreliability.[253] It may further lead to evidence of confession being excluded as a matter of discretion under Section 76 or 78 of PACE.[254] Tape recording of interrogation also ensures that no unfair means of interrogation are used and also ensures the provision of legal assistance. This safeguard works along with the provision of legal assistance to guarantee the fair trial rights of the suspect. However, this safeguard is subject to criticism as pointed out by Roberts and Zuckerman who opine that tape (audio) recording does not capture bodily gestures and only records the events that occur while the recorder was running.[255] This can easily be remedied by the provision of video recording which can be played at the trial if challenged by either party.[256] This was also highlighted by the RCCP mentioning various advantages of video recording over audio recorded interrogations.[257] Amendments have been made in many situations where interrogations are video recorded more often in England and Wales. Since the records are in possession of an independent body there is a certain level of transparency in this procedure of tape recording the interrogation.

3.15 Do suspects request a lawyer?

It is essential to identify the attitude of the suspects amidst all these legislative safeguards to requesting a lawyer. In England and Wales, following the relevant amendments made in PACE and the codes of practice, all the suspects are informed of their right to legal assistance. Thus, even if suspects do not request a lawyer, they are still aware of the provision. Studies have revealed that suspects may refuse legal assistance because they might think this may delay their release.[258] Most of the times when the suspect refuses physical presence of a lawyer, police officers ensure that they get an opportunity to consult one over the telephone. In any case, if the suspect denies legal assistance, this has to be recorded by the police officer in the station diary.

3.15.1 The right in practice

Earlier studies by Sanders and Young indicated that police officers actively discouraged recourse to legal advice.[259] This reluctance might be due to the perception amongst some officers that suspects' access to legal advice is an impediment to their cooperation.[260] However, more recent studies in England and Wales along with other jurisdictions found no trace of suspects being threatened or tricked by the police into waiving their right to legal assistance.[261] There have been allegations that police officers often dissuade the suspect from using a lawyer. However, studies have confirmed that this has decreased in the past few years owing to strict regulation.[262] Continuous and updated research carried out in England and Wales assists in identifying the flaws in practice and rectifying them. In one of the largest study carried out by Professor Pleasence, analysing 30,000 custody records in England and Wales, it was found that there was a decline in use of the right to legal assistance by suspects.[263] Despite this decline, it is noted that the right in practice remains to be used by a majority of suspects.

3.16 Analysis of comparison

The statutory framework in England and Wales regarding the right to legal assistance is coherent and simple. It lays down specifically the time at which legal assistance shall be guaranteed to the suspect, the advisor providing knowledge of this (in this case the police officer), forms of legal aid and the role of the lawyer. While some of these provisions are taken from the EU directives, most others are implemented by the English Criminal justice system.[264] While in India the right to legal assistance is a constitutional guarantee, it has been further interpreted in detail by the Supreme Court. Hence, although the Constitutional enactments mention that a suspect has the right to legal assistance, it does not mention at which stage. The Supreme Court has tried to fill in this lacuna by delivering various judgements mentioning at times that it is available at the time of the arrest.[265] However, there is no unanimity and consistency among the Supreme Court judgements. Certain cases like *Satpathy v. Dani* and *D K Basu* also took precedent from the famous case of *Miranda v. Arizona*.[266] The judgement in this case is criticised as it affirmed the right to counsel only once the suspect had been charged. The case of *Sheela Barse* tried to fill in the gaps left by *Satpathy Dani*'s case.[267] It was affirmed in this case that the right to legal assistance arises when the suspect is charged "at the police station." This raises another question as to what if the suspect is being questioned. The Supreme Court of India has clearly not taken an affirmative stance on this subject. This suggests two major flaws rendering guarantee of fundamental rights far from being practically re-enforced. Firstly, there is a lack of clarity in the legislative enactments. Secondly, the interpretations of the Supreme Court judgements are ambiguous in interpreting the fundamental rights guaranteed under the Constitution. The fact that there is no clear mention of legal assistance at the time of the arrest being mandatory is a basic flaw and is reflected in the interrogatory process. The importance of having legal assistance at the questioning stage in India is to ensure that the suspect's rights are safeguarded from the inception of the interrogation stage. I suggest that there is an urgent need for the right to custodial legal assistance to be incorporated in legislation and in practice.

I suggest that the use of a caution to inform the suspect of his right to custodial legal assistance may be enforced in India. This provision may be assisted if it bears legislative recognition. The legislative provisions of PACE may be taken as a recommendation for implementing this provision in India.

The existence of PACE has been in England and Wales for just over 30 years. Non-availability of legal assistance at the police station is inconsistent with various international conventions.[268] Other precedents may be taken from the English criminal justice system such as changes to the provision of right to silence. While this has been criticised to be ultra-vires of the Constitutional provision, it may be looked at by law commissions, provided suspect safeguards are in place.[269] Authorities have further criticised the English system for drawing adverse inference from the suspect's silence; for instance, the Law Commission recommended that the same contravene the right to life and liberty.[270] In order to justify this, the famous case of *Maneka Gandhi* is always relied upon by the Law Commission.[271] Drawing of adverse inference in court after the interrogation has been conducted in the presence of a lawyer who advises appropriate use of silence is questionable. Having the legal assistance at the time of arrest can ensure the exercise of right to silence and can further extend to reliable evidence.

Among many criticisms involved with the idea of making legal assistance at the police station mandatory, the most debatable is the cost involved. However, it can easily be compensated with the idea of having numerous lawyers in India and the impact it can also reduce the backlog of cases in courts. A pilot programme using the resources available in terms of available lawyers in India using the legislative framework such as PACE may assist in providing a solution to malpractices and further backlog of cases.[272] Lawyers in India will have to engage with the new demands placed before them by statutory right to custodial legal advice. Many empirical studies in England and Wales demonstrate the presence of a system that reflects the principles of PACE with reference to the presence of a lawyer.[273] This report also reflects the unwillingness on the part of suspects to use lawyers at the custodial interrogation stage.[274] However, the present research highlights the system in place, while acknowledging the loopholes in the system. Contrast to this, in India, the lawyers' focus is usually the court, the preparation of the case and client advice. In England and Wales, frequent advisory services are offered by non-qualified or partially qualified staff, in order to maximise profit. However, the depleting aid from the government has threatened the future workability of this provision.

The work of the Runciman Commission and the Phillips Commission is also commended for the recommendations provided, which resulted in the passing of the laws in England. Conversely in India, recommendations by various law commissions over a longer period of time as compared to England and Wales have seen no progress.[275] Why have these recommendations not been considered by the government? While most of these Commissions have aimed at providing recommendations of having legal assistance at police station mandatory, they seem to lack clarity and detail. The report provides no specific reasons for having mandatory presence of legal assistance at the police station.

While the advancement of providing legal aid is undergoing constant progress in India, there is no provision of legal aid at the police station. The Supreme Court has in many cases, starting as early as 1986, highlighted the importance of legal aid, but it was not promptly reflected in any legislative enactments. The amount of time taken by courts to implement this recommendation has resulted in further delays in the trial process and the backlog of cases at courts. While the courts have made the provision of legal aid, it is only available to people who are economically disadvantaged. This practice is arbitrary and lacks a uniformity of application as it is a provision which almost financially penalises those who can afford legal assistance. The provision of legal aid in England and Wales begins from the time of the arrest of the suspect and is provided uniformly regardless of the earning capacity of the suspect. Owing to this, there has been a debate amongst English scholars as the government plans on imposing legal aid cuts, but it is argued that this will not affect the suspect as much as it will affect law firms commercially. However, a system similar to the current provision of legal aid in England and Wales may be adopted and then updated periodically.

The provisions of PACE came into force after numerous cases of miscarriage of justice and public outcry. The public attitude and awareness towards the right to custodial legal assistance in England and Wales are quite different to the public attitude and awareness in India. The awareness amongst the public in England and Wales ensured that governmental pressure surmounted to some legislative action to be taken immediately. This has also been highlighted by the English courts in their decisions. The public attitude in India towards the lack of safeguards such as the right to legal assistance is indifferent. There is no general consensus among the public against the non-implementation of this right in practice. Even the academics have very little to comment about when they address this issue of non-implementation.

England and Wales was thought to be at an advantage of having an authority like the ECHR constantly guarding the suspects' rights. It was answerable to a higher authority and has to follow the norms set by the convention regarding the right to legal assistance. As a result of the pursuance of the ECHR, many other countries have also adopted the mandatory provision of legal assistance at the police station. Precedents may be taken from the ECtHR jurisprudence along with English jurisprudence by the Indian Criminal Justice system. Countries such as Scotland, Belgium and the Netherlands are also adopting similar procedures after seminal judgements such as *Salduz v. Turkey* and *Cadder v. H M Advocate*. This may provide assistance in the procedure to be adopted for mandating the right to legal assistance. However, it may be argued that post-Brexit the certainty of this rule may be considered dubious.

With the presence of the legal assistance at the custodial police interrogation stage, the possibility of using the right to silence may follow and with that the drawing of adverse inferences. As observed in England and Wales, this has drawn huge criticisms as it has its advantages and disadvantages. Quirk notices, "Somehow, subtly, curtailing the right of silence had shifted from erroneous to aspirational—the mark of an advanced criminal justice system—a view enhanced by the lack of objection in England and Strasbourg."[276]

The right to custodial legal assistance has not been researched or implemented in legislation in India over the past few years. As demonstrated in the previous chapter on police interrogation, it is argued that a police officer may fail to implement any suspects' rights. The lack of training of police officers may contribute towards the non-observance of suspects' rights. In the absence of other mechanisms, such as lack of tape recording of the interrogation and ensuring the safety of the suspect, it is argued that the presence of a lawyer at the time of interrogation must be mandatory. Lawyers' introduction at this vital stage can also ensure protection against abuse of police powers. Lawyers may also have a professional interest to protect the suspect during interrogation in India. Hence, I argue that there is some level of urgency in providing the right to custodial legal assistance legislative recognition.

3.17 Conclusion

In conclusion, the current practice of having legal representation present at the time of police interrogation at the police station in India lacks clear legislative interpretation. Immediate and exhaustive reforms must be made in order to interpret this constitutional right. Legislative enactments must reflect mandatory provision similar to those of PACE and its codes of practices. Police officers should be endowed with the responsibility of informing the suspects of their right to legal assistance using "caution." Since the right to legal representation cannot be added to the Constitution of India, a new enactment such as PACE should be adopted.[277] I argue in this chapter that it is due to the lack of essential safeguards in India, such as the right to custodial legal assistance, that a police interrogation is not monitored and is subject to various criticisms. The protective role played by a lawyer at the police station in India is highly undermined and under-researched. The continued abuse of police powers during interrogation highlights the importance of custodial legal assistance. The right to custodial legal assistance needs to be incorporated in legislation as it has been argued that mere Supreme Court legislation is not sufficient. It is also because of this factor that a confession given to a police officer is inadmissible in India. The admissibility of a confession given to a police officer is examined in detail in the next chapter.

Notes

1 H Packer, 'Two Models of the Criminal Process' (1964) 113 U. Penn. L. Rev. 1.
2 Ibid.
3 Article 6 of the ECtHR. Also see, *Salduz v. Turkey* 36391/02 (2008) ECHR 1542.
4 Article 22(1): '(no) person who is arrested shall be detained in custody without being informed, as soon as may be, of the grounds of arrest nor shall he be denied the right to consult, and be defended by a legal practitioner of his choice.' The Constitution of India, available at http://www.constitution.org/cons/india/const.html; Section 154 of the Code of Criminal Procedure, 1973.
5 Section 154 of the Code of Criminal Procedure, 1973; Section 50A(3) Cr.PC—that information regarding the arrest and the person informed about the arrest is recorded in the designated register kept in the police station.
6 Article 22(1) of the Constitution of India.
7 *Broken System: Dysfunction, Abuse and Impunity in the Indian Police*, 2009, Human Rights Watch Report, available at http://www.hrw.org/sites/default/files/reports/india0809web.pdf.
8 Article 22(1), "(no) person who is arrested shall be detained in custody without being informed, as soon as may be, of the grounds of arrest nor shall he be denied the right to consult, and be defended by, a legal practitioner of his choice."
9 Section 303: right of person against whom proceedings are instituted to be defended. Any person accused of an offence before a Criminal Court, or against whom proceedings are instituted under this Code, may of right be defended by a pleader of his choice.
10 Dr B Ambedkar is the architect of the Constitution of India. Further details can be found at http://www.sankalpindia.net/drupal/ambedkar-the-architect-indian-constitution.

11 G Singh, '"Bill of Rights" in the Constitution of India' (2009), available at http://www.newenglishreview.org/print.cfm?pg=custpage&frm=42164&sec_id=44259, accessed on 20 November 2015.
12 Article 22(2) of the Constitution of India. A Judicial Magistrate First Class is equivalent to the District Magistrate at a county level in England and Wales.
13 As observed by B Uma Devi, *Arrest, Detention, and Criminal Justice System: A Study in the Context of the Constitution of India*, OUP, 2012; Law Commission Reports 177 and 184, available at http://lawcommissionofindia.nic.in/, accessed on 15 August 2015.
14 The Law Commission Report and the Justice Malimath Committee Report.
15 K Madan and S Gupta, *Legal Aid in India*, Legal Services India, October 2008, http://www.legalserviceindia.com/article/l261-Legal-Aid.html *in Sheela Barse v. State of Maharashtra* (1988) 1 S.C.R. 210 (India), available at http://www.cscsarchive.org:8081/MediaArchive/medialaw.nsf/%28docid%29/F189008680136C31E5256AC700322FD5.
16 R Mittal, *Legal Aid: Catalyst for Social Change*, Delhi: Satyam Law International, 2012.
17 The term lawyer includes Solicitor. The Indian legal system does not have a mandatory divide between the Solicitor and the Barrister unlike England and Wales. Any member admitted to the Bar Council is called an Advocate or a Lawyer. There are a few qualified Solicitors in India, but they are optional and Solicitor exams are undertaken by choice.
18 A.I.R. 1926 Bom. 551; see also *Hans Raj v. State,* AI.R. 1956 All 641, 642.
19 *AmolakRam v. Emperor* AI.R. 1932 Lah 13.
20 *Tara Singh v. State,* A.I.R. 1951 S.C. 441, p. 452.
21 *State of Punjab v. Surinder Singh,* 1965 Cri.L.T. 161 (P & H).
22 *Janardhan Reddy v. State of Hyderabad,* A.I.R. 1951 S.C. 217.
23 *Miranda v. Arizona*, 384 U.S. 436 (1966).
24 *Satpathy v. PL Dani*, AIR 1978 SC 1025, at para 612.
25 Ibid at para 650.
26 Ibid at para 613 and 614.
27 *Miranda v. Arizona*, 384 U.S. 436 (1966) at p. 623.
28 *Satpathy v. P L Dani*, AIR 1978 SC 1025, at para 612.
29 *Ajmal Amir Kasab v. State of Maharashtra* (2012) 9 SCC 234, *Salduz v Turkey* 36391/02 (2008) ECHR 1542.
30 180th Report, *Law Commission of India, May 2002*, available at http://lawcommissionofindia.nic.in/reports/180rpt.pdf.
31 *Nandini Satpathy v. P L Dani*, AIR 1978 SC 1025.
32 *Sheela Barse v. State of Maharashtra*, A.I.R. 1983 S. C. 378.
33 Ibid at 344 A-D.
34 Article 22(1) of the Constitution of India.
35 D Arnold, *Police Power and Colonial Rule: Madras 1859–1947*, Delhi: OUP, 1986.
36 *D K Basu v. State of West Bengal* AIR 1997 SC 610, these are mentioned in the previous chapter on Police Interrogation.
37 Ibid at para 9.
38 Ibid at para 9–11.
39 These guidelines have been mentioned in Chapter 2.
40 Enforcement Guidelines:

1. The guidelines must be translated in as many languages as possible and distributed to every police station. It must also be incorporated in a handbook which should be given to every policeman.
2. Guidelines must receive maximum publicity in the print or other electronic

media. It should also be prominently displayed on notice board, in more than one language, in every police station.

3. The police must set up a complaint redressal mechanism, which will promptly investigate complaints of violation of guidelines and take corrective action.
4. The notice board which displays guidelines must also indicate the location of the complaints redressal mechanism and how that body can be approached.
5. NGOs and public institutions, including courts, hospitals, universities etc., must be involved in the dissemination of these guidelines to ensure the widest possible reach.
6. The functioning of the complaint redressal mechanism must be transparent and its reports accessible.
7. Prompt action must be taken against errant police officers for violation of the guidelines. This should not be limited to departmental enquiries but also set in motion the criminal justice mechanism.

41 *Miranda v. Arizona*, 384 US 436.

42 *D K Basu v. State of West Bengal* AIR 1997 SC 610. Proceedings under the Contempt of Courts Act, 1971 can be started in any High Court.

43 B Fortman, "Adventurous' Judgments: A Comparative Exploration into Human Rights as a Moral-Political Force in Judicial Law Development' (2006) 2(2) *Utrecht Law Review* 22–43.

44 J Kuhns and J Knutsson, 'Police Encounters in Mumbai' in J Belur (ed), *Police Use of Force: A Global Perspective*, Santa Barbara, CA: Praeger Security International, 2010.

45 For details, see the case of *Anant Brahmachari v. Uoi and Others*, W.P.(CRL) No. 55/2011.

46 *Anant Brahmachari v. Union of India & Others*, W.P.(CRL) No. 55/2011, at para 4.

47 The Inspector of Police, *P Saravanan v. K C Palanisamy* CRL.O.P. (MD). No. 13615 of 2011.

48 *D K Basu v. State of West Bengal* AIR 1997 SC 610.

49 *Anant Brahmachari v. Uoi & Others*, W.P. (CRL) No. 55/2011. For the purpose of this section, the terms arrestee and suspect are used interchangeably and bear the same meaning.

50 *Sundeep Bafna v. The State of Maharashtra*, Criminal Appeal No. 689 of 2014.

51 Section 46 of the CrPC.

52 Decision reported as *Paramhansa Jadab v. State* AIR 1964 Ori 144.

53 One of the main components of Lon Fuller's eight requirements of the Rule of Law. For details, see C Murphy, 'Lon Fuller and the Moral Value of the Rule of Law' (2005) 24 *Law and Philosophy* 239–262, 240.

54 Article 55(2)(d) of the Rome Statute of the International Criminal Court. The Supreme Court of India in the case of *D K Basu v. State of West Bengal*, 18 December 1996, (1997) 2 LRC 1, para 36(10) has recommended the presence of a lawyer during but not throughout the interrogation. Although this seems to be a progressive approach, it still falls short of international standard.

55 *Ramdev Food Products Private Limited v. State of Gujarat*, Criminal Appeal No. 600 of 2007, Decided on: 16.03.2015.

56 *Malimath Committee Report: Committee on Reforms of Criminal Justice System*, Government of India, 2003, mha.nic.in/pdfs/criminal_justice_system.pdf

57 Ibid.

58 Justice V S Malimath is a retired Chief Justice of Kerala, India. This Committee was constituted by the Government of India, Ministry of Home Affairs by an order dated 24th November 2000. The main idea was to examine the fundamental principles of criminal law more particularly with a view to shorten long delays of criminal trials and sentences, thereby restoring confidence in the Indian criminal justice system.
59 *Malimath Committee Report: Committee on Reforms of Criminal Justice System,* Government of India, 2003, mha.nic.in/pdfs/criminal_justice_system.pdf, para 2.16.4.
60 Ibid at para 4.4.
61 Ibid at para 4.5.
62 Ibid at para 5.
63 *Nandini Satpathy v. P L Dani,* A.I.R. 1978 S.C. 1025.
64 *Amnesty International, India: Report of the Malimath Committee on Reforms of the Criminal Justice System: Some Observations*, 19 September 2003, ASA 20/025/2003, available at: http://www.unhcr.org/refworld/docid/3f914cba4.html.
65 B Uma Devi, *Arrest, Detention, and Criminal Justice System: A Study in the Context of the Constitution of India*, OUP, 2012.
66 Second Administrative Reforms Report, Fifth Report, June 2007, Government of India.
67 *Malimath Committee Report: Committee on Reforms of Criminal Justice System,* Government of India, 2003, mha.nic.in/pdfs/criminal_justice_system.pdf, Recommendation no 1–7.
68 Ibid, recommendation no. 3.41.
69 Ibid, recommendation no. 1–7.
70 J Blackstock, E Cape, J Hodgson, A Ogordova, and T Spronken, *Inside Police Custody: An Empirical Account of Suspects' Rights in Four Jurisdictions*, Intersentia, 2014.
71 *Salduz v. Turkey* 36391/02 (2008) ECHR 1542.
72 For a detailed review, please refer to D Giannoulopoulos, 'Strasbourg Jurisprudence, Law Reform and Comparative Law: A Tale of the Right to Custodial Legal Assistance in Five Countries' (2016) 16 *Human Rights Law Review* 1 (forthcoming).
73 In December 2013, the Diplomat provided an estimate of 32 million cases of judicial backlog. http://thediplomat.com/2013/12/justice-delayed-is-justice-denied-indias-30-million-case-judicial-backlog/
74 Criminal Justice Reform in India, Review of the Recommendations made by the Justice Malimath Committee from an International Human Rights Perspective, available at http://www.docs-archive.com/view/fa8ac0be9f7951d55b7f83c572efdf05/Criminal-Justice-Reform-in-India%3A-ICJ-Position-Paper.pdf, 14.
75 Ibid.
76 Ibid, 16.
77 Ibid, 19.
78 Article 39A of the Constitution of India- Equal justice and free legal aid.

> "The State shall secure that the operation of the legal system promotes justice, on a basis of equal opportunity, and shall, in particular, provide free legal aid, by suitable legislation or schemes or in any other way, to ensure that opportunities for securing justice are not denied to any citizen by reason of economic or other disabilities."

79 *Sheela Barse v. Union of India* (1986) 3 SCC 596.
80 *Nandini Satpathi v. Dani,* A.I.R. 1978 S.C. 1073.

81 *Khatri v. State of Bihar* A.I.R. 1981 SCR (2) 408.
82 Ibid, 414.
83 *Khatri v. State of Bihar* A.I.R. 1981 SCR (2) 408.
84 *Mothi Bhai v. State of Rajasthan* 1954 Cri. L.J. 1591.
85 *Khatri v. State of Bihar* A.I.R. 1981 S.C. 928.
86 *Gian Singh v. State (Delhi Admn.),* 1981 Cri. L.J. 100.
87 *Khatri v. State of Bihar* A.I.R. 1981 S.C. 928.
88 *Sheela Barse v. Union of India* (1986) 3 SCC 596, *D K Basu v. State of West Bengal* (1997) 1 SCC 216.
89 *D K Basu v. State of West Bengal* (1997) 1 SCC 216.
90 *Janardhan Reddi v. State of Hyderabad* A.I.R. 1951 S.C. 217.
91 *D K Basu v. State of West Bengal* (1997) 1 SCC 216.
92 Centre for Legal Research and *Another v. The State of Kerala*, AIR 1986 SC 2196.
93 The Legal Services Authorities Act accessed at http://lawmin.nic.in/la/subord/nalsa.htm.
94 *Ajmal Amir Kasab v. State of Maharashtra* (2012) 9 SCC 234.
95 Ibid.
96 For further details, please see http://www.un.int/india/india_and_the_un_hr.html.
97 Bureau of Democracy, Human Rights and Labour, U.S. Department of State Country Reports on Human Rights Practices: India 19 (2010), available at http://www.state.gov/documents/organization/160058.pdf.
98 For details, please see http://www.i-probono.com/.
99 *Mothi Bhai v. State of Rajasthan* 1954 Cri. L.J. 1591.
100 India is a signatory to the United Declaration of Human Rights, thereby aiming to provide the basic human rights ensuring a fair trial to the suspect. For further details, please see http://www.un.int/india/india_and_the_un_hr.html.
101 Interview Transcript PO4.
102 Ibid.
103 *Khatri v. State of Bihar*, AIR 1981 SC 928.
104 J Mathivanan, 'Legal Aid: Issues, Challenges, and Solutions', available at https://www.google.co.uk/url?sa=t&rct=j&q=&esrc=s&source=web&cd=1&cad=rja&uact=8&ved=0CCEQFjAA&url=http%3A%2F%2Fwww.hcmadras.tn.nic.in%2Flegalaid-issues.pdf&ei=CxHaVOiGNsLwatbzgqAI&usg=AFQjCNHP1JZBdzPtO-z-ttRa64kia2qH7Q&sig2=SNMzaWnhnvLuJpp0r9pEiw&bvm=bv.85464276,d.ZWU.
105 *D K Basu v. State of West Bengal* (1997) 1 SCC 216.
106 Ibid, Directive No 11. Proceedings for contempt of court can be initiated in any High Court under the Contempt of Courts Act, 1971.
107 J Vadackumchery, *Indian Police and Equal Justice under Law*, APH Publishing, 1999, India, 80.
108 Article 226 of the Constitution of India, Section 50 of the Code of Criminal Procedure.
109 *Md. Sukur Ali v. State of Assam* (2011) Criminal Appeal No. 546 OF 2011.
110 Article 22 (1): 'no person shall be denied the right to counsel.'
111 A Bewicke, 'Asian Developments in Access to Counsel: A Comparative Study' 2011 10(2) *Northwestern Journal of International Human Rights* 27–53.
112 H M Seervai, *Constitutional Law of India*, 2015, 4th edn, 857.
113 Ibid.
114 Article 20(3) of the Constitution of India reads, 'No person accused of any offence shall be compelled to be a witness against himself'. This is often described as the right to silence.

115 Article 61(1)(g) and 67(1)(g) of the Rome Statute of the International Criminal Court.
116 *D K Basu v. State of West Bengal* (1997) 1 SCC 216, at para 20 of the judgement.
117 *Nandini Satpathy v. Dani*, 1978 AIR 1025, 1978 SCR (3) 608, 644 D-F.
118 F Nariman, *India's Legal System: Can It Be Saved?*, Penguin Publishers, India, 2006.
119 Ibid, Recommendation no. 8.
120 47th Report of the Law Commission of India on the Trial and Punishment of Social and Economic Offences (New Delhi: Ministry of Law and Justice, Government of India, 1972).
121 F Nariman, *India's Legal System: Can It Be Saved?*, Penguin Publishers, India, 2006; Neeta Lal, 'Huge Case Backlog Clogs India's Courts' *Asia Times Online*, 28 June 2008, available at http://www.atimes.com/atimes/South_Asia/JF28Df02.html; Biography of Bijaya Chanda, 2010 Asia JusticeMakers Fellow, International Bridges to Justice, http://justicemakers.ibj.org/fellows/bijaya-chanda/.
122 The Inspector of Police, *P. Saravanan v. K C Palanisamy* CRL.O.P.(MD). No. 13615 of 2011.
123 Committee on reforms of the Criminal Justice System, 57.
124 N Lal, 'Huge Case Backlog Clogs India's Courts' *Asia Times Online*, 28 June 2008, available at http://www.atimes.com/atimes/South_Asia/JF28Df02.html; Biography of Bijaya Chanda, 2010 Asia JusticeMakers Fellow, International Bridges to Justice, http://justicemakers.ibj.org/fellows/bijaya-chanda/
125 B Uma Devi, *Arrest, Detention, and Criminal Justice System: A Study in the Context of the Constitution of India*, OUP, 2012, 60.
126 Bureau of Democracy, Human Rights and Labour, U.S. Department of State Country Reports on Human Rights Practices: India 19 (2010), available at http://www.state.gov/documents/organization/160058.pdf, at 10.
127 Interview Transcript PO7.
128 Interview Transcript PO7.
129 As pointed out in the unpublished thesis submitted by N Kumar titled, 'Human Rights Violation in Police Custody,' available online at https://dyuthi.cusat.ac.in/xmlui/bitstream/handle/purl/927/Dyuthi-T0127.pdf?.11.
130 Interview Transcript PO9.
131 Interview Transcript PO4.
132 Interview Transcript PO5.
133 Interview Transcript PO4.
134 Interview Transcript PO3.
135 Interview Transcript PO7.
136 Article 22 of the Constitution of India and the guidelines provided by the Supreme Court in the case of *D K Basu*.
137 *Ajmal Amir Kasab v. State of Maharashtra* (2012) 9 SCC 234, para 160.
138 Interview Transcript PO5.
139 *D K Basu v The State of West Bengal*, AIR 1997 SC 610, Directive Number 10, 'The arrestee may be permitted to meet his lawyer during interrogation, though not throughout the interrogation.'
140 177th Law Commission Report.
141 J Vadackumchery, *Indian Police and Equal Justice under Law*, APH Publishing, 1999.
142 Interview Transcript PO7.
143 Interview Transcript PP1.
144 Interview Transcript L1.

145 ECtHR 8 February 1996, *John Murray v. UK* No. 18731/91; ECtHR 18 February 2010, *Zaichenko v. Russia* No. 39660/02; ECtHR 13 October 2009, *Dayanan v. Turkey* No. 7377/03; and ECtHR, Grand Chamber, 27 November 2008, *Salduz v. Turkey* No. 36391/02.
146 PACE, Code of Practice C, para 10.5.
147 J Blackstock, E Cape, J Hodgson, A Ogordova, and T Spronken, *Inside Police Custody: An Empirical Account of Suspects' Rights in Four Jurisdictions*, Intersentia, 2014.
148 The Police and Criminal Evidence Act, 1984, which came into effect in January 1986.
149 Section 58(8) of the Police and Criminal Evidence Act, 1984.
150 P Devlin, *The Criminal Prosecution in England*, Oxford: Oxford University Press, 1957, 26–31, 62–66.
151 E Cape and R Young, *Regulating Policing: The Police and Criminal Evidence Act 1984 Past, Present and Future*, Hart Publishing, 2008, 125.
152 Ibid, 126.
153 J Coppen in E Cape and R Young, *Regulating Policing: The Police and Criminal Evidence Act 1984 Past, Present and Future*, Hart Publishing, 2008, 97.
154 K Bottomley, C Coleman, D Dixon, and M Gill, 'The Detention of Suspects in Police Custody; The Impact of the Police and Criminal Evidence Act 1984' (1991) 31(4) *British Journal of Criminology* 347–364, 358.
155 Ibid.
156 P Softley, *Police Interrogation: An Observational Study in Four Police Stations,* Royal Commission on Criminal Procedure, Research Study no. 4. London: HMSO, 1980.
157 M McConville, A Sanders, and R Leng, *The Case for the Prosecution*, London: Routledge, 1991.
158 J Jackson in E Cape and R Young, *Regulating Policing: The Police and Criminal Evidence Act 1984 Past, Present and Future*, Hart Publishing, 2008, 259.
159 J Vadackumchery, *Indian Police and Equal Justice under Law*, APH Publishing, 1999.
160 C Phillips, *Royal Commission on Criminal Procedure: The Investigation and Prosecution of Criminal Offences in England and Wales; The Law and Procedure* (1981), para 4.77.
161 J Rosenberg, 'Miscarriages of Justice' in E Stockdale and S Casale (eds), *Criminal Justice under Stress* (1993).
162 *R v. Paris, Abdullahi and Miller* (1992) 97 Cr App R 99, 102.
163 Ibid, 104.
164 E Cape and R Young, *Regulating Policing: The Police and Criminal Evidence Act 1984 Past, Present and Future*, Hart Publishing, 2008, 262.
165 D Dixon, *Law in Policing: Legal Regulation and Police Practices*, Oxford: Clarendon Press, 1997.
166 A Ashworth, *The Criminal Process,* OUP, 1993, 93; L Campbell, A Ashworth, and M Redmayne, *The Criminal Process*, 5th edn, 2019.
167 M Zander, 'PACE (The Police and Criminal Evidence Act, 1984): Past, Present, and Future' (2011) LSE Legal Studies Working Paper 1–14.
168 The Runciman Committee Report, available at https://www.gov.uk/government/uploads/system/uploads/.../2263.pdf, para 45.
169 Ibid, para 50.
170 A Ashworth and M Redmayne, *The Criminal Process*, 3rd edn, OUP, 2004, 14; L Campbell, A Ashworth, and M Redmayne, *The Criminal Process*, 5th edn, 2019.

171 Ibid, The Runciman Committee Report, 1993 available at https://www.gov.uk/government/uploads/system/uploads/.../2263.pdf.
172 A Hucklesby and A Wahidin, *Criminal Justice*, (ed.) 2nd edn, OUP, 2013.
173 1996 (22) EHRR, 29.
174 E Cape and R Young, *Regulating Policing: The Police and Criminal Evidence Act 1984 Past, Present and Future*, Hart Publishing, 2008, 228, See generally; T Smith and E Cape, 'The Rise and Decline of Criminal Legal Aid in England and Wales' in A Flynn and J Hodgson (eds), *Access to Justice and Legal Aid: Comparative Perspectives on Unmet Legal Need*, Hart Publishing, 2017, available at https://uwe-repository.worktribe.com/output/899612.
175 Ibid, 226, M McConville and Hodgson, 'Custodial Legal Advice and the Right to Silence' RCCJ Study 16, London: HMSO, 1993.
176 *R v. Argent* (1997) 2 Cr App R 27, *R v. Imran and Hussain* (1997) Crim L.R. 754 CA and *R v. Roble* (1997) CLR 346.
177 *Imran and Hussain* (1997) Crim. L.R. 754, CA and *Farrell* (2004) EWCA Crim 597.
178 H Quirk, 'The Right of Silence in England and Wales: Sacred Cow, Sacrificial Lamb or Trojan Horse?' in J D Jackson and S J Summers (eds), *Obstacles to Fairness in Criminal Proceedings: Individual Rights and Institutional Forms*, Oxford: Hart Publishing, 2018.
179 H Quirk and J Robins, 'The Right of Silence and Undermining Legal Representation at the Police Station', in *No Defence: Miscarriages of Justice and Lawyers*, 2013, (ed), 48–51.
180 (2009) 49 EHRR 19.
181 (2010) UKSC 43, 2010 SLT 1125.
182 (2000) SLT 239.
183 (2001) SLT 674.
184 (2009) HCJAC 97, 2010 SLT 73.
185 (2009) 49 EHRR 19.
186 *Salduz v. Turkey* 36391/02 (2008) ECHR 1542.
187 *R v. Alladice* (1988) 87 Cr App R 380; *R v. Mason* (1988) 1 WLR 139; and *R v. Walsh* (1990) Cr App R 161.
188 *Imbroscia v. Switzerland* (1994) 17 EHRR 441, para 441.
189 C Phillips, *Royal Commission on Criminal Procedure, the Investigation and Prosecution of Criminal Offences in England and Wales; The Law and Procedure* (1981).
190 Council of Europe, 'Human Rights Education for Legal Professionals' available at http://www.coehelp.org/mod/glossary/showentry.php?courseid=75&concept=Positive+obligation.
191 *Salduz v. Turkey* 36391/02 (2008) ECHR 1542.
192 ECtHR, *John Murray v. the United Kingdom, John Murray v. UK* No. 18731/91; ECtHR 18 February 2010, 26–28.
193 For further details, see Giannoulopoulos, '"North of the Border and across the Channel": Custodial Legal Assistance Reforms in Scotland and France' (2013) *Criminal Law Review* 369.
194 *Cadder v. H M Advocate* (2010) UKSC 43.
195 *Dayanan v. Turkey* No. 7377/03.
196 Ibid, para 33.
197 *Demirkaya v. Turkey*, 13 October 2009, No. 31721/02.
198 See generally; A Elson, 'The Rushcliffe Report' (1946) 13(2) *The University of Chicago Law Review*; S Hynes and J Robins, *The Justice Gap*, LAG, 2009; T Bingham, *The Rule of Law*, Penguin, 2010, 86–89; Lord Justice Jackson. 'Review of Civil Litigation Costs: Preliminary Report Volume One' May 2009,

available at http://www.judiciary.gov.uk/Resources/JCO/Documents/jackson-vol1-low.pdf.

199 Section 58 of the Police and Criminal Evidence Act, 1984.

200 Also known as Police Station Accredited Representative (PSAR) in England and Wales.

201 This provision also includes the Defence Solicitors Call Centre and the CDS Direct telephonic services.

202 Section 58(4) PACE, Code of Practice C, para 6.5.

203 PACE, Code C, Section 6.

204 E Cape, 'England and Wales Country Report' available at http://www.legalaidreform.org/criminal-legal-aid-resources/item/download/148_3c7d8614d751b7b505c15e59a87b5706.

205 *Hooper v. the United Kingdom* (2005) 41 EHRR 1.

206 E Cape, 'England and Wales Country Report' available at http://www.legalaidreform.org/criminal-legal-aid-resources/item/download/148_3c7d8614d751b7b505c15e59a87b5706, Article 6: The Right to a Fair Trial, Human Rights Review 2012, available at http://www.equalityhumanrights.com/sites/default/files/documents/humanrights/hrr_article_6.pdf, accessed on 12 November 2015.

207 'Legal Aid Reforms: Judge Overturns Duty Lawyer Contracts Cut', available at http://www.bbc.co.uk/news/uk-29283993.

208 A Edwards, 'Do the Defence Matter?' (2010) 14 *International Journal of Evidence & Proof* 119–128.

209 As set out under Sections 34–37 of the Criminal Justice and Public Order Act, 1994.

210 Directive 2013/48/EU/ of the European Parliament and of the Council of October 2013 on the right to access to a lawyer in criminal proceedings and in European arrest warrant proceedings.

211 *Mader v. Croatia*, No. 56185/07; ECtHR 28 June 2011.

212 *Sebalj v. Croatia* No. 4429/09.

213 *Salduz v. Turkey* no. 36391/02, para 54. See also *Pischalnikov v. Russia*, no. 7025/04, para 69.

214 See generally; H Quirk, 'Twenty Years On: The Right to Silence and Legal Advice: The Spiralling Costs of an Unfair Exchange' (2013) 64 *Northern Ireland Legal Quarterly* 465, D Wolchover, 'Serving Silent Suspects-Part 1' (2011) *Criminal Law and Justice Weekly* 71.

215 *John Murray v. United Kingdom* (1996) 22 EHRR 29.

216 Sections 34, 36 and 37 of the Act.

217 *Murray v. United Kingdom* (1996) 22 EHRR 29.

218 T Bucke et al., 'The Right of Silence: The Impact of the Criminal Justice & Public Order Act 1994' (2000) HORS 199 Home Office, available at http://www.homeoffice.gov.uk/rds/pdfs/hors199.pdf, accessed on 11 March 2015.

219 E Cape, 'Defence Services: What Should Defence Lawyers Do at Police Stations?' in M McConville and L Bridges (eds), *Criminal Justice in Crisis (Law in its Social Setting) 186–199*, Aldershot: Edward Elgar, 1994; T Smith and E Cape, 'The Rise and Decline of Criminal Legal Aid in England and Wales' in A Flynn and J Hodgson (eds), *Access to Justice and Legal Aid: Comparative Perspectives on Unmet Legal Need*, Hart Publishing, 2017, available at https://uwe-repository.worktribe.com/output/899612.

220 H Quirk and J Robins, 'The Right of Silence and Undermining Legal Representation at the Police Station' in *No Defence: Miscarriages of Justice and Lawyers*, 2013, (ed), 48–51; H Quirk, 'The Right of Silence in England and Wales: Sacred Cow, Sacrificial Lamb or Trojan Horse?' in J D Jackson and S J Summers (eds), *Obstacles to Fairness in Criminal Proceedings: Individual Rights and Institutional Forms*, Oxford: Hart Publishing, 2018.

221 R Card, and R Ward, *The Criminal Justice and Public Order Act 1994*, Bristol: Jordans, 1994.
222 D Wolchover, 'Serving Silent Suspects: Part 1' (2011) *Criminal Law and Justice Weekly* 71.
223 *Condron v. UK* (2000) 31 EHRR 1, 60.
224 *R v. Betts and Hall* (2001) EWCA Crim 224.
225 *R v. Howell* (2003) EWCA Crim 1.
226 A Choo, *Evidence*, 5th edn, OUP, 2018.
227 *180th Report, Law Commission of India*, May 2002, available at http://lawcommissionofindia.nic.in/reports/180rpt.pdf
228 R Card and R Ward, *The Criminal Justice and Public Order Act 1994*, Bristol: Jordans, 1994.
229 PACE, Code of Practice C, para 10.5.
230 PACE, Code of Practice C, para 11.1.
231 PACE, Code of Practice C, para 3.1.
232 PACE, Code of Practice C, para 10.1 and 11.2.
233 E Cape, Z Namoradze, R Smith, and T Spronken, *Effective Criminal Defence in Europe*, Antwerp: Intersentia, 2007.
234 *R v. Fulling* 1987 2 All E R 65.
235 PACE, Code of Practice G, para 4.
236 As evidenced by a research conducted J Blackstock, E Cape, J Hodgson, A Ogordova, and T Spronken, *Inside Police Custody: An Empirical Account of Suspects' Rights in Four Jurisdictions*, Intersentia, 2014.
237 These have been mentioned in Sections 4.12 and 4.13.
238 See generally; Open Society Justice Initiative, *Community Based Paralegals: A Practitioner's Guide*, New York: Open Society Foundation, 2010.
239 E Cape, *Improving Pretrial Justice: The Roles of Lawyers and Paralegals*, New York: Open Society Foundations, 2012, available at http://www.soros.org/initiatives/justice/articlespublications/publications/cape – ptj –20120416, 19.
240 E Cape, *Improving Pretrial Justice: The Roles of Lawyers and Paralegals*, 2012, Other, New York: Open Society Foundations, available at http://www.soros.org/initiatives/justice/articlespublications/publications/cape – ptj –, accessed on 14 November 2014.
241 E Cape, *Defending Suspects at Police Station, Practitioner's Guide to Advice and Representation*, 6th edn, LAG Publication, 2012, Chapter 1 and Chapter 4.
242 E Cape, *Defending Suspects at Police Station, Practitioner's Guide to Advice and Representation*, 6th edn, LAG Publication, 2012, Chapters 1 and 4.
243 E Cape, *Improving Pretrial Justice: The Roles of Lawyers and Paralegals*, New York: Open Society Foundations, 2012, available at http://www.soros.org/initiatives/justice/articlespublications/publications/cape – ptj –20120416, 77.
244 Ibid.
245 Interview Transcript PP1.
246 Interview Transcript PO3.
247 E Cape, *Improving Pretrial Justice: The Roles of Lawyers and Paralegals*, New York: Open Society Foundations, 2012, available at http://www.soros.org/initiatives/justice/articlespublications/publications/cape – ptj –20120416. pg 25.
248 *Cadder v. H M Advocate* (2010) UKSC 43 at para 48.
249 Committee for the Prevention of Torture, *2nd General Report*, CPT/Inf (92) 3, 36, available at http://www.cpt.coe.int/en/annual/rep-02.htm.
250 Ibid.
251 *D K Basu v. State of West Bengal* (1997) 1 SCC 216.
252 PACE, Code C, available at https://www.gov.uk/government/uploads/system/uploads/attachment_data/file/252903/2013_Code_C.pdf.

253 *R v. Absloum* (1989) 88 Cr. App. R. 332, *R v. Delany* (1989) 88 Cr. App. R. 338.
254 A Choo, *Evidence*, 5th edn, OUP, 2018.
255 P Roberts and A Zuckerman, *Criminal Evidence*, 2nd edn, OUP, 2010; A Choo, *Evidence*, 5th edn, OUP, 2018.
256 S Kassin et al., 'Police-Induced Confessions: Risk Factors and Recommendations' (2010) 34 *Law and Human Behaviour* 3.
257 C Phillips, *Royal Commission on Criminal Procedure: The Investigation and Prosecution of Criminal Offences in England and Wales*; The Law and Procedure, 1981.
258 V Kemp and N Balmer, 'Criminal Defence Services: User's Perspectives' Research Paper No. 21. London: Legal Services Research Centre, 2008.
259 A Sanders and R Young, *Criminal Justice*, OUP, 2007.
260 N Deslauriers-Varin, P Lussier, and M St-Yves, 'Confessing Their Crime: Factors Influencing the Offender's Decision to Confess to the Police' (2011) 28(1) *Justice Quarterly* 113–145.
261 J Blackstock, E Cape, J Hodgson, A Ogordova, and T Spronken, *Inside Police Custody: An Empirical Account of Suspects' Rights in Four Jurisdictions*, Intersentia, 2014.
262 V Kemp and N Balmer, 'Criminal Defence Services: User's Perspectives' Research Paper No. 21, London: Legal Services Research Centre, 2008.
263 See generally; P Pleasence, V Kemp, and N Balmer, 'The Justice Lottery? Police Station Advice 25 Years on from PACE' (2011) *Criminal Law Review* 3–18.
264 Article 3(3)(c) of the ECHR provides that a lawyer must be present at the earliest stage of the criminal proceeding, but does not mention the extent of the role of the lawyer, the duration the lawyer must remain present and extent of advice given by the lawyer.
265 *Tara Singh v. State*, A.I.R. 1951 S.C. 441.
266 *Satpathy v. P L Dani*, AIR 1978 SC 1025; *Miranda v. Arizona*, 384 US 436 (1966).
267 *Sheela Barse v. State of Maharashtra*, A.I.R. 1983 S. C. 378.
268 United Nations Basic Principles on the Role of Lawyers.
269 *180th Report, Law Commission of India*, May 2002, available at http://lawcommissionofindia.nic.in/reports/180rpt.pdf.
270 *Amnesty International, India: Report of the Malimath Committee on Reforms of the Criminal Justice System: Some observations*, 19 September 2003, ASA 20/025/2003, available at http://www.unhcr.org/refworld/docid/3f914cba4.html.
271 *Maneka Gandhi v. Union of India*, 1978 (1) SCC 248.
272 It is intended that an empirical project may be taken up after completion of this present research in this area.
273 P Pleasence, V Kemp, and N Balmer, 'The Justice Lottery? Police Station Advice 25 Years on from PACE' (2011) *Criminal Law Review* 3–18.
274 Ibid.
275 http://lawcommissionofindia.nic.in/reports/48rpt.pdf, accessed on 4 March 2015; *Malimath Committee Report: Committee on Reforms of Criminal Justice System*, Government of India, 2003, mha.nic.in/pdfs/criminal_justice_system.pdf, accessed on 12 February 2013.
276 H Quirk, *The Rise and Fall of the Right of Silence*, Routledge, 2016, 170.
277 The fundamental rights contained in the Constitution of India form the basic structure of the Constitution and cannot be amended or added.

4 Revisiting the absolute ban on evidential uses of confessions made to police officers

4.1 Introduction

Having examined the safeguards required for protecting fundamental suspects' rights at the time of police interrogation, I will now investigate the question of the inadmissibility of confessions given to a police officer when these rights have been violated. Confessions are the most important forms of evidence obtained by police officers during the course of interrogation. Often when a confession is given by a suspect, it usually means the end of an investigation. "*Confessio facta in judicio omni probatio major est*"[1] and "*Confessio in judicio est plena probation*"[2] show the importance of confessions. Obtaining a confession from the suspect was always considered the main, if not the ultimate, motive underpinning custodial interrogation. Under the Indian context, the Indian Evidence Act (IEA) contains all the provisions relating to confessional evidence. This act was promulgated under the auspices of British lawmakers in 1861 and the legislation has been in effect till date. The Supreme Court in as early as 1977 had directed the police that "obtaining a confession by hook or by crook should not be the high-end of an investigation."[3] As confessions are viewed extensively and in detail by psychological studies, this legislation has evolved over time. Some attention has therefore been paid to relevant psychological research in this chapter. This chapter therefore aims to analyse the concepts of confession made to a police officer, and the reasons for its inadmissibility. This chapter also analyses the admissibility of confessions given to a police officer in India and England and Wales and draws upon the differences and similarities. The chapter demonstrates that the main factors affecting the admissibility of confessions are related to the structure of police interrogation and custodial interrogation methods, police training and, importantly, the presence of a lawyer in interrogations. All these factors are examined in order to get a better understanding of why confessions are inadmissible in evidence. This chapter aims to consider whether the status quo needs to be revisited and the relevant provisions adjusted so as to reflect the systematic flaws in custodial interrogation that have been identified in the previous two chapters. The chapter first undertakes an analysis of the use of confessional evidence in India before embarking upon an analytical comparison with England and Wales, the intuition that underpins

DOI: 10.4324/9781003213024-4

this chapter is that subject to important safeguards being provided to the suspect at the custodial interrogation stage, when the emphasis is placed on effectively implementing the right to legal assistance, there would be scope to review the absolute ban on the use of confessional evidence in court. It will also be argued here that any reforms deriving from this line of reasoning should be seen in the light of perennial criminal justice dilemma of achieving balance between due process and crime control values, and the very pragmatic limitations, at the level of resources and at the level of police culture among other things facing the Indian Criminal Justice system.

4.2 The absolute ban on confessional evidence in India

Most legal systems allow a confession made to a police officer to be admissible in evidence. Some countries like South Africa and Kenya allow a confession made to a police officer above the rank of a captain and an inspector.[4] Historically, the evidence acts in these countries were passed on through India in the post-colonial era, but their main provisions were reformed since their inception. The inadmissibility of confessional evidence in India is often associated with being the relic of the colonial past, a cultural understanding that merits attention if one looks more closely at the position of the common law. *Karl Marx* was of the opinion that the British colonial law-making and interrogation was largely affected by use of torture by the police.[5] This principle had an impact on the admissibility of confession, which, inter alia, interfered with the legislation drafted at the time. There are three main kinds of confessions in India that are discussed in this section: judicial, extrajudicial confessions and admissions. The principal aim of discussing these is to understand issues relating to admissibility and the authority which might record them.

4.3 Types of confession

The word “confession” is not defined under the IEA. However, scholars and jurisprudence have referred to the definition provided by *Sir Stephen* as follows: “A confession is an admission made at any time by a person charged with a crime stating or suggesting the inference that he committed a crime.”[6] Sir Stephen’s explanation of a confession also extends to any statement made by the suspect even before he was arrested.[7] There are three types of confessions discussed in this chapter: judicial confession, extrajudicial confession and admissions. The main aim of discussing these is their admissibility and the authority which might record it.

4.3.1 *Judicial confession*

As observed from the previous sections, during an interrogation, a suspect is required to be taken to a magistrate within 24 hours of being arrested. Any confession that is made before the magistrate and in the court is a judicial confession.[8] Judicial confessions are taken at the time of the initial investigation and before the commencement of the trial. A judicial confession made by one accused is applicable to the co-accused in the same investigation.[9] The Supreme Court has held that a judicial confession is highly reliable as no person makes admission against his interest if in his consciousness, it does not prompt him to do so.[10] In ordinary circumstances, the leading authority recording judicial confession is the Magistrate and must exercise due diligence at the time of recording a confession.

4.3.2 Drawbacks of confessions before a magistrate

The most common safeguard to ensure a suspect's well-being and recording of any confession is when the suspect is produced before the Magistrate. This system of waiting to get to the Magistrate in order to render a confession admissible is time consuming. Also, there is a possibility of the suspect changing his mind and refraining from confessing while waiting a period of 24 hours.[11]

Section 164 of the CrPC contains an elaborate set of guidelines that the magistrate must follow prior to recording the confession. This section also allows a magistrate to record a confession even if he does not have jurisdiction in that particular case.[12] A magistrate may record a confession in the course of the investigation under any criminal law and at any stage of the trial. It is at this stage that the magistrate also explains to the suspect that he is not bound to make the confession and also warns him of the consequences of the confession. The most obvious consequences are explained first: that the evidence shall be used against him in the court of law.[13] The magistrate also confirms that the confession is given voluntarily and that it was made in the presence of the magistrate. The magistrate signs a memorandum stating all of the above conditions were met and it is signed and forms a part of the trial papers. If the suspect decides not to make the confession, then the magistrate shall not authorise detention of such person in police custody.[14] In order to ensure further compliance with these provisions, the Supreme Court has provided principles which a magistrate has to ensure have been respected at the time of recording the confession.[15] Along with these guidelines, each state also has its own criminal rules practice manifesto and the two are read together. Noorani claims that the additional step to approach the magistrate is also flawed as it was as good as pinning the suspect down to get a confession and then getting it legitimised by a magistrate.[16] This is a legitimate argument and the magistrate does very little to protect the right of the suspect, as noted in previous chapters when the police officer requests further custody. There have also been instances of using torture to obtain confessions, with the Magistrate failing to intervene.[17] This allows the suspect to withdraw his confession even if it was made before the Magistrate. This provision of confessing before a magistrate fails to act as a safeguard, which is the purpose of its enactment. Since confessions made to a magistrate are also subject to being held inadmissible, it is questioned, why the credibility of a confession given to a police officer would be any different to that given to a Magistrate.

4.3.3 Extrajudicial confession

An extrajudicial confession is a confession made at any place outside of a court or before a magistrate. This can be made to any person or persons and at any given time and by using any mode of communication and may only be used as corroborative evidence. The courts have emphasised on the confessions being voluntary and free and, if either requirement has not been fulfilled, then such a confession fails to form a part of corroborative evidence. A conviction cannot be made on an extrajudicial confession alone. The Supreme Court held that an extrajudicial confession if made freely, voluntarily and in a fit state of mind can be relied upon in court.[18] The test of validity here is the voluntariness of the confession and hence when all the accused made an extrajudicial confession that appeared suspicious, improbable and uncorroborated, it was held inadmissible.[19] The Courts have interpreted that an extrajudicial confession shall not be relied on its own merit alone to be rendered inadmissible. Thus, in a case where the confession was recorded by the Village Administrative Officer and was testified by the Village Assistant, the lower courts were right in relying on such extrajudicial confession.[20] Since this is done in a secure environment of the court, its validity is undoubted.

On perusal of the law reports from 2000, it can be inferred that courts are increasingly relying on the extrajudicial confessions as substantial evidence along with other forms of evidence. In *Ram Singh v. Sonia*,[21] the courts held that a confession was a substantial form of evidence contrary to its precedent cases such as *Rahim Beg v. State of UP*.[22] This constantly changing reliability of extrajudicial confessions appears to lack consistency in application. This was reflected in a recent Supreme Court judgement where the court held as follows:

> There is no absolute rule that an extra-judicial confession can never be the basis of a conviction, although ordinarily an extra-judicial confession should be corroborated by some other material.[23]

It is argued here that the reliance placed on extrajudicial confession is higher than a confession given to a police officer. The admissibility of an extrajudicial confession therefore places less confidence in the interrogating police officers. This is also reflected in the legislative provisions determining confessions at various levels of interrogation. The fact that courts admit extrajudicial confessions and exclude those made in the presence of police officers perhaps shows the level of distrust towards the police. This reinforces my argument for placing emphasis on the right to legal assistance. The system is so flawed that the courts have placed more faith in evidence obtained outside the formal police interrogation system rather than in it. With lawyers at the police station, the Indian Criminal Justice system can aspire to increase faith in police interrogations and the use of evidence obtained therein.

4.3.4 Admission

The term "confession" has not been defined either under the IEA or the CrPC and hence its interpretation has been inferred from foreign judgements or foreign scholarly works.[24] As a result, the term "confession" is also often confused with admission. The underlying principle is that both a confession and an admission are made by a person against his own interest. Sections 17–31 of the IEA deal with the term "admission" generally. Sections 24–30 mention provisions relating to confessions. An admission would usually be associated with civil transactions.[25] An admission is not conclusive evidence in itself unlike a confession. Most commonly known as the "acid test" for distinguishing an admission from a confession is where the conviction can be based on a statement alone. This is a confession. When supplementary evidence is needed to authorise a conviction, then that amounts to an admission.[26] The Bombay High Court also emphasised the difference between admission and confession and suggested a simple test for distinguishing the two. The court observed that if a statement by itself is sufficient to prove the guilt of the maker, it is a confession. But if the statement falls short of it, then it amounts to an admission.[27] While efforts were made by the Supreme Court in differentiating the two terms, a lot of confusion still exists about the understanding of them, especially when they both are of high evidentiary value. The need for clear distinction arises as a confession given to a police officer is inadmissible, whereas an admission made is admissible. It is therefore possible for a police officer to disguise obtaining a confession with an admission.

4.4 Legislative provisions

Any confession given to a police officer is considered "involuntary" and is not relevant for the provisions of this part under the IEA.[28] The divulgence of any information which would implicate him would amount to confession under Section 25. Section 26 of the Indian Evidence Act specifically mentions that any confession given to the police officer is inadmissible unless it is made in the presence of a magistrate.[29] The place where and the person to whom the confession was given under this provision change. In India, only a confession made before a magistrate is admissible in evidence. The test under Section 26 of the IEA is also considering "under what circumstances was that confession made." Even if the confession is made to a police officer in the presence of a magistrate, it is to be excluded.[30] Section 164 of CrPC provides the procedure required for the recording of confession before a competent magistrate. The magistrate also makes sure that the confession is being made voluntarily and freely. Thus, while the provisions of Section 26 make confessions to a police officer inadmissible in evidence, Section 27 may be considered as an exception.

Section 27 of the IEA of this act allows evidence or information obtained by way of confession or related to any confession given to the police officer admissible in court.[31] Section 27 incorporates the "Theory of Confirmation by Subsequent Facts." This allows a statement which may amount to a confession but leads to the discovery of a substantial fact to be admissible in court. Police officers and the courts can choose and accept a part of the confession. This section is a proviso to the provisions of Sections 25 and 26 of the IEA and is confirmed by the theory of finding of facts. A common example of this is, if a suspected thief is tortured into telling the police the whereabouts of a stolen property or such other facts not amounting to confession, the police can seize the stolen property or investigate further and use this evidence against the accused. It is therefore argued here that the code does not protect the suspect against making a confession to a police officer in its entirety. It is a common practice that police officers would seek a confession during an interrogation. Thus, although this information might not be confessional, it leads to evidence that becomes reliable information.[32]

The courts have emphasised the voluntariness requirement for the confession. In *Inspector of Police, Tamil Nadu v. Bala Prasanna*, the Supreme Court held that the prosecution while relying on the confessional statement leading to the discovery of articles under Section 27 has to prove that the statement has been made voluntarily.[33] However, these sections exclude from evidence a confession made to the police officer under any circumstances while in police custody or otherwise. The courts observed this in *R v. Babulal*,

> The legislature had in view the malpractice of police officers in extorting confessions from accused persons in order to gain credit by securing convictions and those malpractices went to the length of positive torture.[34]

Any other information disclosed by the accused which may lead to further investigation but still forms a part of the confession would still be admissible.[35] Thus, if a suspect is accused of murder and he admits to having an affair with the deceased, this information will be admissible under Section 8 of the IEA, which the court sifts through after examination of the statement.[36] Authors have also pointed out that the provisions of Section 27 almost "nullify" the protection provided under Sections 24 and 25.[37] The Supreme Court has almost supported this by deciding, "Discovery of the fact itself therefore substantiates the truth of the confessional statement."[38] The Supreme Court has therefore placed heavy reliance on the discovery of evidence by way of confession or forming a part of the confession. It is pointed out here that the interrogating police officer may aim to obtain a confession using the provisions of this section. As discussed previously, among other issues, this was also considered by the board in the Justice Malimath Committee Report.[39] This report highlights the practice of interrogation being led by the motive to obtain a confession.

4.4.1 *Police custody*

Since the relevant sections revolve around a confession given to a police officer while the suspect is in police custody, it is essential to consider what amounts to police custody. The term is not defined under any act, but the closest explanation is provided under Section 167 of the CrPC. As observed in earlier chapters, the Magistrate authorises police custody and may extend its duration as may be required for the police to undertake additional enquiries. Police custody does not have to mean that a suspect is physically present in the police cell. It includes scenarios such as being under police surveillance, where movements of the suspect are restricted by the police.[40] To take an example, when a confession was made to a press reporter in the presence of an investigating officer while the suspect was in police custody, the confession was rendered inadmissible.[41] One can infer from the relevant provisions that the presence of a Magistrate provides a form of security to the suspect when it comes to recording confessions. However, this is refutable as the police may be granted further custody of the suspect for further investigation if police officers request it.

4.4.2 *Torture and confession*

As observed above, the provisions of Section 27 allow police officers to use any means available to them to interrogate the suspect, which often results in using force and other unlawful methods. This perennial problem is discussed at length in the following chapter. Here it suffices to draw the link between force and the obtaining of confessions by the police. Authors like Ganesan and Grossman have argued that the provisions of Section 27 should be removed as trying to obtain a confession encourage the use of torture and police brutality.[42] Use of torture as a means to extort confession from the suspect remains a common practice all over India. Commentators have highlighted the misuse of power by the police in India.[43] In the case of *Kartar Singh v. State of Punjab*, the Supreme Court observed that they had

> Frequently dealt with cases of atrocity and brutality practiced by some overzealous police officers resorting to inhuman, parabolic,

> archaic, and drastic methods of treating the suspects in their anxiety to collect evidence by hook or crook and wrenching a decision in their favour.[44]

The above-mentioned provisions aim to make it a substantive rule of law that confessions are inadmissible regardless of the place and time made, if made to the police.[45] This issue of inadmissibility of a confession to a police officer has been accepted by scholars as a safeguard against the police resorting to torture and force. While this provision is credible, it is not entirely accepted as the only reason strong enough to make inadmissible a confession to a police officer. No research has been undertaken on contributing factors other than the use of force by the police. It is suggested here that such research may assist in analysing the reasons for the inadmissibility of confessions made to the police in India. Police officers are aware of this connection between the use of torture and confessions,

> Yes we might have to use other means for obtaining confessions. Who in their right mind will confess willingly?[46]

4.4.3 Constitutionality of confession

The Constitution of India does not make specific reference to confessions obtained as a result of custodial interrogation. The provisions of Article 20(3) of the Constitution of India are often drawn along with the validity of confessions in general. There have been issues raised with regard to the constitutional validity of the provisions mentioned herein mainly contained under Sections 24–30 of the IEA. It has been held by the Supreme Court in the case of *State of Bombay v. Kathi Kalu* that the provisions of Section 27 are not unconstitutional and do not violate the rights guaranteed under Article 20(3) of the Constitution of India.[47] The Court subscribed to the principle that "no person shall be compelled to be a witness against himself," but found that this does not prevent a suspect from giving a confession.

The Supreme Court in the same judgement also highlighted the need to balance the security of the nation with the human rights of the accused in this situation:

> The protection and promotion of human rights under the rule of law is essential in the prevention of terrorism. … If human rights are violated in the process of combating terrorism, it will be self-defeating. Terrorism often thrives where human rights are violated, which adds to the need to strengthen action to combat violations of human rights. … The lack of hope for justice provides breeding grounds for terrorism. … In all cases, the fight against terrorism must be respectful to the human rights.[48]

While making these observations the Supreme Court has also suggested the need to make various amendments in the above-mentioned acts. The Central Government has incorporated these amendments guaranteeing safeguards of the suspects, which have been included under Section 32 of POTA. The Court was also satisfied that the Central Government has taken appropriate measures and hence this issue requires no more attention.

4.5 Why confessions are made?

Evidence is imperative to the police, and they often have considerable evidence even before the commencement of an interrogation.[49] The emphasis is more on oral evidence compared to other forms of evidence such as forensic evidence. The propensity of resorting to physical violence therefore increases with the amount of leverage given to conviction resulting from confession. The absolute ban on confessions given to a police officer is well documented in the legislative and executed by jurisprudence in India. However, it must be highlighted that many institutional parties are unaware of this position. This has a twofold implication: the police officer may obtain a confession or the suspect who is aware of the inadmissibility of confessions and the value of confession to a police officer may give a false confession.

4.5.1 Why is a confession inadmissible in India?

The provision of inadmissibility of confessions owes its origin to the pre-Independence era. At the time of the formation of the act, the original lawmakers decided to keep the provisions of Section 24 as they are even today. Commentators have tried to connect the dots of the colonial to the post-colonial period to seek an explanation of the IEA provisions discussed here.[50] Many commentators acknowledge the colonial past as the main contributor to the existing flaw in the legislation. However, after nearly six decades, failure to reform the relevant legislation can no longer be legitimised as a colonial relic. No change has been attempted in this realm and this against the backdrop of Law Commission reports advocating the need for reform.[51] Academic commentators providing analysis of the provision have rather pessimistically accepted that, despite its considerable flaws, these provisions are the only effective safeguard against police lawlessness in this area.[52]

Now a change in perspective is needed for analysing this provision. The Indian criminal justice system has never experimented with the position of admissibility of confessions being made to a police officer. But the potential provision of procedural safeguards that I am arguing for in this volume offers new vistas of possibility for Indian criminal justice. A more intuitive approach, where the effective implementation of new procedural safeguards means an absolute ban on the use of confessional evidence is no longer required and balance can be achieved between convicting the guilty and protecting the rights of the accused, has much to commend it.

With all this in mind, it is also instructive to look at the exceptional circumstances which make confessions given to police officers admissible in evidence.

4.6 Exceptions

There are instances where certain officers are enrolled and vested with the powers of a regular police officer, but do not formally enjoy the status of a police officer. For instance, a Customs Officer is not a police officer and a confession given to a Customs Officer, even if retracted subsequently, can therefore be used against the accused.[53] Another instance of exception is an excise officer, who was not a police officer under Section 25 of the IEA and therefore a confession recorded by the excise officer was admissible at trial.[54] A confession made in relation to killing a bison attracted a conviction under the Wild Life Protection Act. Since this confession was made before a forest ranger, it was also held admissible because a Forest Ranger is not a police officer under the ambit of Section 25 of IEA.[55] Even a confession made before the Officer of Department of Revenue is admissible in evidence.[56] Similarly, a confession made before a police officer in departmental enquiries while in police custody is admissible in evidence and can be proved against such a police officer.[57] Thus, where a delinquent police officer made a confession before the Disciplinary Enquiry Board, it was held admissible and they also decide whether such a confession is voluntary or otherwise.

In view of the above, it can be questioned whether an investigating Police Officer has less credibility than some of the officers mentioned above, who are empowered to record a confession while a police officer cannot. It is also questioned here what is the exact test used by the Supreme Courts and the High Courts to allow these persons to record confessions in contrast to interrogating police officers who are not allowed to do so. One author explains the test that determines who a police officer is if the officer has the power to file a chargesheet under Section 173 of CrPC, as observed in the earlier chapter.[58] A chargesheet is the basis of all the trials and precedes an investigation, this explanation is credible, but this alone cannot be a justifiable reason for excluding police officers to record confessions. There is no other data suggesting any other reason for not letting police officers record confession and neither has this been debated by any academics. It is almost assumed that the only reason to prevent police officers from doing this is that they will use force and threat to obtain a confession.

These exceptions have the capacity to undermine the effect of the absolute ban on the use of confessions given to police officers, depending on how widely some of the concepts central to them may be interpreted in practice.

A confession may also be admissible in evidence even if given to a police officer in cases relating to Terrorism and Disruptive Activities (Prevention) Act, 1987 (TADA),[59] or the Prevention of Terrorism Act, 2002 (POTA),[60] and under the Narcotic Drugs and Psychotropic Substances Act, 1985 (NDPS).[61]

4.6.1 *Possession of drugs and other substances*

A confession made before an officer by a person arrested under the NDPS Act is admissible in evidence.[62] The offences registered under this act relate to the possession and sale of illegal drugs. Matters relating to the seizure of illegal drugs have been given hierarchy in the crime strata by the Indian criminal justice actors. Supreme Court and High Court jurisprudence provide confirmation. The Central Government has also issued a Standing Order empowering the officers of customs, Central Excise, the Directorate of Revenue Intelligence (DRI), etc., to exercise the same powers of "officer in charge of a police station."[63] However, this reference to a police officer is only in relation to powers of search and seizure and not to record a confession. The Supreme Court has also interpreted this provision to allow the recording of confessions under these circumstances to be admissible,[64] explaining that because these confessions are made under the NDPS to a special officer, and not a police officer, they do not amount to statements made under Section 161 of CrPC.[65] In this context, it is only confessions made under threat, duress, force or coercion that are inadmissible, indicating an interesting rapprochement with the English law on the exclusion of improperly obtained confessions. These variations in the admissibility of confessional evidence, which merely depend on the quality of the officer to whom the confession is made, reveal once again that the judiciary does not place trust in police officers when it comes to obtaining, and recording the obtaining, of confessional evidence. Interestingly, if a confession under the NDPS Act is being made to a customs officer who has the powers to investigate and file a chargesheet, it is rendered inadmissible.[66] Thus, this practice of having a confession under the NDPS Act being admissible as compared to other aforementioned offences made to a police officer inadmissible can be said to be arbitrary. The personnel who were interviewed for this research highlighted the importance of confessions in the following manner:

> Of course they will have admissibility of confessions for drugs related cases. There is commercial value above everything else in those cases.[67]

4.6.2 *Anti-terrorism laws*

A confession made to a police officer is admissible in evidence for cases registered under TADA[68] and POTA.[69] These matters relate to cases of terrorism and disruptive activities. Under Section 32 of TADA, any confession made to an officer above the rank of a superintendent was admissible in evidence. This made it possible for a police officer to record a confession using a device or in writing. The Supreme Court held in accordance with the promulgation of the TADA at the time of the Khalistan insurgency that a confession given shall be treated as an exception to Section 25 of IEA. The custodial confessions were challenged for being unconstitutional in the landmark judgement of *Kartar Singh v. State of Punjab*.[70] It was also argued by the state that this violated the provisions of Section 25 of the IEA. The Supreme Court held that the provisions of admissibility of custodial confessions do not violate any constitutional provisions.[71] The Supreme Court also held that the gravity of the problem of terrorism endangering the sovereignty, integrity and security of the nation mentioned in the statement and reason for the act bear higher leverage.[72] In lieu of protecting the human rights of the suspect, the court upheld the test of voluntariness of the confession. The Supreme Court has directed that the other courts apply a double test for deciding the acceptability of confessions made to a police officer; whether a confession was perfectly voluntary and if so, is it trustworthy and true.[73] Considering the gravity of offences listed in this act, confessions from co-accused were also exceptionally admissible and applicable to all the suspects.[74] Further provisions were made to ensure transparency; the confession taken was to be read out to the suspect making this confession.[75] The courts have raised concerns about empowering the Senior Officer to record confessions under the anti-terrorism legislation as follows:

> While the Code and Evidence Act seek to avoid inherent suspicion of a police officer obtaining confession from the accused, does the same dust not cloud the vision of superior police officer?[76]

This act was replaced by the POTA in 2002, which contained similar provisions on terrorism-related offences.[77] The Supreme Court emphasised that procedural rules relating to recording confessions in this context had to be strictly adhered to. The Court also held that "any confession made in defiance of these safeguards cannot be accepted by the courts as reliable evidence."[78] The constitutional validity of the provision of Section 32 was challenged in the case of *People's Union for Civil Liberties v. Union of India*.[79] It was argued that since the suspect is expected to be produced before the Magistrate, the Magistrate should record the confession, not the police officer. IEA's provisions requiring the suspect to be produced before the Magistrate within 24 hours should be applicable in relation to these offences too, and any confession should be recorded at this stage. The Supreme Court reiterated the position of admissibility in *Kartar Singh v. State of Punjab*, accepting as the main rationale the urgency of the situation.[80] The Court added that presenting the suspect before the Magistrate was just an additional safeguard. The provisions of POTA were alleged to be depriving the suspect of his human rights in the case of *State (NCT of*

Delhi) v. Navjot Sandhu.[81] The conviction of the accused in this case was solely based on the confession obtained, which resulted in an unfair trial.

After a period of sustained criticism over the abuses carried out by the armed forces under POTA, it was repealed in 2004 and the Unlawful Activities (Prevention) Act, 2004 (UAPA) was legislated. One of the major changes brought about by this act was that confessions given while the suspect was in custody were no longer admissible in evidence.[82] The example of the Central Government was followed by the states. After the repeal of POTA, many state governments enacted their own anti-terrorism legislations. The Maharashtra Control of Organised Crime Act, 1999 (MCOCA), provided that where confessions had been made in custody, they were admissible against the accused and the co-accused.[83] This lack of consistency in legislative provisions and jurisprudential interpretation has attracted considerable criticism with the focus being on the risk of unfair practices towards the suspect. The Supreme Court responded to criticism by highlighting the *sui generis* nature of terrorist offences justifying the need for the exceptional measures employed,

> Parliament has explored the possibility of employing the existing laws to tackle terrorism and arrived at the conclusion that the laws are not capable. It is also clear to Parliament that terrorism is not a usual law and order problem.[84]

The severity of using confessions has not been questioned in this research. However, the means of using such confessions in terrorism-related cases are criticised. But as understood and demonstrated by a personnel interviewed for this volume, this is a matter of necessity,

> Do you expect the police or any other officer to show any mercy to a terror suspect? Have you not seen what happened in Kasab's case?[85]

4.6.2.1 Signing of false confession

One of the most common features of custodial interrogation in India is the "signing of forced confession."[86] The police enjoy large powers to obtain such statements under the terrorism acts. Many commentators question the legitimacy of the admissibility of confessions in terrorism-related cases.[87] It is also felt that the absence of an exclusionary rule for confessional evidence in terrorist cases explains the level of police lawlessness at the custodial interrogation stage in India, offering a useful contrast to common law jurisdictions where the exclusion of improperly obtained evidence primarily serves a deterrent function.

Both of these provisions are commonly referred to in the Indian context as "taking a departure from the provisions of Section 25 of the IEA." The reason for discussing the above provisions at length is to highlight the gravity of the offence and the evidentiary value of a confession. In the NDPS, the TADA and the POTA, different authorities are given responsibility for taking confessions. Terrorism offences require a confession to be taken by a police officer ranking higher than an investigating police officer. The Supreme Court and the lower courts have endorsed this practice, which raises the important question of why the practice could not be extended to all other offences.

In light of the above, it can be argued here that relying on higher ranked police officers, in addition to potentially attaching more weight to the voluntariness criterion—which I will be examining below—may be the way forward for the Indian law on the use of improperly obtained confessional evidence in trial.

4.6.3 Removal of threat, inducement or promise

The IEA provides for the removal of any influences which may cause a confession inadmissible. Section 28 of the IEA provides that if a confession is obtained after removal of any threat, inducement or promise from the initial confession, then it is admissible in evidence. The court may use such confession if it is explained that it was obtained after removing any such oddity. There may be instances where the confession might have been obtained after the threat ceased or before the threat started. This would imply that the entire confession would not be dismissed in the presence of the above-mentioned features. The court may choose to select that part of the confession which it may believe has been obtained after removal of any threat. The burden of proof is on the prosecution to prove if the confession was voluntary or involuntary. Authors like Vadackumchery mention that this provision is in place so that police officers do not offer any promise or threaten the suspect.[88] However, the practical application of this provision is different to the legislation. In the present research, one of the police personnel notes,

> The police officers are aware of the provisions of Section 25. But this is not regularly applied in practice and we see many police officers trying to get a confession from a suspect.[89]

Equally problematic is the fact that Section 29 of the IEA allows for the admission of confession even in the face of deception and secrecy or of confessions that are obtained when the suspect was drunk, if the confession is otherwise relevant to the matter on trial. It is of course puzzling that confessions obtained under such circumstances are deemed voluntary and therefore admissible evidence in criminal trials in India. Here we can paint a strong contrast with exclusionary doctrines in England and Wales and other parts of the common law world. The argument that naturally follows is that this practice must be urgently revisited and appropriate attention must be paid to whether the taint of threats, inducements or promises can in reality ever be removed from a confession or whether they should in fact be seen in line with relevant comparative perspectives, as factors prohibiting the use of the tainted confessional evidence.

4.6.4 Exclusion of involuntary confessions

As seen above, the scope of Sections 24 and 25 of IEA clearly specify the removal of any inducement, threat or punishment from a confession. The Supreme Court also draws a sketchy image of the interpretation of these provisions. The court held in *State v. NMT Joy Immaculate* that a confession made to a police officer and the recovery of incriminating articles pursuant to the confession cannot be excluded merely on the ground that it was obtained illegally.[90] It is unclear to determine if the courts are undermining the recovery of articles, which form an exemption under Section 27 or the provisions of Section 25 may be subject to interpretation. The other provisions relating to confessions made before a Magistrate do not act as conclusive proof either, as the suspect may withdraw his confession, which has already been discussed. Again, it is questioned here, if this is still excluded at trial by the Magistrate, then why would this be any different to a confession given to a police officer? If this is done solely on the ground of preventing police officers from misusing their power, then this may be subject to criticism.

4.7 Adversarial features

The Indian criminal justice system is accusatorial in nature when it comes to investigation and preparing the case for prosecution. The adversarial nature of policing is attributed to the post-colonial law-making impact on the IEA.[91] The police have exclusive responsibility for obtaining criminal evidence, and providing reasonable grounds for extending the detention of a suspect in order to obtain additional evidence. However, a confession is only admissible if given in the presence of a Magistrate. Thus, the Magistrate also plays a part in gathering evidence, thereby departing from the adversarial role. A clear demarcation of adversarial duties needs to be legislated in terms of recording the confession. Alexander argues that it is this nature of the system which almost coerces the police to resort to all kinds of illegalities in order to gather confession.[92] It is argued here that this shared responsibility between the Magistrate and the police officer to test the validity of the confession and to interrogate respectively causes delay in the process. There have been various recommendations from the law commissions suggesting a shift towards the inquisitorial system, which might assist in clarifying the demarcation of roles.[93]

4.8 Law Commission reports on confession

Law Commission reports have stressed the need for reforming the IEA for nearly 50 years. In the 48th Report, the Law Commission suggested that a confession given to a police officer of the rank of a Superintendent should be admissible in evidence.[94] This should be accompanied by the safeguard of providing the suspect with a lawyer at the time of recording such a confession. Similar recommendations were made in the 69th Law Report, which were not taken into consideration by the criminal justice actors.[95] Some of these recommendations were adopted in the TADA and the POTA relating to the admissibility of confessions extending to the co-accused. However, the basic structure of the confessions made to a police officer remains unchanged. The Malimath Committee Report also suggested similar recommendations to revise the provisions of the IEA.[96] A common feature in all these commission reports was that a confession made before a police officer should be admissible in evidence. This can be justified by providing safeguards such as the presence of a lawyer, requiring that a confession be recorded by a police officer of a higher rank, and that the confession must be recorded in writing. Reference was being made to international practices while providing these recommendations. It is evident that none of these have been implemented till date. Authors and criminal justice actors fail to address the reason for this non-implementation. While the use of force and the infringement of the right against self-incrimination by the police account for institutional and political reluctance to implement these recommendations,[97] the evidentiary potential of confessions given to police officers militates for urgently revisiting. This is also in line with Law Commission recommendations advocating a greater role for Magistrates in the "quest for the truth."[98]

Baxi has criticised Law Commission reports for being undemocratic in their inception, ignoring the need for safeguards in the criminal justice system.[99] This criticism is moving in the right direction, as any changes relating to the admissibility of confessional evidence in India should necessarily be followed by wide institutional and procedural reforms equipping suspects with appropriate safeguards. As previously argued, cementing the right to legal assistance has a very important role to play in that respect.

4.9 Police interrogation and confession

The rationale for excluding confession made to police officer at the time of interrogation is to protect the suspect from the coercive atmosphere inherent in police interrogation. In using an absolute ban for confessions made to police officers in custodial interrogation, the Indian lawmaker almost presumes that the police will use force to obtain the confession. Kalra points this out by highlighting the damaging effect on the reputation of police officers who are seen as inherently unable to refrain from the use of coercive practices at the police station and ensure the lawfulness of any confessions made in that context.[100]

Unfortunately, this pessimistic view of police attitudes in custodial interrogations finds support in the empirical work demonstrating that despite the absolute ban on the use of confessions made to police officers, these continue to resort to the use of force in order to obtain such confessions.[101] Perhaps there are important comparative lessons here for advocates of the deterrent rationale as the main basis for the exclusion of improperly obtained evidence.

4.9.1 Confessions and FIR

As observed in the previous chapter, the FIR records the information received by police officers and it may also contain a record of the confession if it was given during an interrogation. Whether this is given by the suspect with or without the knowledge of the provisions of Section 24, a confession is recorded in the FIR. However, only that part of the statement which contains the confession is excluded and the relevant portions containing further information are retained. This other information not amounting to confession is admissible in evidence and is used for further interrogation. The courts are capable of eliminating the confession and retain that part which provides further information.[102] The court also held that if the FIR is confessional in nature, the portions leading to the discovery of certain facts may be retained.[103]

Admissions made in the FIR are relevant and may be proved against the maker.[104] It may be pointed out here that the task of sieving through a confession looking for other information is with the police officer. It is therefore not a difficult task for a police officer to aim for a confession under the guise of obtaining an admission or other related information.

As observed in the previous chapter, there are discrepancies in the recording of the FIR, such as the police officer refusing to record the FIR owing to a number of reasons.[105] There is a possibility under such circumstances that an FIR may not contain a confession or other information. It is suggested here that stringent measures for recording an FIR may also assist in increasing the credibility of a confession given to a police officer.

4.9.2 Police training and confession

The Police Act which provides for the training received by police officers for interrogating a suspect makes no mention of the inadmissibility of confessions. The police officer is expected to have the knowledge of the CrPC and the IPC. In the absence of specific training for interrogation, police officers are expected to know that confessions given to them are inadmissible, and the various exceptions to this rule. Many police officers feel the need for periodic and updated training of laws and practices. One of the participants in the empirical survey undertaken in this volume pointed out that

> [t]he law is clear on all aspects. ... More police officers need to get training to identify what is a confession while they are interrogating a suspect.[106]

In the absence of any such periodic and updated training, it is difficult to determine if police officers have the awareness required to comply with the provisions of the IEA. There is an urgent need to provide police officers with comprehensive interrogatory training and highlight the importance of a confession. Police officers should receive periodical training about recording a confession and its implications.

4.9.3 Are police officers aware of the inadmissibility of confessions?

Most of the police personnel I have interviewed mentioned that they were aware of the provisions of Section 25 as provided at the time of training.[107] However, an interesting observation can be made that none of them mentioned that they were "not allowed to record confessions." This provides a useful insight into why putting pressure to obtain confessions in a police interview is still very much an ongoing concern in India. The Indian criminal procedure paradox of having an absolute ban on using confessions made to the police, on the one hand, and considerably relying on police officers to interrogate suspects, on the other hand, merits attention. It is counter-intuitive to separate the process of police interrogation from the process of obtaining incriminating evidence and subsequent question as to the use of such evidence in court. The fact that a part of the confession and, to some extent, evidence deriving from that, *can* be used in evidence qualifies somewhat the previous statement, but do not reduce its force altogether.[108]

In any case, if Indian criminal procedure is serious about implementing the absolute ban on the use of confessions made to police officers, there needs to be a renewed focus on raising awareness about this ban. But as things stand, we are currently very far from achieving this objective. As the current empirical study demonstrates, most police officers, and especially those operating in rural areas, are still focusing their energies on getting a confession from the suspect. More specifically, 5 out of the 15 police officers interviewed mentioned that they "aim" to get a confession from an interrogation and, in the process of doing so, some of them might go as far as "resort to third degree torture to get a confession."[109] As illustrated in the dramatic account offered by one of the interviewees,

> The law is clear on all the aspects. But then there are police officers would resort to third degree torture to get confession. More police officers need to get training to identify what is a confession while they are interrogating a suspect. But nowadays because of media and court it is not very easy to manhandle the accused and use third degree.[110]

> Indian police wastes no time in torturing the suspect for information about the crime and obtain a confession. The Indian police will not go to court to seek permission to hit the suspect. So they allege the suspect of stealing or committing a crime and almost compel him to accept the allegation and charge.[111]

Another police officer explained that police officers are normally aware of the inadmissibility of confessions under Section 25 of the IEA,[112] and then noted, in an equally dramatic tone,

> You see extortion in India police officers use third degree therefore the confession is inadmissible. Does the suspect know this? Of course not.[113]

In general, police officers gave mixed responses on the issue of awareness around inadmissibility of confessions. Some of them were confident that police officers are expected to know about the provisions of Section 25, while others remained silent on this point, while one of the participants characteristically said that police officers rely on confessions because they don't know how else to carry out an investigation.[114]

4.9.4 *Lack of trust in the police*

This provision of inadmissibility demonstrates the lack of trust in the police placed by Indian lawmakers and has also restricted the powers of the police to a great extent. Authors like Verma also argue on this attempted restriction placed on the police and the system's distrust in the police.[115] This confused reliance placed by the judiciary on police officers when it related to confessions is under-researched and hence difficult to assess. While the lawmakers gave police officers wider powers in relation to arrest and preventive arrests, and search and seizure, it would be unreasonable not to empower the police with recording of confession at the time of interrogation.

4.9.5 *Confession and conviction*

This section aims to analyse how the current practice of inadmissibility of confessions may change provided certain changes are made to the current practices. The courts and the lawmakers do not want to place reliance on police officers to record a confession. However, from the above provisions, it is also clear that they do not want to rely on the magistrate to record confessions.[116] It may also appear that the courts and jurisprudence rely heavily on the voluntariness as compared to the actual truth of the confession. It may be argued that the truth of a confession as opposed to the voluntariness is easier to prove at trial. For a confession to be made reliable and secure a conviction, certain safeguards may be provided to the suspect, which might result in a fair conviction. One of the ideas proposed by the Supreme Court and the Law Commission reports is the presence of a lawyer.

4.10 Confession and the presence of a lawyer

Despite the directions given by the Supreme Court in *D K Basu* being clear on the presence of a lawyer, it is not implemented in practice. Therefore, confession to a police officer and the presence of a lawyer is discussed romanticising the concept to be implemented in the future. The confession is recorded before the Magistrate and this is where the suspect is supposed to be provided with legal assistance. It is no doubt that the presence of a lawyer at the police station interrogation will be a way of ensuring the voluntariness of the confession. A volunteer working with the Bangalore Police informed Human Rights Watch that there was a common procedure to follow to extract a confession out of the suspect.[117] This involved using coercive methods, including third degree, to extract a confession can be stopped with the presence of a lawyer at the time of interrogation.

In order to ensure the implementation of the right to legal assistance in its entirety, there should be equal observance of the provision of legal aid. As observed in the previous chapter, the concept of legal aid is developing at a slow pace and legal aid is granted at a much later stage in the trial. In *Babubhai Parmar v. State of Gujarat*, the Supreme Court made it evident that the principles provided to the Magistrate, which were meant to be honoured in letter and spirit, failed to do so. Failure to provide legal aid, discrepancies in the case of prosecution and confession and irregularities in the recording times of the confession rendered the confession given to a magistrate inadmissible.[118] This judgement has received similar treatment as the practical implication the judgement of *D K Basu* had on the procedure of interrogation and presence of a lawyer.

It is a hypothesis here that the presence of a lawyer may assist in legitimising the reasonability of a confession. This will also assist in determining the fairness and reliability of a confession and ensure that police officers adhere to a fair interrogatory process.

4.11 Confession and police torture

As observed, it is confirmed by the courts and academics that the fear of police officers using force and other unlawful methods to obtain a confession renders it inadmissible. The judiciary has time and again placed reliance on the non-admissibility of confessions made to a police officer on this fact alone. This is discussed at length in the next chapter.

Justice Ramaswamy mentions that the provisions of Section 25,

> Rests upon the principle that it is dangerous to depend upon a confession made to a police officer which cannot extricate itself from the suspicion that it might have been produced by the exercise of coercion.[119]

Confessional laws that have not changed since their inception during the colonial era are now in dire need for amendment. It has been an assumption for over five decades that confessions made to police officers are inadmissible in order to safeguard the suspect against the ill-treatment by the police. However, despite the provisions, it has been observed that police officers in certain parts of India still interrogate to get a confession. Similar practices may be followed in other rural villages and smaller towns, which have not been explored. Senior police officers have admitted that interrogations are being carried out with a view to obtaining a confession, making the law in practice different to the law in theory. In a study conducted by Human Rights Watch, a police officer mentioned that the police seek confessions instead of gathering evidence because it is time consuming. A comparative analysis of the confession laws in England and Wales may assist in providing recommendations for the legislative provisions.

4.12 Comparing India with England and Wales

The law of confessions in England and Wales has undergone many changes since the 1700s. In the second half of the eighteenth century, untrustworthy confessions were rejected. In the nineteenth century, exclusion of confession became the rule and inclusion of the confession was an exception. As Langbein notes,

> If there had been any massive use of torture before the records began to evidence it in 1540, or after they cease to disclose it in 1640, or omitted from the records for the intervening century, literary and other sources would alert us.[120]

Blackstone concludes, "(torture) was occasionally used as engine of state, not of law, more than once in the reign of Queen Elizabeth."[121] However, in the second half of the nineteenth century, the law relating to confession underwent a change, where the criminal justice system adopted a rights-based approach. Towards the end of the nineteenth century, the rule of exclusion was firmly established and confessions were rarely read in evidence. International human rights regimes make it compulsory for confessions be voluntary as a part of a fair trial.

4.12.1 Judges' Rules and confession

Before the Judges' Rules, exclusion remained confined to the judicially determined cases and the acts by the police to obtain these confessions were not taken into account. In the beginning of the twentieth century, there was an almost exclusionary rule for confessions obtained by the police. This was severely criticised by authors such as Wigmore and is said to be the contributing reason for recommendations in the Judges' Rules.[122] Wigmore was also of the opinion that confessions and the status of the accused were factors closely affecting one another. Hence, if a suspect belonged to a disadvantaged or a lower class of society, he was bound to make a confession.[123] This categorisation of crime based on the class ideology is adopted from Stephen's Digest.[124] This had a lot of impact on the decisions made by the judiciary on the legitimacy of confessions given and the reliance placed on police officers.

Judges' rules were framed so that police activities could be regulated over their method of obtaining confession. The Judges' Rules introduced rules, which had the similar impact as provisions of law and were meant to be enforced by the police superiors in order to render fair administration of justice. The rules were enforced bearing in mind the rights of the "citizens." The word "citizen" was referred to because the police had the power to interrogate any person, whether they were suspect to a crime or otherwise and if they were in custody or a witness. These rules guaranteed the right to consult a solicitor privately before being interrogated. A statement of confession was to be accepted only if it had been obtained without any fear, prejudice or oppression. These rules also laid down a procedure to be followed by the police officer to record the confessions. In the absence of any other rules, it was assumed that police officers would follow the Judges' Rules as a part of their duty. The courts are also said to have placed reliance on the evidence of police officers against the evidence of the suspect.

This has been argued by many critics of the time who argue that the police culture and police powers often negate the high reliance placed upon them. Fisher rightly points out that the police do not see it as their duty to follow up lines of enquiry to exonerate the suspect.[125] An illustration of this was received in the *Confait* case where police officers were attempting to negate an alibi rather than analyse the case for countervailing evidence.[126] As a result of these critical views, many steps were taken by the Law Commissions, who were trying to amend the provisions relating to confessions making it rights based while also trying to preserve the adversarial element.

4.12.2 Pre-PACE

The period before the enactment of PACE and just after the Judges' Rules provided a detailed regulation to be followed by the police at the time of interrogation. The remark of Lord Scarman in *R v. Sang* explains this subtle rule of exclusion, "The Judges' Rules are not a judicial control of police interrogation but notice that if certain steps are not taken, certain evidence otherwise admissible may be excluded at trial."[127] The decision in *R v. Voisin* also recognised the discretion to exclude confession that was obtained in breach of the Judges' Rules.[128] This substantiates the evidentiary value and the process of police interrogation to obtain a confession held by the judiciary was in alliance with the Judges' Rules. It was common to abrogate the right to legal advice and essential note-keeping during the police interrogation.

With the existence of the word of the suspect versus the word of the police, during this period of course the word of the police gained preference. The suspect has often been at a structural disadvantage before the judge at a trial in claiming the voluntariness of his confession against the word of the interrogating officer. Despite this, the suspects were often able to claim the protection of the voluntariness rule because the judiciary were often aware of the usual non-observance of the Judges' Rules by the police. A subtle comparison is made here with the Indian judges who are aware of similar non-observance of rules. A plethora of judgements given by the Indian courts discussed above reflect similar views of the English courts during this pre-PACE era.

The creation of the Crown Prosecution Services in 1985 is also said to have attributed to the existing confusion on the implementation of Judges' Rules and paving a path for PACE. Police officers were no longer responsible for prosecuting cases in court and only entrusted with the investigation. As Zuckerman observes, owing to the trustworthy attitude of the courts, the suspects were often left to the mercy of police officers.[129] The excessive power held by the police also has an adverse impact on the confession-making ability of the suspect. This has been observed by Reiner who mentions that the police had become "lionised" by the broad spectrum of power.[130] This excessive faith in police may have been the reason for the delayed implementation of the rules for exclusion of confession. This further resulted in the continued practice of non-exclusion of confessions in the absence of observing Judges' Rules or the right to legal assistance.

4.12.3 RCCP and confession

The RCCP in their report highlighted the impact of police interrogation and police attitude on confessions and hence provided various recommendations around improving police practices to improve the reliability of confessions. There existed a culture of considering the constable a "citizen in uniform," which was propagated by the government and given effect by the judiciary. This aimed at making the police officer aware of his power and at the same time the responsibility over citizens as opposed to the suspect. However, authors such as Dixon referred to this practice as a myth, and advised that the courts needed to intervene in order to regulate the practices relating to confessions.[131] Dixon also points out that it is imperative for the judiciary to be willing to exclude confessional evidence in order to control police powers.[132] The RCCP also observed that considering police officers as citizens in blue is far from reality. The RCCP recommended therefore that any rules regulating police investigation must be framed in a way that the police can discharge their duties, while the suspects' rights are also protected.[133] This recommendation has been described by authors to be a "watershed consolidating and clarifying the changes in formal powers and concrete practice ... separating the police officer from the ordinary citizen."[134] Various commissions in India such as the Malimath Committee and Law Commissions have suggested reforms that can render confessions admissible. However, this has received criticism from various authors who fear the misuse of power by the police. This may also be the reason why there is reluctance by lawmakers to incorporate this recommendation in practice.

4.12.3.1 Verbal confessions

The report also expressed concerns over the increase in political and social controversy surrounding policing and the growing public concerns thereafter in the late 1970s. This report addressed another concern of "verballing," which was an increasing phenomenon in criminal trials, where the police officer would allege the suspect of giving oral confessions. This was no doubt refuted by the suspect at trial, causing further delays in the trial or reliance being placed by the judiciary on the police officer.[135] J Hodgson also argued that admitting a confession which was submitted by police officers, falling in the verbal category would put the suspect at a disadvantage. Relying on such evidence would result in wrongful conviction and therefore an unfair trial.[136] It was suggested that all these could be easily averted by police officers recording all the confessions made to them at the police station. It was also highlighted that there should be a legislative provision mandating the recording of the confession along with the provision of safeguards for the suspect, which was paving a way for PACE. This was followed by a series of misuse of powers by police personnel, leading to disbanding of groups such as the "West Midlands Serious Crime Squad."[137] Since confessions made to a police officer in India have never been admissible in evidence, there is no issue about such verbal confessions. However, the information leading to discovery of evidence in a confession is admissible and it may be given verbally. In the absence of any legislation in India requiring such a confession or other information to be recorded in writing, there is a similar problem with confessions. This practice is subject to similar criticism in England as pointed out by authors.[138]

4.13 Post-PACE

PACE was an attempt to balance the ideology of police effectiveness and individual liberty of the suspect. The main provision relating to confession also provides an elaborate definition of a confession, which was contained in Section 82 of PACE.[139] Section 76 describes the admissibility of confessions and which parts can be excluded. It is pointed out here that the policy adopted by PACE is not entirely of total exclusion or inclusion of a confession and its admissibility depends on factors contained therein. Authors like Zander have mentioned that the provisions of PACE have made the obtaining of confessions more difficult than under the Judges' Rules. However, studies show that the rate of confessions in the post-PACE era is almost the same as in the pre-PACE era. This may also be because police officers had to adhere to legislative norms also protecting suspects' rights.

PACE placed the burden of proof on the prosecution to prove any disputes regarding the confession raised by the suspect. In order to ensure transparency and at the same time reduce the pressure on the courts, the system of *voire-dire* was introduced by PACE.[140] This system facilitates both parties to call upon their evidence in order to support their argument.

The significance of PACE was expressed by authors commenting in the case of *R v. Samuel*, stating that "Samuel sent shockwaves through the police as it came to be realised painfully that PACE would be interpreted much more stringently than the Judges' Rules."[141] In this case, the police were alleged of delaying legal assistance to the suspect accused of robbery and using his confession in court. It was held that denying the suspect legal assistance was a breach of his fundamental right and hence the confession was rendered inadmissible.[142] PACE brought with it a disciplined approach to be followed by the courts in cases of evidence obtained in breach of its procedures. After the enactment of PACE, the judiciary were convinced that they formed a syndicate of due process and ensure its compliance. They were also in charge of excluding any evidence that was a result of the unfairness of the police interrogation, which could have a direct impact on the fairness of the trial. The importance of following the procedure of fairness was interpreted by the judiciary efficiently. The courts held that the trial judges were wrong in admitting confessions obtained after having disregarded the safeguards.[143] The judicial attitudes towards the "verbal" confessions were also thought to be a "significant and substantial" breach of the PACE code. The testimony of the police that the confession was given to them verbally was no longer accepted in evidence.[144] Very soon with the enactment of PACE, the credibility of verbal confessions seemed to fade.

4.13.1 Police interrogation and confessions

As observed, in England and Wales, the history of confessions has been seen to change with the changing practices and the introduction of legislation. The abuse of police power by the interrogators to obtain a confession in order to secure a conviction has caused judicial scepticism. Even the courts have inferred that the police value confessions as they are an easy route to conviction and are likely to devise their interrogation accordingly.[145] It is important to analyse the following elements pertaining to police interrogation in the backdrop of confession: creditworthiness of confessions, reasons why a suspect may confess and false confessions. In the pre-PACE era and the initial few years when PACE was introduced, certain police tactics used at the time of interrogation rendered confessions unreliable. This was also raised by the Criminal Law Revision Committee in 1972.[146] It is rightly pointed out by Baldwin that the police are concerned with the future and not the past events.[147] Their motive is far from gathering evidence to ascertain the truth, which should be the ideal characteristic of an interrogation. The police are also alleged to use the vulnerability of certain suspects to their advantage when aiming to obtain a confession.[148] Knowledge of the PACE legislation is mandatory for an interrogating officer and this ensures knowledge of consequences of methods used by police officers. Most of the times the suspects would confess either because of the authority of the police or because they were uninformed about their rights. Wrongful conviction based on false confessions is highlighted by many researchers such as Kassin. Kassin associates two factors with false confessions: personal (psychological) vulnerability of an individual, and the use of accusatorial investigative methods.[149] However, this practice has ceased with the inception of PACE and its codes of practices.[150] The inception of PACE also introduced certain safeguards which assisted in ensuring police officers followed these safeguards while obtaining a confession.

4.13.2 Training and confession

Police officers are made aware of all the exclusionary provisions relating to a confession both in the initial training and in the periodical training thereafter. With the changes in legislation and training procedures, the police are trained to interrogate with an open mind and not just to obtain a confession. The training provided by the PEACE model reflects a more due process approach adopted by England and Wales.[151] Many studies carried out in England and Wales have confirmed this and have further helped in providing better training to the police for carrying out interrogation. Many countries like Norway and Sweden are adopting the PEACE model to change the police interrogation procedure for recording a confession.

There is an ever-standing issue about police culture and practice resorting to unlawful means when the evidence is not strong. As J Hodgson writes,

> In cases where the rest of the evidence is weak or non-existent, that is just the situation where the temptation to do what the provisions are aimed to prevent is greatest and the protection of the rules most needed.[152]

The dynamic relation between the police officer and the suspect has also been highlighted in a research study by McConville et al.[153] This study concluded that any confession given in an interrogation would be a result of this dynamic relation. However, this dynamicity causes a power imbalance between the police and the suspect, which may be the reason why the police will always be bound to use unlawful measures to obtain a confession and training may not be sufficient. However, in the present circumstances, it is fair to say that there has been considerable change in the admissibility of confessions, due to periodic and elaborate training provided. Since the present provision of admissibility of confessions in India is prone to similar criticism as in the pre-PACE era in England and Wales, it is suggested here that training may be provided for recording a confession. Elaborate training for the police offices along with other safeguards may render a confession admissible in evidence in India.

4.13.3 Exclusionary rule

PACE introduced the provisions of exclusionary rules ensuring that the police do not use unfair means to obtain a confession during their interrogation. Section 76(2) of PACE serves as a safeguard to exclude confessions which are inadmissible. The exclusionary rule is adopted in legislation because the interrogating police officers have been threatening or inducing to obtain a confession. Confessions may be excluded on the grounds of unreliability, unfairness or oppression. The court also has to be satisfied beyond "reasonable doubt" that a confession was not obtained in the aforementioned circumstances.[154] It is the responsibility of the Prosecution to prove the reliability and fairness of the confession. As mentioned by Cape, courts are often reluctant to exclude evidence of confessions under these provisions.[155] However, jurisprudence confirms the use of this exclusionary rule at numerous occasions highlighting the impetus attached to the fairness of an interrogation.

4.13.3.1 Unreliability, unfairness and oppression

The courts must exclude any confession that might be unreliable owing to the nature in which it was obtained. The most common before the enactment of PACE were the inducement methods used by police officers such as offering bail and smaller charges. Procedural fairness was of utmost importance after the enactment of PACE and a series of judgements displays this. In many cases such as *R v. Keenan, R v. Walsh* and *R v. Quinn*, the courts observed that even highly reliable confessions obtained using unfair means are inadmissible.[156] Thus, the appeal courts criticised the trial courts' decision to wrongly admit a confession obtained using unfair means.[157]

The other factor which was considered unfair was recording confessions made by vulnerable suspects. In *R v. Delaney*, the courts observed that the vulnerability of the suspect rendered the confession unreliable.[158] These have been illustrated further in the judicial interpretation of the provisions of Section 76(2). Instances such as a confession obtained from a suspect with learning difficulties, who was interrogated for a span of 13 hours over a period of five days, were held inadmissible.[159] However, the demeanour of the police officer for instance being "rude and discourteous" had no impact on the admissibility of confession.[160] But in a case where a confession was obtained after denying the suspect any access to a doctor was held inadmissible.[161] Since a confession is placed before the jury, its reliability is of paramount importance and very little is left for the jury's discretion. Thus, it is pointed out that the process is kept transparent and the preparations to ensure the fairness of the trial begin at the interrogation stage making sure these elements are avoided to obtain a confession. The workability of Section 76(2) has been questioned by Mirfield, who doubts that the police practices having the tendency to produce unreliable confessions will be influenced by court decisions.[162] However, the practice of tape recording of the police interrogation and continual training received by police officers might be stated in the counterargument.

It is concluded that the focus of the provisions of Section 76(2) of PACE apply to any confession and is not affected by the possibility of the confession being true. Section 76(2) has a deterrent rationale where it seeks to rule the inadmissibility of a confession depending on the behaviour of the police officer. It is fair to assume that if police officers aim to get a reliable confession, then they must follow the procedure laid down in PACE and avoid all the provisions of Section 76(2). The courts are also seen to interpret the provisions fairly and consistently throughout the past years and have considered sensitive matters in the reliability of confessions. The potential risk of "false confession" during custodial interrogation has been extensively discussed by Gudjonsson.[163] Gudjonsson argues that the lack of interviews played back at the trial prevents the jury to realise that false confessions can be made.[164] He writes that the giving of confessions is affected by various psychological factors and legislative implications. While much emphasis has been placed on attributes of police training by Gudjonsson, he also suggests various methods in which this can be reformed.[165] A lot of research has been based on this study and legislative reforms have been suggested to minimise the use of coercive interrogation techniques.

4.14 The ECHR and confessions

The ECHR has had a significant impact on English laws and jurisprudence. The ECHR has under Article 6 para 1, banned close-ended or deception and confirmatory questions being used to interrogate suspects. Various derelictions have occurred as observed in the case of *Chiti v. Zambia*, where the author's husband was a military officer arrested as a suspect in an attempted *coup d'e´tat* and convicted and sentenced to death for treason.[166] The husband was deprived of food, severely beaten and forced to sign a confession. The HRC found this use of the confession at trial violated the right to a fair trial. The ECHR have emphasised that the voluntariness of a confession guarantees fair trial rights and this has been interpreted by the ECtHR in a plethora of judgements. It was held in the case of *Gerasimov v. Kazakhstan* that any confession obtained by the police using force or threat affected the domestic right guaranteed for a fair trial.[167] In the case of *Nechiporuk and Yonkalo v. Ukraine*, the ECHR confirmed the provisions of Article 6 rendered a confession inadmissible if obtained while denying safeguards to the suspect.[168] While the ECtHR has always associated the protection of safeguards (such as presence of a lawyer during interrogation) paramount to a confession, the two have always been considered synonymously. In the case of *Pishchalnikov v. Russia*, where it was argued that the confession of the accused acted as a waiver to the right to legal assistance, it was dismissed by the ECtHR.[169] On analysis of various judgements of the ECtHR, it is inferred that reliance is placed on the right to legal assistance on the suspect making a confession. In order to ensure a fair trial, all measures are taken to ascertain the right to legal assistance prior to a confession being made by the suspect. The discretion of the courts to exclude unreliable confessions as set by the ECHR was imported into domestic law under The Human Rights Act, 1998. The cases relating to unreliable confessions were resolved under this act and the need to approach the ECtHR ceased. Thus, the provisions contained under Section 76 of PACE would be dealt with under the Human Rights Act in accordance with the provisions of Articles 3 and 6 of ECHR.

Many countries such as England and Wales, Norway, Australia and New Zealand have since the inception of this practice modified their interrogatory practices to gather information.[170] This practice of the ECHR and the ECtHR ensuring the safeguards to the suspect and its impact on confessions is being adopted by many countries even outside European borders. It is concluded that the enforcement mechanism has been adopted by England and Wales and is being taken into consideration by the English courts.

4.15 The right to legal assistance and confessions

After considering many recommendations made by various law commissions, another safeguard was put in place to ensure that if a confession was made to the police, it was voluntary and free from coercion. The Right to Legal Assistance as discussed in the previous chapter was put in place by PACE and was beginning to show great results. Studies have shown that the presence of a lawyer at the police station has resulted in the suspects' deciding not to admit or confess.[171] Since the introduction of PACE, the awareness of the right to legal assistance has also increased having an impact on the amounts of confessions made to a police officer. The courts have mandated the presence of a lawyer in the light of any confession given to a police officer. Thus, in the case of *R v. McGovern*, Lord Farquharson held that a confession given in the absence of a lawyer was dismissed altogether as it violated the provisions of this Act.[172] Thus, the aim of the PACE enactors who wanted to ensure the balance between the due process and the crime control system seems closer than it was during any previous rules. The courts have highlighted the importance of a lawyer more vehemently in cases involving vulnerable suspects. The importance of having a mandated right to custodial legal assistance may also assist in ensuring the suspect's rights, while he is making a confession. Authors such as J Chalmers point out similar concerns of the absence of guidance to the right to legal assistance post-Cadder.[173]

4.15.1 Legitimacy of confessions

The legitimacy of confessions in England and Wales has been a topic of concern among scholars as much as the topic of exclusion of unfairly obtained evidence. The legitimacy of a confession is often said to have a direct relation to the due process model propagated by Packer.[174] The ever-standing dilemma between ensuring the suspect the right against self-incrimination and the punitive responsibility cast upon the state by way of a confession stands on the brink of the due process model. It can also be argued that from its inception, the law of confessions has been on the basis of exclusion more than a positive duty. For instance, the exclusion of confession obtained under oppression was emphasised under the Judges' Rules. The attitude of the courts towards the police being more biased has been evidenced in the pre-PACE era. Since the lawyers, judges and prosecution rely on the confession obtained by the police interrogation, a lot relies on the combination of intuition and corroboration of the interrogator. Thus, for a confession to be legitimate, a combination of this has to be identified. As Ashworth notes, a suspect whose rights have been infringed upon should not be put to a disadvantage by ensuring at the trial that no improper means were used to obtain a confession.[175] Thus, if a confession is provided where the safeguards of the suspect were protected and without any duress and unfair means used by the police, it passes the legitimacy test.

4.15.2 Tape recording of confessions

Following the enactment of PACE which became a part of the provision of a fair trial, tape recording of the interview and any confession became mandatory. The practice of recording on tape the confession obtained during interrogation seems to legitimise the reliability of the confession and its authenticity. Baldwin has described the requirement to have tape recording of the interviews as the "single most important reform of the criminal justice system in the recent years."[176] This requirement is undeniably the most effective way of verifying many facts and refuting any arguments raised by the maker of the confession or the police. This not only makes it possible to check the validity of the confession but also reduces the work of the trial judge. Any threats relating to the legitimacy of confessions may be addressed easily if the taped interrogation is examined. Any alleged miscarriage of justice based on a false confession can also be cross-examined by the court by playing the recorded interview. In the wake of a series of cases of miscarriage of justice based on false confessions, this practice would adduce evidence in favour of a speedy trial. Gudjonnson has also acknowledged this system to aid criminal justice academics to study the behaviour of suspects and the police and provide useful recommendations.[177]

Further developments by way of video recording may also assist the judge and the jury at trial determine the authenticity of the confession. An analysis of the video tape may help determine any alleged misconduct on the part of the interrogator and can also be examined if challenged by the suspect. This caused a twofold problem: the judiciary would be wasting their time if they had to go through the procedure to obtain a confession, or the public faith in the criminal justice system would dwindle. This was also queried by the court in the case of *AT & T Istel v. Tully*, where the court emphasised on the following:

> Ill treatment of prisoners and fabrication of confessions can only be prevented by better organisation, selection, training, supervision and remuneration of the police force coupled with stringent rules for access to independent legal advice and a bar on confessions obtained in the absence of that representation. If fewer convictions result, this is a price which must be paid and a price which the police force as at present trained are unable to accept.[178]

The practice of tape recording has been commended by many countries and by various academics. Authors like Griffin have described this effort made by England and Wales as "righting miscarriages of justice" in light of various cases of pre-PACE.[179] The courts have also emphasised the use of tape recording of the interrogation to assist while determining the reliability of confessions.[180] While not all tapes are played back in the court, a transcript called ROTI (Record of Taped Interview) is produced in court and is sometimes redacted. Many other jurisdictions like the United States have recently emphasised on recording confessions and the entire police interview, as observed in *Commonwealth v. DiGiambattista*.[181]

One of the criticisms attributed to this practice is the practice of not having all the interrogations tape recorded. A confession obtained from a non-taped interrogation is still likely to be subject to scrutiny and further delay at the trial. This would also include any "off the record" chat between the police officer and the suspect, which might not be on tape. A confession made in these circumstances will also be subject to scrutiny simply for not following the appropriate practice. Authors like Baldwin have criticised the practice of providing transcripts as opposed to playing the recorded interviews in court, as the transcripts can easily be manipulated.[182] It may be agreed here recommending the practice of having all the interviews recorded and no confessions to be taken while "off the record."

4.15.3 Constitutionality of confessions

The constitutionality of confessions obtained is clear from the position set by the ECHR and interpreted into The Human Rights Act, 1998. The regulators of an interrogation need to be assured that a confession is a product of a fair and regular procedure. A doubt about the fairness of the confession alleged or otherwise is put to test under Section 76. The constitutionality of a confession undergoes two tests: voluntariness, and right to legal assistance test. These two elements help in establishing the due process followed in recording a confession. In the presence of clear guidelines provided for both police officers and the prosecution, it is easy to test the confession at the trial stage.

The philosophy of a confession acts against the privilege of the right against self-incrimination and the right to silence. Thus, it must be ensured that a suspect wishing to make a confession was both aware of these rights and given a choice to act against them. As a feature of the adversarial legal system, the burden of proof is on the prosecution to prove beyond reasonable doubt that the suspect has confessed to a crime. It is therefore the duty of the prosecution to ensure that these rights have been wilfully ignored by the suspect under no coercion or unfair methods. At the same time, the prosecution also needs to ensure and answer any allegations (raised by the suspect) about the unfair procedure to obtain a conclusion. The other test of constitutionality about the right to legal assistance has already been discussed above. Both of these rights must coexist in order to prove the constitutional validity of the confession obtained.

4.16 Analysis of comparison

As observed, there are distinct similarities and differences between both these systems and a reformative model may be suggested based on the English criminal justice system. The scope of Sections 25, 26 and 27 of the IEA were inserted in the original act in 1861 to protect the suspect against custodial torture. No other jurisdiction apart from the Indian Criminal Justice system discourages confessions from being made to a police officer. The only justification reflected in jurisprudence and academics' work is to discourage police officers from using force at the time of interrogation. While this has been a provision instituted by the British at the time of the inception of the Indian Evidence Act, no reform or change has been brought about in the act. There has been little effort in reforming the system by providing better training facilities in India, along with providing safeguards such as the presence of a lawyer and the recording of the interrogation.

The provision of allowing other information to be used from a confession almost seems to negate the provisions of Section 25. This is because the interrogating officers have a good reason to interrogate to get a confession which contains relevant information. It is suggested that confessions given to a police officer were never admissible in evidence, except in cases relating to terrorism and possession of illegal substances. A lesson can be taken from the English Criminal Justice system as it has reformed its laws regularly. Legislations such as PACE have provided coherent provisions for police officers to record a confession. As observed, PACE has decreased the number of miscarriages of justice by use of confessions obtained inadmissibly also. The rules which are also safeguards for the suspect can be said to have been observed by police officers. While there have been occasions of lapse by police officers, overall, the provisions of PACE can be said to have been observed. The evidentiary value of confessions is further tested by the judges, jury and prosecution at the trial stage. The verification is provided by the tape-recorded CCTV footage of the entire interrogation.

It is presented in this research that there is a certain culture of acceptance by the general public and academics in India that has prevented any reform from changing the admissibility of confessions to a police officer. On the contrary, in England and Wales, efforts were made by the RCCP and various other commissions in changing the practice of admissibility and issues surrounding false confessions. This was also assisted by research studies carried out periodically assessing the cases of miscarriage and methods used by the police to obtain a confession. This has resulted in various legislative amendments and change in practices relating to admissibility of confessions. Systematic steps are taken following the directions of the ECHR and the judgements passed by the ECtHR, which have also assisted in taking due process steps towards fair trial.

The following hypothesis has been presented: mandated use of video-recorded police interrogations will assist in analysing the accuracy of a confession and render it admissible. The efforts made by the English Criminal Justice system are commendable when it comes to recording the interrogation and are in fact a step ahead of the ECHR. While the ECHR emphasises on the presence of a lawyer to legitimise a confession, the need for recording the interview is widespread in England and Wales. If the recent judgement of the Bombay High Court regarding the installation of CCTV in police stations is implemented, confessions to police officers can easily be admissible.

The other hypothesis is presented here: the presence of a lawyer can ensure fairness in obtaining a reliable confession. This can be a safeguard for the confessing suspect against the unfair methods used by the police officer. The emphases of the presence of a lawyer and the value of confession have been highlighted by the ECHR under Article 6. This is also reflected in the ECtHR jurisprudence. There has been consistency in the judgements of both the English courts and the ECtHR on the presence of a lawyer at the time of confession, highlighting its importance. This can also be gathered from the various systems around the world which are adopting these procedures. Since the Indian Constitution also provides for the presence of a lawyer at the time of interrogation, this can be incorporated in the pretrial stage making the confession to a police officer admissible.

The provisions of Section 76 of PACE may be taken as precedence to test the fairness and validity of confessions in the Indian criminal justice system. Various miscarriages of justice in England and Wales persuaded the lawmakers to incorporate this provision. The steps taken by various law commissions and research studies in England and Wales in the wake of these cases have been commendable. The tests that confessions are put at the trial are also constitutional and ensure the legitimacy of the confessions. The test of exclusion is already being used in the Indian cases relating to terrorism and possession of unlawful substances. Many jurisdictions such as Scotland, who have recently adopted the mandatory presence of a lawyer at the police station, are still unclear on the provision of a mandatory tape recording of the interview. It is contended, however, that this is a working example of a system that can be put in place, which provides for safeguards such as the right to legal assistance.

4.17 Conclusion

This chapter has highlighted the fundamental differences as to the position on the admissibility of confessional evidence given to a police officer in India and England and Wales. The inadmissibility of confession in India has been a relic of the past and is in need of urgent reform. The admissibility of confessions in cases relating to terrorism and possession of unlawful substances is arbitrary. While these are admissible in India, no safeguards are provided to the suspect making a confession and hence its voluntariness and fairness are subject to criticism. But if the appropriate safeguards were adopted, modelled upon the English experience with the use of improperly obtained evidence only when certain procedural criteria are satisfied, Indian criminal justice could reinvent its jurisprudence on the matter, eventually also forcing a change from the part of the legislature.

Notes

1 Meaning 'A confession in a judicial proceeding is greater than any other proof.'
2 Meaning 'A Judicial confession is the absolute proof.'
3 *Dagdu v. State of Maharashtra*, A.I.R. 1977 SC, 1579.
4 Section 217(1) of the Criminal Procedure Act, 1977 (South Africa); Section 29 of the Evidence Act, 1963 (Kenya).
5 K Marx, 'The British Rule in India' (25 June 1853), *New York Daily Tribune*.
6 Sir J Stephen, *A Digest of the Law of Evidence*, New York Publishers, 1829–1894, available at https://archive.org/details/chasedigestoflawof00step, accessed on 23 March 2015.
7 Ibid.
8 Section 164 of the CrPC.
9 Section 27 of the IEA.
10 *The State (NCT) of Delhi v. Navjot Sandhu*, 2005 (11) SCC 600.
11 As observed earlier, the police officers are allowed to wait up to a period of 24 hours to get the suspect to the nearest Magistrate.
12 Section 164(1) of CrPC.
13 Section 164(4) of CrPC.
14 Section 164(3) of CrPC.
15 *Dara Singh v. Republic of India*, 2011 (2) SCC 490.
16 A Noorani, 'Teaching Human Rights to the Police' (October 1993) XXVIII(42) *Economic and Political Weekly* 2252.
17 *Surendra Koli v. The State of Uttar Pradesh*, 2011 (4) SCC 80.
18 *The State of Rajasthan v. Raja Ram*, 2003 (8) SCC 180, also see *Alok Nath Dutta v. State of West Bengal*, 2007(12) SCC 230, *Chattar Singh v. State of Haryana*, AIR 2009 SC 378.
19 *Surinder Kumar v. The State of Punjab*, AIR 1999 SC 215.
20 *Pakkirisamy v. The State of Tamil Nadu* (1997) 8 SCC 158.
21 *Ram Singh v. Sonia*, 2007 (2) SCC (Crl) 1.
22 *Rahim Beg v. The State of UP*, 1972 (3) SCC 759.
23 *Sansar Chand v. The State of Rajasthan* (2010) 10 SCC 604.

24 The Supreme Court has relied on the judgement in the case of *Miranda v. Arizona* and referred to scholars like Sir Stephen.
25 Section 17 of IEA.
26 *Ram Singh v. The State*, AIR 1959 Crim. L. J. 1134.
27 *Satyawan Pagi v. The Union of India*, 2006 Crim. L. J. 2181.
28 Section 25 of the IEA.
29 Section 26 of the Indian Evidence Act, 187:

> Confession by accused while in custody of police not to be proved against him—no confession made by any person whilst he is in the custody of a police officer, unless it be made in the immediate presence of a Magistrate 1, shall be proved as against such person.

30 *Ariel v. The State*, AIR 1954 SC 15.
31 Section 27 of the Indian Evidence Act, 1872:

> How much of information received from accused may be proved—provided that, when any fact is deposed to as discovered in consequence of information received from a person accused of any offence, in the custody of a police officer, so much of such information, whether it amounts to a confession or not, as relates distinctly to the fact thereby discovered, may be proved.

32 *Bodh Raj v. State of Jammu and Kashmir*, AIR 2002 SC 16.
33 *Inspector of Police, Tamil Nadu v. Bala Prasanna* (2008) 11 SCC 645, at p. 652.
34 *R v. Babulal*, 1884 (6) A 509, at 523.
35 *Sandeep v. The State of UP*, 2012 (6) SCC 107.
36 Ibid.
37 R Kumar, A Singh, A Agrawal, and J Kaur, *Reduced to Ashes: The Insurgency and Human Rights in Punjab*, Nepal: South Asia Forum for Human Rights, 2003.
38 *Madhu v. The State of Kerala*, 2012 (2) SCC 399.
39 *Malimath Committee Report: Committee on Reforms of Criminal Justice System,* Government of India, 2003, mha.nic.in/pdfs/criminal_justice_system.pdf, accessed on 12 February 2013.
40 As interpreted from the jurisprudential interpretation of the term police custody, for further details see *The State of Andhra Pradesh v. G Satya Murthy*, 1997 CRI LJ 744 (SC).
41 *Ram Chander v. State of Rajasthan*, 2003 Cri LJ 2485.
42 A Ganesan and P Grossman, *Police Abuse and Killings of Street Children in India*, Human Rights Watch, 1996, 34.
43 A Verma, *The New Khakhi: The Evolving Nature of Policing in India (Advances in Police Theories and Practice)*, CRC Press, Taylor and Francis Group, 2012.
44 *Kartar Singh v. State of Punjab*, 1994 3 SCC 569.
45 M Monir, *Textbook on the Law of Evidence*, New Delhi: Universal Law Publication, 2011.
46 Interview Transcript PO16.
47 *The State of Bombay v. Kathi Kalu* AIR 1961, 1808.
48 *People's Union for Civil Liberties v. Union of India*, 2004 SCC 580, 591.
49 P Softley et al, *Police Interrogation: An Observational Study in Four Police Stations*, Home Office Research Study No. 61, April 1980, available at http://library.npia.police.uk/docs/hors/hors61.pdf, accessed on 10 January 2015; A Choo, *Evidence*, 5th edn, OUP, 2018.
50 See e.g. J Lokaneeta, *Transnational Torture: Law, Violence, and State Power in the United States*, New York University Press, 2011.

51 *Malimath Committee Report: Committee on Reforms of Criminal Justice System*, Government of India, 2003, mha.nic.in/pdfs/criminal_justice_system.pdf, accessed on 12 February 2013.
52 See generally; G Pelly, *State Terrorism: Torture, Extra-Judicial Killings, and Forced Disappearance in India*, New Delhi: Human Rights Law Network Publication, 2009; C A Meissner, A D Redlich, S Bhatt, and S Brandon, 'Interview and Interrogation Methods and Their Effects on True and False Confessions' (2012) 8 Campbell Systematic Reviews 1–53, Campbell Collaboration; S Sarangi and A Wright, 'Human Rights Is Not Enough: The Need for Demonstrating Efficacy of an Ethical Approach to Interviewing in India' (2008) 13 *Legal and Criminological Psychology* 89–106.
53 *The State of Punjab v. Barkatram*, AIR 1962 SC 276; *Surjit Singh Chandra v. Union of India*, 1996 (8) Supreme 374.
54 *Badkujoti v. State of Mysore*, AIR 1966 SC 1746.
55 *Forest Range Officer, Changathara II Range v. Aboobacker*, 1989 Crim LJ Kerela 2038.
56 *Rajkumar Kanwal v. Union of India*, AIR 1991 CRI LJ SC 97.
57 *Kuldip Singh v. The State of Punjab*, AIR 1997 SC 82.
58 V Sithannan, *Police Investigation: Powers, Tactics, and Techniques*, Chennai: Jeywin Publication, 2013.
59 Under Section 15 of TADA.
60 Under Section 32 of POTA.
61 Under Sections 53 and 67 of the NDPS.
62 Section 67 of NDPS.
63 Central Government Standing Order No. 822 (E).
64 *Husen Bhenu Malad v. State of Gujarat,* 2003 Cri L J 5070.
65 *Kanhayalal v. Union of India*, AIR 2008 SC 1044.
66 *Raju Premji v. Customs*, 2009 (16) SCC 496.
67 Interview Transcript PO16.
68 The Terrorism and Disruptive Activities Act.
69 The Prevention of Terrorism Act.
70 *Kartar Singh v. State of Punjab*, AIR 1994 (3) SCC 569.
71 Ibid.
72 Ibid.
73 *Gurdeep Singh v. State (Delhi Administration)*, AIR 1999 SC 3646.
74 *Jameel Ahmed v. State of Rajasthan*, 2003 (9) SCC 673.
75 TADA Rules 15(2).
76 *Kartar Singh v. The State of Punjab* 1994 (3) SCC 569.
77 Under Section 32 of POTA, a confession made to a high-ranking police officer can be used as evidence against the maker of such confession.
78 *Ayyub v. State of UP*, AIR 2002 SC 1192.
79 *People's Union for Civil Liberties v. Union of India*, 2004 SCC 580.
80 *People's Union for Civil Liberties v. Union of India*, 2004 SCC 581.
81 *State (NCT of Delhi) v. Navjot Sandhu,* 2005 (11) SC 600.
82 Section 64-66 UAPA Act, 2004.
83 Section 18 MCOCA.
84 *People's Union for Civil Liberties v. Union of India*, 2004 SCC 580, p. 590.
85 Interview Transcript PO15.
86 *Kartar Singh v. The State of Punjab* 1994 (3) SCC 569.
87 See generally; U Baxi, *The Future of Human Rights,* 2nd edn, Oxford University Press, 2006.
88 J Vadackumchery, *Indian Police and Equal Justice under Law*, India: APH Publishing House, 1999.
89 Interview Transcript PO2.

90 *State v. NMT Joy Immaculate*, 2004 Cri LJ 2515.
91 V Karan, 'A Case for a "Cultural Revolution" of India's Police' in J Guha Roy (ed.), *Policing a District*, Delhi: IIPA, 1992.
92 P Alexander, *Policing India in the New Millennium*, New Delhi: Allied Publishers, 2002.
93 J Lokaneeta, *Transnational Torture: Law, Violence, and State Power in the United States*, New York University Press, 2011.
94 *48th Report, Law Commission of India*, May 2002, available at http://law commissionofindia.nic.in/reports/48rpt.pdf, accessed on 4 March 2015.
95 69th Law Commission Report, available at lawcommissionofindia.nic.in/re ports/185threport-partii.pdf, accessed on 5 April 2015.
96 *Malimath Committee Report: Committee on Reforms of Criminal Justice System,* Government of India, 2003, mha.nic.in/pdfs/criminal_justice_sy stem.pdf
97 P Alexander, *Policing India in the New Millennium*, New Delhi: Allied Publishers, 2002.
98 J Lokaneeta, *Transnational Torture: Law, Violence, and State Power in the United States*, New York University Press, 2011.
99 U Baxi, *The Future of Human Rights,* 2nd edn, Oxford University Press, 2006.
100 K Kalra, *Be Your Own Layer: Book for Layman*, New Delhi: Vij Books Publication, 2013.
101 ACHR's Actions against Torture and Other Forms of Human Rights Violations in India (New Delhi: ACHR, 2009), all reports available at http://www.achr-web.org/, accessed 15 July 2014.
102 *Bharosa v. Emporer*, 1941 Nag 86.
103 *Agnou Naagesia v. The State of Bihar*, 1966 Crim L J 100 SCC.
104 Section 21 of IEA.
105 This is discussed at length in chapter titled 'Police Interrogation: A Comparative Analysis between India and England and Wales.'
106 Interview Transcript PO7.
107 See generally; Transcript PO1, 2, 4, 5, 8 and 10.
108 The provisions of Section 26 and 27 of the IEA.
109 Interview Transcript PO7.
110 Interview Transcript PO7.
111 Interview Transcript PO3.
112 Interview Transcript PO8.
113 Interview Transcript PO8.
114 *Broken System: Dysfunction, Abuse and Impunity in the Indian Police*, 2009, Human Rights Watch Report, available at http://www.hrw.org/sites/default/fi les/reports/india0809web.pdf, accessed on 24 January 2013.
115 A Verma, *The New Khakhi: The Evolving Nature of Policing in India (Advances in Police Theories and Practice)*, CRC Press, Taylor and Francis Group, 2012.
116 A reference here is made to the concept of retracted confession.
117 Human Rights Watch interview, other details withheld. These practices are reflected in the testimony of dozens of victims of police torture and ill-treatment, gathered by People's Watch and its local partners, and in media reports and complaints collected by ACHR.
118 *Babubhai Parmar v. State of Gujarat,* 2007 Cri LJ 786.
119 *Kartar Singh v. The State of Punjab* 1994 (3) SCC 569, 724.
120 J Langbein, *The Origins of the Adversary Criminal Trial*, OUP, 2003.
121 W Blackstone, *Commentaries on the Laws of England*, San Francisco: Bancroft Whitney, 1916.
122 J Wigmore, *A Treatise on the Anglo American System of Evidence in Trials at Common Law*, Boston: Little Brown Company, 1940.

123 Ibid.
124 Sir J Stephen, *A Digest of the Law of Evidence*, New York Publishers, 1829–1894, available at https://archive.org/details/chasedigestoflawof00step, accessed on 23 March 2015; A Choo, *Evidence*, 5th edn, OUP, 2018.
125 Sir Henry Fisher, 'Report of an Inquiry by the then Sir Henry Fisher into the Circumstances Leading to the Trial of Three Persons on Charges Arising Out of the Death of Maxwell Confait and the Fire at 27 Doggett Road, London SEC' 1977.
126 Ibid.
127 *R v. Sang* (1980) AC 402.
128 *R v. Voison* (1918) 1 KB 531.
129 A Zuckerman, *The Principles of Criminal Evidence*, OUP, 1989.
130 R Reiner, *The Politics of the Police*, 2nd edn, OUP, 1992.
131 D Dixon, 'Revising 'Police Powers': Legal Theories and Policing Practices in Historical and Contemporary Contexts' in L Noaks, M Levi, and M Maguire (eds), *Contemporary Issues in Criminology*, 1995.
132 Ibid.
133 C Phillips, *Royal Commission on Criminal Procedure, The Investigation and Prosecution of Criminal Offences in England and Wales*; The Law and Procedure 1981, para 2.21.
134 R Reiner and L Leigh, *Police Power, in Individual Rights and the Law in Britain*, C McCrudden and G Chambers (eds), 1994.
135 R Reiner, *The Politics of the Police*, 2nd edn, OUP, 1992.
136 J Hodgson in the judgement of *R v. Keenan* (1990) 90 Cr App R 1.
137 A Ashworth and M Redmayne, *The Criminal Process*, 3rd edn, OUP, 2004; L Campbell, A Ashworth, and M Redmayne, *The Criminal Process*, 5th edn, 2019.
138 R Reiner, *The Politics of the Police*, 2nd edn, OUP, 1992.
139 Section 82 of PACE

82 Part VIII— interpretation.
(1) In this Part of this Act—

"confession", includes any statement wholly or partly adverse to the person who made it, whether made to a person in authority or not and whether made in words or otherwise;

"proceedings" means criminal proceedings, including [service proceedings]

"Service court" means the Court Martial or the Service Civilian Court.

(3) Nothing in this Part of this Act shall prejudice any power of a court to exclude evidence (whether by preventing questions from being put or otherwise) at its discretion.

140 Section 76 of PACE, 1984.
141 R Reiner and L Leigh, *Police Power, in Individual Rights and the Law in Britain*, C McCrudden and G Chambers (eds), 1994; J Chalmers, 'Recording of Police Interviews' in J Chalmers, F Leverick, and A Shaw (eds), *Post-Corroboration Safeguards Review Report of the Academic Expert Group*, Edinburgh: The Scottish Government, 2014.
142 *R v. Samuels* (1988) 1 QB 615.
143 See generally; *R v. Keenan* (1990) 90 Cr App R 1, *R v. Quinn* (1990) Crim L R 581, and *R v. Walsh* (1989) 91 Cr App R 161.
144 *R v. Keenan* (1990) 90 Cr App R 1.
145 *R v. Mackenzie* (1993) 96 Cr. App. R. 98.

146 The Criminal Law Revision Committee, 1972, available at http://www.ncbi.nlm.nih.gov/pubmed/5076843, accessed on 13 August 2014.
147 J Baldwin, 'Police Interview Techniques: Establishing Truth or Proof?' (1993) 33(3) *British Journal of Criminology* 325–352.
148 S Kassin and G Gudjonsson, 'The Psychology of Confessions: A Review of the Literature and Issues' (2004) 5 *Psychological Science in the Public Interest* 33–67.
149 S Kassin et al., 'Police-Induced Confessions: Risk Factors and Recommendations' (2010) 34 *Law and Human Behaviour* 3.
150 S Soukara, R Bull, A Vrij, M Turner, and J Cherryman, 'What Really Happens in Police Interviews with Suspects?: Tactics and Confessions' (2009) 15 *Psychology, Crime & Law* 493–506.
151 The provisions of the PEACE model are discussed in the chapter marked 'Police Interrogation: A Comparative Analysis between India and England and Wales.'
152 *R v. Keenan* (1990) 90 Cr App R 1.
153 M McConville, A Sanders, and R Leng, *The Case for the Prosecution,* London: Routledge, 1991.
154 Section 76 of PACE, 1984.
155 J Blackstock, E Cape, J Hodgson, A Ogordova, and T Spronken, *Inside Police Custody: An Empirical Account of Suspects' Rights in Four Jurisdictions*, Intersentia, 2014.
156 *R v. Keenan* (1990) 90 Cr App R 1, *R v. Walsh* (1989) 91 Cr App R 161, and *R v. Quinn* (1990) Crim L R 581.
157 *R v. Keenan* (1990) 90 Cr App R 1.
158 *R v. Delaney* (1988) 86 Cr App R 18.
159 *R v. Paris, Abdullahi and Miller* (1993) 97 Cr App R 99.
160 *R v. Emmerson* (1991) 92 Cr App R 284.
161 *R v. Crampton* (1990) 92 Cr App R 369.
162 P Mirfield, 'The Future of the Law of Confessions' (1984) *Criminal Law Review* 70.
163 For details see, G Gudjonsson, *The Psychology of Interrogations, Confessions, and Testimony,* New York: John Wiley & Sons, 1992.
164 G Gudjonson, 'False Confessions and Correcting Injustices' (2012) 46 *New England Law Review* 689–710.
165 Ibid.
166 *Chitti v. Zambia*, CCPR/C/105/D/1303/2004.
167 *Gerasimov v. Kazakhstan*, CAT No. 433/2010 (2012). For further details, please also see *Aboufaied v. Libya*, HRC No. 1782/2008 (2012).
168 *Nechiporuk and Yonkalo v. Ukraine* Application no. 420/04 (2011), 175.
169 *Pishchalnikov v. Russia*, 7025/04 (2009) ECHR 1357.
170 S Soukara, R Bull, A Vrij, M Turner, and J Cherryman, 'What Really Happens in Police Interviews with Suspects?: Tactics and Confessions' (2009) 15 *Psychology, Crime & Law* 493–506.
171 S Moston, G Stephenson, and T Williamson, 'The Effects of Case Characteristics on Suspect Behaviour during Police Questioning' (1992) 32 *British Journal of Criminology* 33.
172 *R v. McGovern* (1991) 92 Cr. App. R.
173 J Chalmers, 'Recording of Police Interviews' in J Chalmers, F Leverick, and A Shaw (eds), *Post-Corroboration Safeguards Review Report of the Academic Expert Group*. Edinburgh: The Scottish Government, 2014.
174 H Packer, *The Limits of the Criminal Sanction,* Herbert L Packer (ed.), Stanford University Press, 1968.
175 A Ashworth and M Redmayne, *The Criminal Process*, 3rd edn, OUP, 2004; L Campbell, A Ashworth, and M Redmayne, *The Criminal Process*, 5th edn, 2019.

176 J Baldwin, 'Police Interviews on Tape' (1990) 11 *New Law Journal* 662.
177 J Pearse and G Gudjonsson, 'Police Interviewing and Legal Representation: A Field Study' (1997) 8(1) *The Journal of Forensic Psychiatry* 200–208.
178 *AT&T Istel Ltd v. Tully* (1993) AC 45.
179 L Griffin, 'Correcting Injustice: Studying How the United Kingdom and the United States Review Claims of Innocence' (2009) 41 U. Tol. L. Rev. 107.
180 *R v. Keenan* (1990) 90 Cr App R 1.
181 *Commonwealth v. DiGiambattista* 813 N E 2d 516 (Mass 2004).
182 J Baldwin, 'Police Interview Techniques: Establishing Truth or Proof?' (1993) 33(3) *British Journal of Criminology* 325–352.

5 Suspects' rights in context

Tackling the use of force and torture in custodial interrogations

5.1 Introduction

This chapter revisits evidence demonstrating the recurrent use of force and torture in custodial interrogation in India. As it emerged from the discussions in Chapters 3 and 4, in the absence of proper safeguards for the suspect, including any form of legal assistance, the police continue to resort to these methods when interrogating a suspect. Research conducted by international human rights NGOs proves this point. This chapter approaches these questions with the underpinning hypothesis that the provision of adequate safeguards could significantly deter the use of torture and unlawful force at the police station. The example of the English transition from the pre-PACE to the post-PACE era provides support to this idea.

5.2 Excessive use of force and torture

Historically, the use of torture in India has been associated with colonial rule. Excessive use of force and torture methods by the British-recruited police officers confirms the use of force by the Indian police and excludes the influence of the British. Foucault describes the transformation of power from the use of torture to a power based on control through discipline in society.[1] HLA Hart and Dworkin opine, which is also asserted by Hobbes, that law based on coercion is replaced in modern societies by law based on rules and principles.[2] This is one of the reasons why theorists assume violence occupies the secondary position in legal process.[3] Often the blame of using force is put on the native police officers, and this allegedly is one of the reasons why a confession made to a police officer is inadmissible in evidence. The use of force by police officers is of utmost concern because it not only affects the citizens but also changes their attitude towards the government.[4] It is the responsibility of the government to regulate the use of force by the state actors. Torture, the use of force and other methods have not been defined in any of the criminal codes. The use of excessive force and brutality by the police has led to custodial deaths in the past few years. The government has failed to take proper measures to curb this practice.

DOI: 10.4324/9781003213024-5

This inaction of the government has been criticised by various human rights organisations and the Supreme Court.

5.2.1 *The legislative framework*

This section analyses the provisions in the domestic legislation in India for the use of force and torture by an interrogating police officer. Section 29 of the Indian Police Act specifies that if evidence suggests that a police officer has inflicted harm on any person in his custody, he shall be liable to pay a fine and or imprisonment.[5] Sections 330 and 331 of the IPC prohibit voluntarily causing hurt and grievous hurt respectively to a suspect in police custody in order to extort a confession or to compel restoration of stolen property. This action is punishable by imprisonment up to seven and ten years, respectively, and shall also be liable to a fine. Sections 50, 54, 56 and 57 of the CrPC also try and restrict the use of unfair means in order to avoid human rights violations.

Further safety measures are taken in the form of Section 50, which mentions that the person arrested shall be informed of the grounds of his arrest. This section also includes informing a member of the family of his arrest and details relating to the arrest. Section 54 provides the suspect in police custody the right to medical attention to assure no physical harm is inflicted upon the suspect by the police. While most of these sections ensure the suspects' well-being, none of them are punitive measures that could be applied upon police officers breaching custodial interrogation duties. Finally, Section 176(a) of the IPC makes it mandatory for the magistrate to enquire into any custodial death.

5.2.2 *The courts' response*

In *Niranjan Singh v. Prabhakar Rajaram* case, the Supreme Court emphatically observed that "The police instead of being protector of law, have become engineer of terror and panic putting people into fear."[6] It is noted here that as early as 1980, the Supreme Court acknowledged the use of force by the police at the time of interrogation. The courts have further criticised the use of excessive force by the police and its impact on the fairness of the trial. The Supreme Court has emphasised the gravity of this section and has in the case of *Sheela Barse v. The State of Maharashtra* held as follows:

> The Magistrate before whom an arrested person is produced shall enquire from the arrested person whether he has any complaint of torture or maltreatment in police custody and inform him that he has a right under Section 54 to be medically examined.[7]

In *Kartar Singh v. The State of Punjab* case, a constitutional bench remarked the following:

> We cannot avoid but saying that we—with the years of experience both at the Bar and on the Bench—have frequently dealt with cases of atrocity and brutality practised by some overzealous police officers resorting to inhuman, barbaric, archaic and drastic methods of treating the suspects in their anxiety to collect evidence by hook or by crook and wrenching a decision in their favour. We remorsefully like to state that on a few occasions even custodial deaths caused during interrogation are brought to our notice. We are very much distressed and deeply concerned about the oppressive behaviour and the most degrading and despicable practice adopted by some of the police officers.[8]

In the landmark judgement of *D K Basu*, the Supreme Court held as follows:

> Custodial violence, including torture and death in the lock-ups, strikes a blow at the rule of law, which demands that the powers of the executive should not only be derived from law but also that the same should be limited by law. ... Transparency of action and accountability perhaps are two possible safeguards which this Court must insist upon.[9]

Even in the most recent cases where the suspect was beaten and raped in a police station, the Supreme Court held as follows:

> It is in that context the High Court held that the so-called beating could have meant to shake off their inhibition and fear, to make them free to say what they wanted to say. In the given facts and circumstances of this case, beating will mean to remove the fear psychosis and to come out with truth. We do not find any infirmity in the concurrent findings recorded by both the courts below on this court.[10]

From this contextual standpoint, the Supreme Court questioned the credibility of the criminal process' ability to implement the rule of law and ensure the effective administration of criminal justice.[11] The courts have emphasised the need to eliminate "dehumanising torture, assault, and death in custody," but it can be seriously doubted whether their jurisprudence can in itself exercise the systemic influence required considering the culture of violence inherent in Indian criminal investigations. *Sube Singh v. The State of Haryana*, on the other hand, emphasised that there is a remedy for the victims in both civil and criminal laws.[12] But it is also felt that these are not enough.

5.2.3 Ratification of international conventions

Owing to the growing instances of police torture, killings and the use of force, many international human rights institutions have taken interest in the situation in India. The following section looks at some of the international conventions which might be applicable here.

5.2.3.1 Universal Declaration of Human Rights, 1948

India is one of the signatories to the UDHR, thus having legal obligations to protect, promote and fulfil human rights treaties under Article 5 of the UDHR. The convention requires member states to take effective legislative, administrative, judicial and other measures to prevent acts of torture under their jurisdiction,[13] and provides that member states should not condone the use of torture under any circumstances. Important obligations for India derive from the UDHR but there is no evidence demonstrating that the country has sought to effectively address these.

5.2.3.2 ICCPR

India has ratified and incorporated the ICCPR rights in the Indian Constitution and, in particular, Articles 19, 16 and 22. A very important provision that has been recognised by the Indian government is the issue of forced disappearance as a violation of the right to life reflected under Article 14 of the Indian Constitution.

However, India has signed but not ratified other conventions such as United Nations International Convention for the Protection of all Persons from Enforced Disappearances, 2006. Under Article 5 of the convention, enforced disappearance of a suspect in custody is an international crime. It encourages member states to enforce this in their domestic legislation. This convention also makes it the responsibility of the member state to ensure the victims get a form of redress and compensation. The courts have also confirmed that the (Indian) constitutional provisions of Article 21 reflect the provisions of Article 7 of the ICCPR and guarantee the protection against torture, cruelty and inhuman or degrading treatment.[14] Authors have written that India has constantly been breaching the provisions of Article 7 of the ICCPR.[15] This further impacts the reluctance of the Indian government to incorporate the provisions of the convention, affecting its customary international law. Despite the similarity in the provisions between Article 7 and the above-mentioned articles of the Constitution, it paints a completely different practical picture.

5.2.3.3 The United Nations Convention Against Torture and Other Cruel, Inhuman and Degrading Punishment or Treatment, 1984

The CAT defines torture as follows:

> Any act by which severe pain or suffering, whether physical or mental, is intentionally inflicted on a person for such purposes as obtaining

> from him or a third person information or a confession, punishing him for an act he or a third person has committed or is suspected of having committed, or intimidating or coercing him or a third person, or for any reason based on discrimination of any kind, when such pain or suffering is inflicted by or at the instigation of or with the consent or acquiescence of a public official or other person acting in an official capacity. It does not include pain or suffering arising only from, inherent in or incidental to lawful sanctions.[16]

CAT provides for each signatory state to take effective measures to prevent torture and similar treatment from being practised. The states are expected to redress and compensate for those who have been the victims of torture by the actors of the state. India signed the CAT but is yet to ratify the convention. This convention includes a ban on evidence obtained as a result of torture, and requires states to investigate allegations, and compensate the victims, of torture.[17] This convention has been ratified by 117 countries. India is one of the few countries which has signed but not ratified it. Many commentators have criticised the Indian government's reluctance to ratify this convention.[18] The prohibition of torture is *jus cogens*, hence legally binding to all states, irrespective of whether they have been signatories or not.

Even as just a signatory to this convention, India is liable to invite a UN Special Rapporteur on Torture to facilitate preparing of a report. However, this has never been done in practice.[19] Constant reports have been filed by the UN Special Rapporteur on Torture based on the information they have received from other sources over a number of years. This did not seem sufficient even for the UN Rapporteur and they still insist on visiting the country to carry out various studies to file adequate reports. This report has only estimated with the size and population of the country the use of force and its consequences.[20] In conclusion, the report mentioned that the impunity of police officers along with the tolerance of the use of torture throughout the department is what causes the continued existence of this malpractice.[21] This indicates that urgent measures need to be taken to ratify this convention in order to reform the existing practice of torture.

5.3 Forms of torture

This section discusses the forms of torture used at the time of police interrogation and the level to which the use of force can be considered legitimate. The main forms of torture that are discussed here are torture as a tool of interrogation, use of force and beating, encounter, custodial violence and custodial death. These are analysed in light of their impact on police interrogation and the reasons why they go unnoticed or unreported.

5.3.1 *Torture as a tool of interrogation*

Torture is most commonly used at the time of police interrogation. Torture goes unreported because there is no mandatory requirement by the police to record the use of torture. Singhvi, an amicus curie appointed by the Supreme Court, in a case on the use of torture during police interrogation mentioned that

> Unlike custodial deaths, the police are not mandatorily required to report cases of torture which do not result in deaths to the NHRC. Hence the number of reported cases of torture is a fraction of the actual incidents.[22]

The position of the police is authoritative in nature and hence requires the use of some form of force, which easily leads to torture. The continued use of torture and oppression by those in position to threaten suspects at the time of interrogation has been exacerbated by the lack of accountability and regulation. Amnesty International has expressed its concern in various reports suggesting that torture is still being used as a tool for interrogation and is an "evil endemic."[23]

The period of 24 hours between the initial detention and taking the suspect to the magistrate is sufficient time to inflict torturous methods on the suspect under the guise of interrogation. During this time, there is no safeguard in practice which can protect the suspect from any potential use of torture by the police. It is a fact that the vulnerability of the detainee is at its peak during this period and it is easy for the police officer to torture. This has been confirmed by a testimony given by a police officer to Human Rights Watch:

> They say, "investigate within 24 hours" but they never care about how I will do [that], what are the resources. ... There is use of force in sensational cases because we are not equipped with scientific methods. What remains with us? A sense of panic surrounds our mind that if we don't come to a conclusion we will be suspended or face punishment. We are bound to fulfil the case, we must cover the facts in any way.[24]

A similar theme was detected in an interview carried out for the present research:

> Twenty-four hours are more than enough to do what the police please or want to do.[25]

Even a lawyer noted that the initial period before the suspect is presented before a magistrate, the police are at an advantage:

> The initial time is more than enough for them (police) to do what they please or want to do.[26]

Many studies carried out in various states and villages in India have revealed the implication of the use of torture by police officers. In an empirical research carried out by Pelly, instances of pregnant women losing their babies, loss of sight, use of electric shocks, laying the suspect on ice are some instances of torture used by the police under the guise of interrogation.[27] The use of such torturous methods is a country-wide phenomenon and is not restricted to the urban areas or villages. Many studies have also indicated the use of torture on individuals who are "poor, and socially and politically marginalised."[28] It is evident from Pelly's study that this allegation has some credibility and the police use more torturous method with certain disadvantaged categories of the population. Waldron notes, "The rule against torture is archetypal of a certain policy having to do with the relation between law and force, and the force with which law rules."[29] Thus, law is non-brutal in itself but the methods employed by police officers display the brutal nature of law. There is a worldwide acceptance that the police are expected to use force at the time of interrogation. However, this use of force is expected to be monitored and regulated by external agencies.

5.3.1.1 Law commissions on torture

The law commission recognised this problem of the use of torture in what is allegedly the only report on torture and custodial crime.[30] This report identified the main reason for the continued use of torture as long hours of duty and other duties leaving little time for interrogation.[31] However, these reasons have condoned the use of torture by the police and have therefore not urged the government to take effective punitive measures to curb this. In the absence of scientific interrogation methods which might speed up the interrogation, police officers are under pressure to produce results. The law commission recognises this issue as one of the reasons but has not provided any measures for eradicating this practice.

5.3.2 Use of force and beating

Policing in general involves adapting a rigorous approach towards police interrogations, which are the most demanding duty carried out by the police. There is no doubt that police officers are authorised to use force, but, as Kleinig points out, there is little consideration by the police in the type and level of force.[32] The use of force and beatings by the police are two very different concepts and the police fail to distinguish between them. The most common forms of beating in India under the guise of interrogation are the use of *lathi*, fists, baton, beating on the suspects' sole or using electric shocks. Various incidents range from excessive beatings using the above methods. Police officers are also infamous for using a kind of torture called "third degree" in an effort to produce results. This was noted by one personnel interviewed as follows:

> The police tells such offenders usually thieves that you accept that you've done this crime also and we won't beat you up. So that poor

> fellow who is too afraid to be beaten up again, just accepts the crime. He as well as the police know that the punishment is the same for committing one crime or two or more crimes.[33]

The lack of accountability and training for fundamental human rights are the main reasons why torture is still used as a tool of interrogation. Some of them have been recorded by the Asian Human Rights Committee.

The justified use of excessive force such as beating is left for the police officer to prove, therefore giving it an element of subjectivity. The determination of the excessiveness of force depends on the person judging the use of force.[34] Belur distinguishes the acceptance of the excessiveness of the use of force when determined by a judge from that of police managers.[35] This may one of the many undiscovered reasons for the justification of beating during a police interrogation. The sophisticated distinction between a human rights approach and professional standards approach towards the excessive use of force is thought to be most appropriate. Police interrogation nonetheless is one of the most feared aspects of policing as evident from a police officer's perspective: "People would prefer not being in the police station for any reason, let alone for an interrogation."[36] It is suggested that this unsupervised use of force and beating during police interrogation results in unfortunate incidents such as custodial deaths.

5.3.3 Custodial death and violence

Various forms of custodial violence follow from the use of excessive force by police officers as discussed above. There is a fine line between the use of force and custodial violence. Custodial violence includes various other forms of violence such as sexual violence, threats and forms of bribery.[37] Police officers are able to carry out any or all of the above forms of custodial violence because of the lack of supervision and vulnerability of the suspect. The absence of any regulation or monitoring makes this an easy task for a person in the position and power of a police officer, very simple.

An interrogation attracting the use of violence results in an atrocity such as custodial death. The attitude of police officers towards custodial deaths has received criticism from the courts and international organisations equally. Constant cases of custodial deaths surface in the media, but there are also cases that are often unreported. Official figures confirm that there have been 11,820 custodial deaths in the country in the last five years.[38] A total of 61 custodial deaths have occurred in India as reported on the official database.[39] It was alarming when in the state of Maharashtra 35 people died in 2014 and not a single police officer was convicted or tried in relation to these deaths.[40] Similar figures exist in other states in India however; many authors and human rights organisation claim that these may not be the correct figures.[41]

5.3.3.1 Constitutional provisions and custodial violence and death

The constitutional provision makes it mandatory for medical attention to be provided to the suspect at the time of arrest.[42] This provision aims at safeguarding the suspect against such practices of custodial violence. However, this is rarely complied with by the hospital or medical examiners in doing their duty. A detailed medical report may assist in providing any incidents of custodial torture, preventing death, but this is rarely reflected in practice. Many NGOs have urged medical professionals to highlight the instances of police brutality.[43] Often NGOs supporting the victims of custodial torture are unable to prove this police brutality in court due to the lack of a detailed medical report. The great divide between the class of the victim and the police also causes hindrance in gathering evidence and proving custodial violence in court.[44]

The police have known to quote the custodial deaths as "suicides." There has also been a parliamentary acknowledgement of this alleged malpractice.[45] However, no exact reasons or further details have been given for this malpractice or of its continuance. The Asian Centre for Human Rights (ACHR) have highlighted in their report through various case studies that calling custodial deaths suicides is common practice in many states in India.[46] Despite this constitutional safeguard of producing the suspect before a magistrate, the continuing rate of custodial deaths reflects the flaw in practice.

5.3.4 Encounters

The use of firearms by police officers also results in the use of deadly force. A common practice, which gained fame notoriously, was shooting a suspect at the time of interrogation. In Mumbai, a metropolitan city of India, it was a usual practice of shooting the usual suspects at the time of police interrogation. Very often these suspects were well-known criminals and were known to have deep-rooted connection with the infamous criminal underworld. Between the period of 1900 and 2001, police officers were alleged of "shootouts" involving regular offenders or notorious criminals. In a series of articles written by Belur, she tried to answer the question, why police officers use this kind of force.[47] In the analysis it was established that the police justified such killings as necessary owing to either peer or public pressure.[48] This practice was condoned in a city like Mumbai and the police were notoriously acclaimed initially for their efforts by the public and media alike, as observed by Belur.[49] The lack of faith by the public in the Indian judiciary was partly responsible for the acceptance of this practice by police officers. The fact that most of these suspects were associated with the infamous underworld provided further justification. However, it was pointed out by one of the personnel interviewed that there was a certain geographical limitation on this:

> There was a nuisance of these police encounters, not here of course, that sort of thing happens in big cities.[50]

Even if the public did not condone these encounter killings, they thought this was the only "practicable" solution.[51]

The two main reasons why the police in India are thought to resort to this is possessing a firearm and self-defence. Since most of the police officers in India are allowed a firearm, they feel the need to use it either owing to pressure or if the suspect misbehaves. Under Section 100 of the IPC, the police are allowed to defend their body and person as per the procedure followed by law as long as it does not result in death. However, little care and caution is used by police officers while exercising self-defence in the name of encounters.[52] It is suggested that this is merely an excuse used by police officers. This is facilitated by the lack of any mechanism holding them accountable for such severe action during interrogation. Despite the jurisprudential acknowledgement about the use of excessive force resulting in brutal acts by the police, there has been no further action to remedy this practice. It is essential to analyse the view taken by the judiciary on this subject.

5.4 Lack of faith by the judiciary

The criminal justice system works on the interdependence of all the actors of the system. The judges have provided guidelines to police officers over the past few decades highlighting the consequences of the use of torture during interrogation. Most of these guidelines address similar issues as a result of which they seem repetitive. Owing to their disruptive activities and their terror on society, Mullah has referred to police officers as "the biggest organised gunda (goons) force."[53] While the academics and judges refer to this behaviour to exist since colonial times, it is contradicted to be the only reason for its existence. Despite the continuous and sometimes repetitive efforts made by the judiciary to provide guidelines, they seem to be lacking in effect.

5.5 Lack of faith in the judiciary

Police officers in India lack the faith in judiciary just as the judiciary lacks faith in the police. It is not uncommon for police officers to act out of duty because of the inefficiency of the judiciary. This creates a lack of authority for the police officer, who does not fear the judiciary for the consequences of his actions.

The backlog of cases before all the courts in India also affects the reputation of the judicial system, which automatically leads to police officers not taking them seriously. One police officer has expressed his lack of faith in the judiciary as follows:

> The Indian law is so bad and ineffective that we are compelled to do so. The courts are slow even if a case comes before the court it takes ages for it to get resolved.[54]

Many other studies carried out by various academics have reflected this lack of faith in the Indian judiciary. Most of these police officers have mentioned that the real reason police officers have to become proactive to carry out killings is because of the inefficiency of the Indian legal system.[55]

5.6 Why do police officers use force?

Despite the legislative provisions and being a signatory to the above international conventions, the government has failed to take adequate steps to reduce the use of torture and hold the actors accountable for their actions. Bayley describes the types of police brutality in his eight-point classification and why police officers use force and torture.[56] Amongst these, it is suggested that the continued use of force is due to tolerance and the culture of acceptance. There is mutual acceptance on the part of the public and the police officers in general. Police officers have taken the theme "brutality is in the eyes of the beholder" in its literal sense.[57] Because of the sensitivity of the subject, illegal violence used by the police is difficult to document scientifically.[58] Hence, other sources to ascertain this data and to find the reasons why they use force are considered here. Some of the main reasons why the police use force are discussed here. In India the acts of police officers are explained using Merton's Anomie theory, which relies on police officers using a means-ends approach to fulfil any crime control goals set by the organisation.[59] This theory fits in well with the explanation that police officers are under constant pressure and in the absence of infrastructure and resources, they resort to the use of force.

5.6.1 Peer pressure

Police officers in India work under a hierarchical structure of power and as a team at the same time. As a result, there is interdependence and interreliability among the junior and senior police officers. Many authors have pointed out that there is usually a lot of pressure from within the team to deliver results. Police interrogation is a vital matter which demonstrates performance of a police officer. Since most of the police promotion is performance based in practice, many senior officials pressurise the juniors to get effective results. This only means securing more convictions and confessions at the time of interrogation. As one police officer notes:

> Sometimes the political pressure is also high on the pending cases. The seniors also pressurise us saying what are you doing, don't you know so many cases are pending. How can you carry on with this? So they catch

> usual offenders and just tell them to accept something that is pending along with what they have done previously. The police tell such offenders usually thieves that you accept that you've done this crime also and we won't beat you up. So that poor fellow who is too afraid to be beaten up again, just accepts the crime. He as well as the police knows that the punishment is the same for committing one crime or two or more crimes.[60]

5.6.2 Public pressure

Police officers face a twofold pressure from the public: one is where the public fear police officers, and the other is where the public urge police officers to find speedy results. Many police officers have acknowledged that the latter is also one of the reasons that compel them to use force and torturous methods. One of the officers interviewed mentioned that the police are compelled to use force when the public expect the interviewed suspect to reveal some information:

> The public will not be happy if we follow procedure where we arrest an individual and produce him before the court and the court grants him bail and he is acquitted. General perception of the public is that the police arrested the person and they let him go. Hence we have to display to the public that we used force and torture on the suspect and he still revealed nothing.[61]

Pursuant to the Merton-Anomie theory, the cultural explanation of a practice propounded by Durkheim also explains the public pressure.[62] The public perception of the police expecting them to fulfil the needs of the public also contributes. This is displayed by an observation made by a police officer:

> Suppose if you consider that you have filed a complaint with us, say someone broke into your house and say you tell us who the suspect is. We arrest them then interrogate them. The first question you will ask us is, have we found out yet? The second question you will ask us is, Did you beat him enough? How do you know he isn't lying?[63]

Many other police officers interviewed also had a similar defence quoting public pressure for the use of torture and force. The public pressure in a certain way encourages the police to use torture and force in order to facilitate their gain.

5.6.3 Work overload

Many officers are of the view that the workload on police officers is unjustified and unmanageable. Along with this, police officers are also expected to carry out other miscellaneous activities, which has an adverse impact on the interrogation. Many other officers feel that the workload is manageable if police officers are only allocated investigative duties and not miscellaneous duties as they currently carry out.[64] This police officer also points out:

> Well here in India you know we have "other duties" which are paramount. The police officer's main aim should be prevention and detection of crime. But this is left aside and we pay more attention to other duties eg overlooking the religious functions. This counts as extra duty for the police. I know this is important as well but this is time consuming for police officers. There should be an extra force deployed for this sort of work. There should be a clear demarcation of duties here.[65]
>
> First of all they should stop the police from taking any other duties like providing security to the politicians, guarding temples during festivals etc.[66]

Many Indian academics and media personnel have highlighted this situation where police officers are entrusted with duties other than investigation and are forced to prioritise the former. As a result, there is little time for investigation which then compels the police officer to use force and other methods to lead to a speedy interrogation. This is where it is important to consider the reforms suggested by various Law Commissions about a separate investigation wing in the police department.[67] This recommendation has not been taken into consideration by the Indian government and hence has failed to reflect in legislation. It is suggested that there is a greater responsibility on police officers to justify the use of their powers.

5.6.4 Power v. *responsibility*

It is argued that police officers are empowered with wide powers of arrest and interrogation. While they have been provided with these powers, there is very little to ensure that they also understand the responsibility that accompanies this power. In the absence of any accountability measures or constant supervision, this power can easily corrupt any police officer. An interesting note has been made by a police officer who observed that the police and the public are equally responsible:

> You see self-regulation should come from people and police equally. I always say every citizen is a policeman without uniform. Every policeman is a citizen with a uniform. Now everybody is not a police officer. I use all the rights, I don't have liberties. It is understood that your powers are given with a responsibility. Government and the Indian citizens want to use the power but either of them doesn't want to be responsible.[68]

Thus, if no efforts are being made by the government to ensure police officers understand their powers and responsibility, they will continue to use force and torture to get the conviction they desire. In the absence of any mechanism, officers continue to blame the public for being ignorant of their responsibilities. While the National Human Rights Commission (NHRC) and various State Human Rights Commissions (SHRC) are set up to ensure police accountability, this has failed to deliver any positive result. Thus, the absence of accountability mechanism and regulation authority has encouraged the police to use force and torture. It is suggested that the lack of safeguards during a police interrogation has also contributed towards this continued use of force.

5.7 Safeguards

In light of the current practice among the police to use force, it is essential to consider the current safeguards that might ensure that the police are held accountable for their actions. As observed in the previous chapter, there are insufficient safeguards at the time of police interrogation. This allows police officers to investigate in a manner they deem fit and necessary. For instance, the police tend to record confessions even when the law does not deem such a confession admissible. In the absence of any mechanism ensuring the regulation of an interrogation, such practices go unnoticed and continue to prevail. Lokaneeta observed that obtaining forceful confessions was a colonial practice used by the native police officers.[69] It was because of this practice that the British while codifying the law suggested the inadmissibility of confessions. The only safeguard against the use of torture by the police officer is approaching the NHRC and the SHRC, as observed in Chapter 2. This section aims to discuss the provision of three specific safeguards hypothetically. The three main safeguards which will be discussed here are the right to legal assistance, tape-recording of interrogation, an external regulatory body, and constitutional provisions.

5.7.1 The right to legal assistance

The importance of the right to legal assistance and the presence of a lawyer are discussed at length in Chapter 3. It is concluded that the right to legal assistance in India does not extend to the pretrial stage and this is clearly reflected in practice.[70] There is no lawyer present at the time of interrogation unless one is requested by the suspect. In the absence of such an important right, the police have unquestioned authority and power over the suspect. It is suggested here that if a lawyer remains present at the pretrial interrogation, the use of any unfair means by the police can easily be monitored and avoided. The lack of willingness for the mandatory presence of a lawyer at custodial interrogation is also criticised.

5.7.2 Tape-recording of interrogation

The initiation of the practice of tape-recorded interviews may also act as a safeguard to discourage police officers from using any force or torture.

As observed in the previous chapters, there is a great potential to safeguard a suspect's right by the installation of tape recorders at the police station. More particularly, using them to record an interview will have evidence of any torture or may assist in denying any claims for torture. However, there has only been one judgement from the Bombay High Court directing the installation of CCTVs at police stations.[71] Despite this judgement, there has been no implementation of this direction as highlighted by a police officer:

> The High Court judgement doesn't apply to other states. So there is no legal mandate. But some states as a proactive measure are in the process of installing CCTV but certainly not in the interrogation room.[72]

It is concluded that even if the CCTVs are installed in the police stations, it is highly unlikely that they will be installed in the interrogation room. This defies the purpose of protection against the use of torture by the police at the time of interrogation.

5.7.3 External regulatory body

The actions of police officers have to be regulated by an external body as opposed to the current practice where any complaint against police officers is investigated internally. This practice does not hold the police officer accountable for his use of force and is not transparent. In order to render police officers accountable for their action and to curb the use of torture and force, an external regulatory body must be created. The characteristic of the NHRC and the SHRC lacks authority and has not had the desired impact on police officers. As observed in the previous chapters, an external regulatory body must be created under legislation, which is binding on police officers. An external body may assist in ensuring a transparent procedure is followed not only for police officers but also for the public.[73]

5.8 Remedies

The legislation and the judiciary have attempted to interpret the provisions of the criminal codes and the Indian Constitution considering the consequences of the use of force by the police. After numerous cases, judicial activists have been successful in establishing the practice of compensation under Article 32 of the Indian Constitution.[74] The cases of police atrocities are never limited to a few or random instances, but have been an ongoing phenomenon. The Supreme Court awarded compensation to a suspect who was wrongfully and unlawfully detained for 14 years in the case of *Rudul Shah v. The State of Bihar*.[75]

However, the practicality of these remedies reaching a common man on a regular basis is far from achievable. As noted by Kalhan et al., the process of approaching a High Court and the Supreme Court to seek these remedies is beyond the "means" of many victims.[76] It is further noted by these authors that even with the assistance of a counsel, the time and travel to approach the judiciary limit the ability to seek recourse to justice. The continued cases of violence on the human rights attorneys, victims and witnesses discourage them to approach the courts for remedies.[77] Any litigation process is therefore not a practical remedy for victims of police torture.

Even the Law Commission of India has observed that in cases of false encounters and custodial deaths, the Supreme Court and the High Courts have been awarding:

> Token, ad-hoc amounts towards damages in proceedings under Article 32 and 226 of the Constitution of India, leaving the aggrieved parties to a suit for damages where the proper damages awardable would be determined.[78]

This route towards a civil suit for claiming damages in India is a time-consuming process and is judicially impractical. However, similar efforts are being made by the various Human Rights Commissions set up as a safeguard to any infringement of fundamental rights.

5.8.1 NHRC

The NHRC was established in 1993 and has contributed significantly to the protection and promotion of Human Rights in India. It was also a mandatory requirement at the time of the inception of the act to study international instruments on human rights and make recommendations. The NHRC has been trying to recommend the ratification of various international conventions. The NHRC is a complaints mechanism for anyone who has suffered violation of human rights from the police or similar actors. The NHRC has done a commendable job in maintaining a separate body of complaints administration. It has made efforts to improve human-rights-based governance in India and has written various guidelines to the State Human Rights Commissions. It has also directed the State Human Rights Commissions to pay compensation to victims of torture and violation of their human rights. The NHRC requires state governments, district magistrates and police officials to send a report of any custodial death within 24 hours of its occurrence to the NHRC. The NHRC can request a further follow-up on the investigation of any case or can investigate into a custodial death on its own. After taking over this role, the NHRC has provided recommendations to the government on increasing accountability and reform the criminal justice system overall. Some of the important recommendations were detailed post-mortem reports of the custodial deaths and video recording of the autopsy. In the absence of such basic amenities, the NHRC could not provide a detailed report to the government on such dire matters. The NHRC has criticised the continued practice of state killings by the police and has even mentioned that this has now become a part of the "State Policy."[79] However, none of these recommendations have been adopted by the state or the centre and hence this has hindered the work of the NHRC. There seems to be a never-ending interdependent loop where the NHRC and the government hold each other responsible for the non-implementation of reforms and where the NHRC has failed to proclaim the individuals' fundamental rights.

In practice, very few cases are administered by this body and the website only displays cases to the year 2005.[80] Another criticism is that the cases listed with this body are not open to public for perusal or academic study. During my visit to Mumbai, I approached the State Commissions and the NHRC. I enquired about the cases and also if I was allowed access to the ongoing or past cases. I was told that they were private matters and public has no access to them. I have been informed that there is an ongoing Public Interest Litigation in the High Court of Bombay under the Right to Information Act, demanding that the general public have access to the records of the NHRC and the State Commissions. Because this Public Interest Litiga tion is pending, there are no official records of this case. Hence, there is no way of analysing whether this body has been successful in performing the duties it was created for and whether justice is "seen" being done to the victims. There is also very little evidence to decipher whether police officers tried for misdemeanour have received appropriate punishment.

There are instances where the NHRC has noticed discrepancies in the functioning of the government and noted "the government has tried to conceal the truth of underplay the accountability of those involved for the death in custody due to custodial violence or negligence."[81] The NHRC is often riddled with issues over jurisdiction and has been unable to access cases which are pending before other tribunals such as the SHRC. The NHRC has also been criticised for lacking the authority necessary to be taken seriously by the government or the courts.[82] Over the period of time, this commission has also been criticised for not taking enough action as its inception promised to do and has become an institution that holds "seminars like any other debating forum."[83]

5.8.2 SHRC

Various commissions have been set up in the states in India with parallel powers as the NHRC. Hence, the most potent power possessed by the SHRC is taking the petitions before the High Courts, but are seldom known to do so. All of these commissions have their offices set up in the capital city of each state and this is where the hearings are held. This is one of the reasons why it is inaccessible for the victims who are placed away from the city or cannot afford to come to the city for hearings. The victims are also rarely notified of the hearing and all updates regarding the hearing are clearly not followed up by the SHRC. There is also a jurisdictional hindrance where the SHRC cannot take cognizance of a case already initiated by the NHRC or which is pending before the NHRC. The lack of funds and manpower make it difficult to update the complaints and follow up with the petition in the High Court. The backlog of cases before the SHRC is similar to the backlog in courts in each state.[84] The cases before the SHRC are also private matters and are not open to public scrutiny or academic study. The SHRC also releases a periodic report giving a vague number of disputes solved and compensation received by victims. It does not provide any further details of these cases or whether police officers are being prosecuted or any action taken against them. This lack of transparency has been criticised by academics and authors such as Gammon.[85]

5.9 Politicisation of police and the use of force

It has been emphasised throughout this volume how important and urgent police reforms are. Authors like Subramanian have stated that police administration has been evolving since Indian independence.[86] However, very little has changed since then and this is mainly due to the political interest in not reforming the police practices. The author further explains why the need for complete reform "bottom-up and not from up-bottom" is needed.[87] This is mainly because the attitude of the superior officers is often unchallenged by the subordinate officers. This strategy seems very promising as it is practical and efficient to have a reformative movement which reforms the junior staff who are in direct contact with the public and interrogate them. Along with this, it is also essential to remove the influence and control of the political representatives from the police duties of interrogation. Most of the times, police officers use torture due to political pressure, which serves the latter's personal interest.[88]

5.10 Public perception

Dhillon has criticised the tolerant attitude of the public in India as follows:

> Blessed with unlimited capacity for patiently suffering indifference, callousness and hypocrisy from their rulers, has made the task of the political and bureaucratic classes so much easier.[89]

The public perception of the police is a direct result of the impression that the police create or a direct encounter with the police. This tension is heightened by the media, by misreporting an incident or being unable to provide the right support to the suspects. The public at large is convinced that the police use force and violence during interrogation. The public are also aware that police officers cannot be held accountable for their actions.[90] In the absence of any mechanisms, this allegation put to police officers has more merit than one can argue. There is a general lack of trust between the public and police officers. As Verma writes:

> The hostility that police personnel encounter from the citizens further sponsors a feeling of us versus them. This attitude develops into a culture of silence, where police officers are reluctant to turn against their own colleagues.[91]

The public perception of the police also influences the impact it has on the rule of law. The public are of the assumption that the law applies differently to the rich and the poor. This is supported by the opinion expressed by one police personnel:

> Now see in Salman Khan's (Bollywood actor) case, because he is a rich person he could hire a fleet of lawyers and get bail immediately. So this option is available to those who are rich and are willing to spend a lot of money. So there is justice in India but it is available to those who are rich and not for the poor.[92]

5.10.1 Corruption

Nalla and Nadan, in their empirical research on the public perception of police, concluded that there was a less than favourable attitude towards the police owing to police corruption.[93] Owing to the issue of corruption in the police, the public have very little faith in them. Policy reforms need to be devised in a manner that prioritises the public perception of the police and reduces corruption in policing. The author emphasises on a valid argument that all negative perceptions of the public need to be diverted to the positive by the government. This ought to be done at the earliest and must be seen to be taking effect by the public. There are also instances where the general public has had to resort to political help in order to avoid police torture. This was concluded from the interview of a police personnel who observed:

> Strictly speaking you are aware of your rights. See if you're produced before a Magistrate and he asks "Did this police torture you?" The fear is so high that even if the police tortured him, he will say no. You can't help it. How much protection can you give citizens? People are afraid. I'll quote a case of Manisha Koirala (an actress). There was a contempt case against her. She has a right to move a Writ Petition, all Indians have the right to move the court to a Writ Petition. This lady moved a Writ Petition, she wasn't able to enforce the judgement of the Bombay High Court. She went to Bal Thackeray (a politician) for help.[94]

5.11 Reforms

Urgent need for police reforms have been highlighted in each chapter of this volume and has also formed an underlying theme. While the Supreme Court has suggested the Model Police Act in response to urgent legislative reform, it is criticised by authors like Grover. She criticises the Act for giving police officers wider and unacceptable powers.[95] The Act's weak accountability mechanism is displayed as the prosecution of police is almost totally avoided. As rightly pointed out, this purported action by the Act is to subvert the rule of law by decreasing the accountability while equipping the police with unlimited power.

Another area which seeks urgent reforms is the working conditions of police officers and other factors affecting it such as pay scale, living conditions and working conditions of police officers. It is unfair obviously to blame police officers for using force and torture but not considering their plight which makes them take such action. Of course, this does not condone the actions taken by police officers but only seeks to reform them in order to avoid the use of torture and force.

As observed throughout this research, Supreme Court guidelines have been issued for protecting the suspects' rights and ensuring suspect safety while in police custody. It is argued here that little or no attempts are made to incorporate legislative reforms to protect suspect detained from torture, violence, rape and death in police custody. Despite clear guidelines issued by the Supreme Court, there has been an indefinite and unexplained delay in incorporating these guidelines in practice, as noted earlier in the case of D K Basu.[96]

The lack of technology also up to some extent delays the interrogation compelling police officers to use unfair means to resort to a speedy interrogation. The lack of both infrastructural facilities and technology has been an impediment to a fair interrogation. Many police officers are of the opinion that increased use of scientific technology will assist the police in interrogation:

> The law is clear on all the aspects. But then there are ... police officers would resort to third degree torture to get confession. But nowadays because of media and court it is not very easy to manhandle the accused and use third degree. But then the option is open that we should go for other avenues of interrogation such as use of forensic laboratory and lie detector test.[97]

The existence of the concept of coercion over governance in police organisations in India has been criticised for standing in the way of reforms. The government does not want to accept responsibility of the actions of police officers by taking active steps to impose the reforms. Dire police reforms and better safeguards for the suspect will ensure the reduction of the use of force and torture by the police.

5.12 Comparing India with England and Wales

The way police officers treat suspects at the time of interrogation has been under scrutiny for a long period of time. One of the many consequences of the growing awareness of the use of force by police is the initiation of PACE, 1984. PACE also introduced various safeguards which assist in ensuring that police officers do not use torturous and unfair methods to interrogate. Manning has suggested that British policing can be associated with a "legal monopoly on violence and is protected to the point of legal sanctioning for the use of fatal force."[98] Authors like Belur have refuted this use of force by the police in England and Wales and have defended them saying "they have greater powers than ordinary citizens."[99] In the UK, the use of force has been associated with the pre-PACE era. Although the use of force still exists, the magnitude of cases that have surfaced in recent years is fairly less. Many countries are taking lessons based on infrastructure of institutions and policy of England and Wales. The ECtHR distinguished between torture and unreasonable force and its effect causing serious and cruel suffering and this is reflected in the English legislation.[100]

5.12.1 ECHR and the use of force and violence

The ECHR has two main provisions for the use of force and torture by the police, which are applicable to the police in England and Wales: Articles 2 and 3. Section 6 of the Human Rights Act, 1998, ensures that the police act in compliance with the provisions of the convention.

5.12.1.1 Article 2 of the ECHR

Article 2 of the convention stipulates the right to life and use of lethal force by police officers. Article 2(2) further extends to unintended death by the use of force. The need for the use of force and the determination of the test of reasonable force had to be proved to be "absolutely necessary." In the case of *McCann and others v. United Kingdom*, the court held that the test of reasonableness provided under Section 3 of the Criminal Law Act 1967 could be compatible with the convention.[101] This had a binding effect on the domestic courts in England and Wales to impose the test of reasonable use of force to fit in with the convention. Article 2 also imposes a positive obligation on the states to take measures to investigate any deaths resulting from the use of force.

The ECHR has in the past severely criticised the procedure adopted for conducting enquiries into custodial deaths.[102] This has also been affirmed by authors like Sanders who hold PACE responsible for having loopholes which let the police get away without enquiry.[103] However, these comments were made a while ago and a quick examination of the IPCC's work may reflect on the progress made recently.

5.12.1.2 Article 3 of the ECHR

Article 3 of the ECHR provides for the prohibition of torture, inhuman and degrading treatment or punishment. Torture is regarded as *"jus cogens"* in international law and is ratified by international treaties such as the ICCPR, UNCAT and the European Convention against Torture (ECAT). When an individual is in police custody, he is in the protective custody of the state and this enhances the state's responsibilities.[104] This also casts a positive responsibility on the state, inter alia, the police to prove the necessity of the use of force. In a recent case of *Gafgen v. Germany*, the Grand Chamber emphasised the prohibition of the use of ill-treatment, but distinguished between real evidence obtained directly from ill-treatment violating Article 3 and the indirect evidential fruits of such violations.[105] This questionable stand taken by the court has been criticised for being ambiguous on the validity of the evidence obtained using ill-treatment. This admissibility of evidence has been referred to as "pragmatism before principle" by authors such as Ashworth.[106] Ratifying these conventions into the domestic legal system has assured the recognition and compliance of the ECHR. However, authors like Davies have raised the issue as to whether common law standards will merge with the standards of the convention.[107] It is pointed out here that while some form of assistance may be provided by the ECHR, it may also lead to confusion. The standards of reasonable force may differ between the two and hence result in a clash between domestic legislation and international conventions. Here, the ECtHR acts as an appellate body deciding any conflicts on the issue of the use of force and torture. The IPCC ensures that the provisions of Articles 2 and 3 are enforced in the domestic legislations.

5.12.2 Domestic legislation and the use of force

The general position for the use of force by the police is described in Section 3 of the Criminal Law Act, 1967. The initiation of PACE brought with it better safeguards for the suspect and created positive responsibility on police officers to provide the suspect with the safeguards mentioned therein. There might be cases of the police using force or brutality, but they are usually limited to a few or a one-off incident. All officers have an individual responsibility of being aware of the relevant legislation and the scope of their powers and its application. There is a great deal of responsibility and accountability for the use of force in achieving the objectives of a police officer. While there is recognition that the police ought to use some force in carrying out these objectives, they are also expected to adopt a human-rights-based approach towards public safety.[108] It is concluded that there is a greater responsibility of caution placed on police officers in England and Wales. This may serve as an example for placing similar responsibilities on the Indian police officers. There is a noticeable difference between the two comparative systems about police responsibilities.

Section 117 of PACE provides that a police officer may use reasonable force if necessary to exercise any power not subjected to the consent of the suspect. This use of reasonable force also extends to effecting an arrest or restraint of an arrested person or to stop and search. The use of more than reasonable force often constitutes police brutality. However, this justification of what constitutes more than reasonable force is a matter of judgement in the circumstances of each case. This was confirmed by Lord Woolf in *Castorina v. Chief Constable of Surrey* that the test for reasonable use of force is objective.[109] This use of force during police interrogation may lead to dire consequences such as custodial death.

5.13 Custodial death

With the issue of reasonability of the use of force being subjective, the use of force has resulted in many custodial deaths even post-PACE. The use of reasonable force very easily turns into torture at the time of interrogation. During the period of 1990 and 2002, nearly 600 people died in police custody and none of the police officers were prosecuted.[110] Authors like Sanders have inferred that fallacies on the part of police officers led to custodial deaths.[111] A Home Office study into custodial deaths at that time failed to hold police officers responsible for these custodial deaths.[112] This has changed in recent years. During 2002–2014, there have been nearly 380 deaths in police custody as a result of police shooting and other incidents.[113] The reduction of custodial death rate is hugely due to the regulatory body IPCC.

5.14 IPCC

The IPCC has delivered to its optimum potential in all matters relating to holding the police officer accountable and serving the victim with a proper reprisal method. Authors like Sanders have confirmed that the number of custodial death have decreased owing to the inception of the IPCC.[114] However, there were instances where the procedure for approaching the IPCC was time consuming and resulted in very few convictions of police officers. The IPCC has also been criticised for not taking initiative. They were also alleged for blaming other factors, which prevented the IPCC from carrying out investigation.[115] In a latest recorded case, the IPCC gave a written warning to a police officer who had used excessive force on an elderly gentleman.[116] The work of the IPCC has been commended by a few authors who believe that it is far more effective than the Police Complaints Authority.[117]

However, lately, the effectiveness of the IPCC has been confirmed by various cases where it has held police officers accountable for their actions. One such case is the shooting of Mark Duggan, where the IPCC successfully held police officers responsible for the shooting by reopening the enquiry.[118]

The highlight of this decision was that it was a result of a public outcry and was investigated by the IPCC. After a thorough investigation, the IPCC held police officers accountable. This has also restored public faith in the police and has ensured that the victims are assured justice by holding police officers accountable. The independence of the IPCC from the police further confirms the transparency in proceedings.

If the figures of custodial death between India and England and Wales are compared, they demonstrate a huge difference. The working of the IPCC compared with the progress made by the NHRC and the SHRC assists in comparing based on the merits of their cases decided. The IPCC is transparent in providing case-related information to the public and all the information is available on its website. The IPCC also displays the action taken against the police officer. On the contrary, the NHRC and SHRC do not display this kind of transparency by withholding all the information from the public and displaying very little on their website. The IPCC also makes accessibility for the general public very easy and approachable, which is an eminent issue with the NHRC and the SHRC. As noted above, most of the SHRCs are located in the cities and this makes it difficult for the infringed public to approach it. This also deals with the issue of police accountability as the IPCC ensures that police officers are accountable for their actions.

5.15 Safeguards

Two main safeguards that are provided to the suspect on being arrested and which have an impact on the use of force and violence by the investigating police officer are discussed here.

5.15.1 Tape-recorded interviews

The tape-recording of interviews is one of the most important safeguards, which prevents the use of torture and use of force by the police at the time of interrogation. It was the result of tape-recorded interviews that in the case of *R v. Paris, Abdullahi and Miller*, the Court of Appeal expressed its "horror" as follows:

> The officers were not questioning him so much as shouting at him what they wanted him to say. Short of physical violence, it is hard to conceive of a more hostile and intimidating approach by the officers to the suspect.[119]

It is evident that the tape-recording of the interviews discourages police officers from using force or torture. With the introduction of PACE, it was a statutory requirement to have the interrogations audio and in some cases video recorded. The fact that CCTVs are placed everywhere throughout the police station also discourages police officers from using force. Any allegations of ill-treatment or abuse by the police made at the trial can easily be examined by the judge and the jury by referring to the tapes. This ensures transparency for both the parties with regard to any claim being made. This along with the efficient working of the IPCC ensures that police officers have some form of accountability and responsibility.

5.15.2 Presence of a lawyer and torture

The second important safeguard provided to the suspect is the mandatory presence of a lawyer at the time of interrogation. It is an obvious observation that the presence of a lawyer has a "monitor" impact on the police, which would discourage the police from using force or torture. The presence of a lawyer is guaranteed from the time the suspect is arrested and hence enjoys the privilege of registering the use of force by the police to his lawyer. In the present legal aid scheme, even when the lawyer is not known to the suspect, police officers are obliged to avoid using any inhuman treatment while interrogating the suspect. A report has shown that the presence of a lawyer acts as a safeguard against the use of torture.[120]

Article 14(3)(b) of the ICCPR stipulates that the presence of a lawyer ensures a fair trial and is a minimum guarantee in a criminal proceeding. This has also been confirmed by the courts in *Salduz v. Turkey* case discussed in the previous chapters. This provision has been incorporated in the domestic legislation by England and Wales and is being adopted by various other countries such as France, Scotland and the Netherlands. The UN Special Rapporteur also emphasises on the presence of a lawyer as an important safeguard as the absence invites potential use of torture.[121]

The presence of a lawyer also assures a balance of power between the police and the suspect in many aspects. Firstly, there is a balance of power of the knowledge of law and hence awareness of the consequences of the use of force and torture. Secondly, there is an assurance of evidence or witness to any force or torture used by the police or to provide a record of an alternative account to that of the police. The UN Subcommittee on Prevention of Torture and other Cruel, Inhuman, or Degrading Treatment or Punishment also emphasises the presence of a lawyer for "preventive" purposes. This can also act as a preventive measure for the police against allegations of torture owing to the independent nature of the lawyer.

5.16 Legitimisation of the use of force

The state exists to protect the natural rights of an individual, which, inter alia, meant preventing anyone from infringing any person's right. In order to do this, the state had to use force, and Webber suggests that this philosophy legitimises the use of force in common law.[122] This culture is said to have spread over Europe and various other common law systems. Drawing from this, it is pointed out that the police have the "just, fair, and valid basis of legal authority."[123] Waddington and Wright also recognise that police officers often struggle with legitimising the use of force.[124] Since the use of force has a direct impact on the admissibility of confessions and conviction at trial, the use of force must be legitimised by the police. Hence, police officers must be able to prove at trial that their use of force was reasonable. Any repressive tactics used by the police are often viewed as unfair and this leaves a long-term effect on the victim and the institution as a whole.[125] It is highlighted here that the social climate of tolerance towards violence does not emerge in such circumstances. An interesting observation made by Jackson et al. is that "a climate that condones or supports violence has weak normative barriers to use the force."[126] When compared to the Indian police officers, there is a greater degree of tolerance among the public which legitimises their use of force.

5.16.1 Accountability and the use of force

Since police officers are likely to use force and violence, robust mechanisms are in place to hold the police accountable. This is also necessary for the government to gain public confidence and trust in the institution in its entirety. PACE and various codes of conduct are the mechanisms in place to ensure that the police are held accountable for their actions. The IPCC is responsible for the compliance towards police accountability and measuring the reasonableness of the use of force. Police training in England and Wales through the codes also ensures police accountability on the issue of use of force and violence.

5.17 Public perception

Many studies carried out by the Home Office have confirmed that in order for the public to trust the police entirely, they must engage with the public and explain their decisions taken. This will help build trust between the two and also improve the public perception of the police use of violence and force. In a study conducted by Cebulla and Stephens, it was observed that police reforms from 2006 to 2010 have helped form a positive opinion of the police.[127] It is fair to say that constant efforts are being made to reform the public opinion of the police by the government and the police equally. It is also evident that from the inception of PACE and a reaction towards the plethora of miscarriages of justice preceding PACE, public perception is paramount. In order to gain public faith in policing, legislation and judiciary have implemented various safeguards of the suspect.

The public perception on the issue of the use of force at the time of interrogation plays a vital role in the implementation of periodic reforms in England and Wales. The public uproar about the use of force in many cases persuaded the government to take positive action. Even the latest cases decided by the IPCC were a result of the public uproar. When comparing this attitude with the attitude of the public in India, there is a striking contrast. The most obvious is the lack of trust in the police and culture of acceptance of the use of force. This is also legitimised by the power displayed by the Indian police. It is thus a standing question that this inaction of the public also condones atrocities like custodial death and encounters by the Indian police.

5.18 Analysis of comparison

It may be argued that the use of torture has declined in England and Wales over the past few years because it is easy to manage a country geographically small in size compared to a country such as India. However, there is no initiative taken towards legislating the use of torture and uniformly imposing it throughout the country in India. In the absence of a complaints mechanism that actively functions, it is easy for the police to use excessive force and get away without any consequences. Non-compliance by the police towards the guidelines issued by the Supreme Court of India on various occasions has also contributed towards the existing use of torture by the police. When comparing the authority of the Supreme Court to that of the ECtHR, the English police officers follow the guidelines in the judgements, whereas the Indian police officers fail to implement the Supreme Court guidelines. It is unclear whether there is a lack of authority or lack of implementation mechanisms in India which causes the use of force and violence by the police. The lack of resources and data leads to under-research on this important topic and pave a way for further and elaborate research. The use of violence in England and Wales despite various ECtHR judgements is undeniable. However, it is the number of cases displaying the use of force and violence by the police that proves the efficiency of the authority. The lack of faith by the judiciary in the police and vice versa does not assist in implementing reforms for the regulation of the use of force and torture. The lack of faith in the judiciary also does not help in implementing the guidelines provided in the Supreme Court judgements.

The recognition and ratification of international treaties and conventions also differs between the two countries. While India has ratified certain conventions and is yet to ratify the most important ones, there is no mechanism to ensure compliance with the provisions. Despite the constitutional measures prohibiting the use of force in India, this still exists in a great magnitude. Despite the international pressure from various organisations in the light of the increased use of violence, very few measures are taken by the Indian government. A lot of responsibility is taken over by NGOs, but this does not seem enough in the wake of the current crisis of the use of excessive force and violence. While England and Wales have ratified the relevant and at times similar conventions to those signed by India, it has incorporated the provisions in legislation. The provisions of the Human Rights Act in England and Wales reflect compliance with various conventions norms. It also gains the advantage of the ECHR provisions and judgements of the ECtHR, which are also incorporated in British legislation.

On the issue of tolerance, it is quite clear that the public and the government condone the use of violence and force by the police in India. Even extreme acts such as encounters are tolerated if not encouraged by the public and the government in India. In the absence of strict regulation and compliance methods, tolerance is an acceptable norm in India. While the tolerance among the public in India is high, sometimes even leading to ignorance, the tolerance for the use of violence among the British public is comparatively low. As a result, there are constant protests made by the British general public in order to reform the police practices as needed. This low level of tolerance results in constant police reforms and monitoring of the compliance measures. Tolerance has been embedded in the police and the public in India alike. The lack of tolerance from the public urged the government in England and Wales to take action legislatively and to implement rules in policing.

The most guiding factors in England and Wales for the decreased use of force are the provisions of safeguards: the right to lawyer and the right to legal assistance and tape-recording of the interrogation. The presence of a lawyer as observed is a fundamental safeguard against ill-treatment and also enables the lawyer to be a witness to any ill-treatment. This is a very important safeguard and needs to be adopted in the Indian criminal justice system to prevent any ill-treatment. Owing to the neutral position of the lawyer, he can be a witness for both the police and the suspect alike, this safeguard should be incorporated by the Indian system. This in itself is a safeguard with little adverse consequence if adopted by India. The other safeguard is the tape-recording of the interrogation which can facilitate any allegations of the use of force and violence by the police.

Many inquisitorial systems such as the United States are now taking precedents from England and Wales, rethinking fundamental approaches to policing. The above amendments appear in the English legislation and are implemented to prevent any misuse of power and authority by the police. The faith of the public in the police is of prime importance, and safeguards adopted by the English legal system should be considered by the Indian criminal justice system.

5.19 Conclusion

The use of force in India at the time of police interrogation has attracted high levels of criticism from outside the country, but more awareness from within India is now required. The absence of important safeguards such as the presence of a lawyer at the time of custodial interrogation along with the lack of tape-recording of interviews condones this practice of use of force. While the NHRC and the SHRC are expected to play the role equivalent to the IPCC, they lack the necessary authority to tackle the use of force and torture. Certain legislative provisions may be adapted from PACE along with the procedure adopted by the English criminal justice system to combat the use of force and torture.

Notes

1 M Foucault, 'Discipline & Punish' (1975), Panopticism, available at http://dm.ncl.ac.uk/courseblog/files/2011/03/michel-foucault-panopticism.pdf
2 T Hobbes, *Leviathan*, D Johnston (eds), New York Press, The Norton Library, 2020.
3 J Lokaneeta, *Transnational Torture: Law, Violence, and State Power in the United States*, New York University Press, 2011.
4 W Geller and M Scott, 'Deadly Force: What We Know' in C Klockars and S Mastrofski (eds), *Thinking about Police: Contemporary Readings*, New York: McGraw-Hill, 1991.
5 Section 29 in The Police Act, 1861:

> Penalties for neglect of duty, etc.—Every police officer who shall be guilty of any violation of duty or wilful breach or neglect of any rule or regulation or lawful order made by competent authority, or who shall withdraw from the duties of his office without permission, or without having given previous notice for the period of two months, or who, being absent on leave, shall fail, without reasonable cause, to report himself for duty on the expiration of such leave, or who shall engage without authority in any employment other than his police duty, or who shall be guilty of cowardice, or who shall offer any unwarrantable personal violence to any person in his custody, shall be liable, on conviction before a Magistrate, to a penalty not exceeding three months' pay, or to imprisonment with or without hard labour, for a period not exceeding three months, or to both.

6 *Niranjan Singh v. Prabhakar* AIR 1980 SC 785.
7 *Sheela Barse v. Union of India* A.I.R. 1983 S. C. 378.
8 *Kartar Singh v. The State of Punjab* 1994 (3) SCC 569.
9 *D K Basu v. State of West Bengal* (1997) 1 SCC 216.
10 *Kamalanantha v. The State of Tamil Nadu*, 2005 5 SCC 194.
11 *Dalbir Singh v. The State of Uttar Pradesh*, W P Crim 193 of 2006.
12 *Sube Singh v. State of Haryana and Others*, AIR 2006 SC 1117.
13 Article 2(1) of the UDHR.
14 *Francis C Mulin v. The Union Territory of Delhi*, AIR 1981 SC 746.
15 A Weisburd, 'Customary International Law and Torture: The Case of India' (2001) 1 *Chicago Journal of International Law*, Article 6.
16 Article 1.1 of the CAT, 1984.
17 Article 5, 12, 13 and 15 of the CAT.
18 India may pass an anti-torture law, available at http://www.hindustantimes.com/newdelhi/india-may-pass-an-anti-torture-law-finally/article1-274992.aspx.
19 Amnesty International Public Statement, 26 June 2007.
20 Report of the Special Rapporteur on Torture, Sir Nigel Rodley, submitted in pursuant to the Commission on Human Rights Resolution No. 2000/43, UN Doc E/CN.4/2001/66.

21 Ibid.
22 A Public Interest Litigation has been filed by A. Singhvi in the case of *D. K. Basu v. The State of West Bengal* for the non-implementation of procedural guidelines to reduce custodial violence.
23 Amnesty International's concerns and consequent recommendations for reform in this area are comprehensively set out in its report, India – Words into action: recommendations for the prevention of torture, January 2001, AI Index: ASA 20/003/2001.
24 Human Rights Watch interview, details withheld, Varanasi, January 2009.
25 Interview Transcript PO15.
26 Interview Transcript L6.
27 G Pelly, *State Terrorism: Torture, Extra-Judicial Killings, and Forced Disappearance in India*, New Delhi: Human Rights Law Network Publication, 2009.
28 Ibid.
29 J Waldron, 'The Torture and Positive Law: Jurisprudence for the White House' (2005) 105(6) Columbia Law Review 1681–1750.
30 Law Commission of India, '152nd Report on Custodial Crimes' 1994, available at http://lawcommissionofindia.nic.in/101169/Report152.pdf, para. 13.3.
31 Ibid.
32 J Kleinig, *The Ethics of Policing*, Cambridge: Cambridge University Press, 1997.
33 Interview Transcript PO2.
34 J Belur, *Permission to Shoot: Police Use of Deadly Force in Democracies*, New York: Springer Publications, 2010.
35 Ibid.
36 Interview Transcript PO7.
37 ACHR, *Torture in India 2009*, New Delhi: Asian Centre for Human Rights, 2009.
38 For further details, please see http://timesofindia.indiatimes.com/india/11820-custodial-deaths-in-five-years/articleshow/26283098.cms; http://www.afternoondc.in/rti/state-registers-highest-number-of-custodial-deaths/article_115964.
39 For further details, please see http://ncrb.gov.in/.
40 For details, please see http://www.afternoondc.in/rti/state-registers-highest-number-of-custodial-deaths/article_115964.
41 N Shah and M Ganguly, *Broken Systems: Dysfunction, Abuse, and Impunity in the Indian Police*, Human Rights Watch, New York Publication, 2009.
42 Article 21 of the Constitution of India, 1960.
43 *Broken System: Dysfunction, Abuse and Impunity in the Indian Police*, 2009, Human Rights Watch Report, available at http://www.hrw.org/sites/default/files/reports/india0809web.pdf, accessed on 24 January 2013.
44 N Shah and M Ganguly, *Broken Systems: Dysfunction, Abuse, and Impunity in the Indian Police*, Human Rights Watch, New York Publication, 2009.
45 The malpractices of the police highlighted in the speech of Shivraj Patil, Home Minister of India, on 12 March 2008.
46 For further details, please see ACHR, *Torture in India 2009*, New Delhi: Asian Centre for Human Rights, 2009.
47 J Belur, 'Why Do the Police Use Deadly Force? Explaining Police Encounters in Mumbai' (2010) 50 *British Journal of Criminology* 320–341.
48 Ibid.
49 Empirical Research in J Belur, *Permission to Shoot: Police Use of Deadly Force in Democracies*, New York: Springer Publications, 2010.
50 Interview Transcript PO15.

51 Empirical Research in J Belur, *Permission to Shoot: Police Use of Deadly Force in Democracies*, New York: Springer Publications, 2010.
52 J Belur, 'Why Do the Police Use Deadly Force? Explaining Police Encounters in Mumbai' (2010) 50 *British Journal of Criminology* 320–341.
53 *The State of Uttar Pradesh v. Mohammad Naim*, AIR 1964 SC 703.
54 Interview Transcript PO3.
55 J Belur, 'Why Do the Police Use Deadly Force? Explaining Police Encounters in Mumbai' (2010) 50 *British Journal of Criminology* 320–341.
56 D Bayley, 'Police Brutality Abroad' in W Geller and H Toch (eds), *Police Violence: Understanding and Controlling Police Abuse of Force*, New Haven: Yale University Press, 1996.
57 Ibid.
58 U Baxi, *The Crisis of the Indian Legal System: Alternatives in Development Law*, New Delhi: Vikas Publications, 1982.
59 R Merton, 'Social Structure and Anomie' (1938) 3(5) *American Sociological Review* 672–682.
60 Interview Transcript PO2.
61 Interview Transcript PO1.
62 E Durkheim, *Suicide: A Study in Sociology*, New York: Free Press, 1897.
63 Interview Transcript PO2.
64 Interview Transcript PO1.
65 Interview Transcript PO1.
66 Interview Transcript PO1.
67 *180th Report, Law Commission of India,* May 2002, available at http://lawcommissionofindia.nic.in/reports/180rpt.pdf.
68 Interview Transcript PO8.
69 J Lokaneeta, *Transnational Torture: Law, Violence, and State Power in the United States*, New York University Press, 2011.
70 For further details, please see Chapter 3, 'The Right to Legal Assistance: A Comparative Analysis between India and England and Wales'.
71 *Leonard Valdaris v. The Officer in Charge, Wadala Police Station, Mumbai and others,* WP/2110/2014/Bom.
72 Interview Transcript PO3.
73 CHRI, 'Police Complaints Authority in India: A Rapid Study' available at http://www.humanrightsinitiative.org/index.php?option=com_content&view=article&id=182&Itemid=511, 2012.
74 *Sheela Barse v. Union of India* A.I.R. 1983 S.C. 378.
75 *Rudul Shah v. The State of Bihar* 1983 4 SCC 141.
76 A Kalhan, G Conroy, M Kaushal, S Miller, and J Rakoff, 'Colonial Continuities: Human Rights, Terrorism, and Security Laws in India' (2006) 20(1) *Columbia Journal of Asian Law* 93–234.
77 Ibid.
78 The 177th Report of the Law Commission of India 2001.
79 K Saxena, 'Report on Prevention of Atrocities against SCs and STs, 2002' available at http://www.ambedkar.org/NHRCReport/prelim.pdf, accessed on 20 May 2015.
80 For further details, please see http://nhrc.nic.in/cdcases.htm#No43, accessed on 19 July 2015.
81 NHRC Annual Report 2004–2005.
82 K Balagopal, 'Terrorism of the Police Kind' (July-August 2007) 6(4) *Combat Law*.
83 Ibid.
84 J Gammon, 'A Meek, Weak NHRC' (July-August, 2007) 6(4) *Combat Law*.
85 Ibid.

86 G Pelly, *State Terrorism: Torture, Extra-Judicial Killings, and Forced Disappearance in India*, New Delhi: Human Rights Law Network Publication, 2009, full deposition of K Subramanian at p. 399.
87 Ibid.
88 Ibid.
89 K Dhillon, *Police and Politics in India: Colonial Concepts, Democratic Compulsions: Indian Police 1947–2002*, New Delhi: Manohar Publications, 2005.
90 Ibid.
91 A Verma, 'A Uniform Betrayal' *India Together,* June 2004, available at http://indiatogether.org/betray-government, accessed on 12 June 2015.
92 Interview Transcript PO7.
93 N Unnithan (ed.), *Crime and Justice in India*, Sage Publishing, 2012, 152.
94 Interview Transcript PO8.
95 V Grover, 'Recipe for Impunity' (July-August 2007) 6(4) *Combat Law Journal.*
96 For eg, *D. K. Basu v. The State of West Bengal*, 1997 1 SCC 416.
97 Interview Transcript PO7.
98 P Manning, *Police Work*, Cambridge, MA: MIT Press, 1977.
99 J Belur, *Permission to Shoot: Police Use of Deadly Force in Democracies*, New York: Springer Publications, 2010.
100 *Ireland v. United Kingdom* (1978) 2 EHRR 25.
101 *McCann and Others v. United Kingdom*, 1996 21 EHRR 97.
102 A Ashworth, 'The Exclusion of Evidence Obtained by Violating a Fundamental Right: Pragmatism before Principle in the Strasbourg Jurisprudence' in P Roberts and J Hunter (eds), *Criminal Evidence and Human Rights: Reimagining Common Law Procedural Traditions*, Hart Publishing, 2012; A Choo, *Evidence*, 5th edn, OUP, 2018.
103 A Sanders and R Young, *Criminal Justice*, OUP, 2007.
104 *Aksoy v. Turkey* (1996) 23 EHRR 553; *Tomasi v. France* (1992) 15 EHRR 1.
105 *Gafgen v. Germany*, 2011 52 EHRR 1 (Grand Chamber).
106 A Ashworth, 'The Exclusion of Evidence Obtained by Violating a Fundamental Right: Pragmatism before Principle in the Strasbourg Jurisprudence' in P Roberts and J Hunter (eds), *Criminal Evidence and Human Rights: Reimagining Common Law Procedural Traditions*, Hart Publishing, 2012; L Campbell, A Ashworth, and M Redmayne, *The Criminal Process*, 5th ed, 2019.
107 H Davies, *Human Rights and Civil Liberties*, Willan Publishing, 2003.
108 G Slapper and D Kelly, *The English Legal System*, 16th edn, Routledge Publishers, 2015.
109 *Castorina v. Chief Constable of Surrey* (1988) 138 NLJ 180.
110 G Vogt and J Wadham, *Deaths in Police Custody: Redress and Remedies*, London: Civil Liberties Trust, 2003.
111 A Sanders and R Young, *Criminal Justice*, OUP, 2007.
112 A Leigh, G Johnson, and A Ingram, *Deaths in Police Custody: Learning the Lessons*, Home Officer Police Research Series Paper 26, London Home Office, 1998.
113 For further details, see http://www.inquest.org.uk/statistics/deaths-in-police-custody.
114 A Sanders in E Cape and R Young, *Regulating Policing: The Police and Criminal Evidence Act 1984 Past, Present and Future*, Hart Publishing, 2008; T Smith and E Cape, 'The Rise and Decline of Criminal Legal Aid in England and Wales' in A Flynn and J Hodgson (eds), *Access to Justice and Legal Aid: Comparative Perspectives on Unmet Legal Need*, Hart Publishing, 2017, available at https://uwe-repository.worktribe.com/output/899612.

115 Independent Police Complaints Commission, *Corruption in the Police Service in England and Wales – First Report,* London: IPCC, 2011, available at https://www.gov.uk/government/uploads/system/uploads/attachment_data/file/229007/9780108510991.pdf, accessed on 15 March 2015.
116 IPCC, May 2013, article available at https://www.ipcc.gov.uk/news/final-warning-police-officer-who-used-excessive-force-grandfather.
117 A Sanders in E Cape and R Young, *Regulating Policing: The Police and Criminal Evidence Act 1984 Past, Present and Future*, Hart Publishing, 2008; T Smith and E Cape, 'The Rise and Decline of Criminal Legal Aid in England and Wales' in A Flynn and J Hodgson (eds), *Access to Justice and Legal Aid: Comparative Perspectives on Unmet Legal Need*, Hart Publishing, 2017, available at https://uwe-repository.worktribe.com/output/899612.
118 For a timeline of events on the Mark Duggan incident, please see https://www.ipcc.gov.uk/page/mark-duggan-investigation-timeline.
119 *R v. Paris, Abdullahi and Miller* (1992) 97 Cr App R 99.
120 Report on the Situation of Human Rights of a Segment of the Nicaraguan Population of Miskito Origin, OEA Ser.L/V/11.62, doc. 10, rev. 3, 1983, at 100.
121 Report on the Mission of the Special Rapporteur to the United Kingdom, UN Doc. E/CN.4/1998/39/add.4, 5 March 1998.
122 M Weber, 'The Theory of Social and Economic Organization' (1948), by A M Henderson, Talcott Parsons Review by S E Thorne, 57(4) *The Yale Law Journal* 676–678.
123 A Papachristo, T Meares, and J Fagan, 'Why Do Criminals Obey the Law? The Influence of Legitimacy and Social Networks on Active Gun Offenders' (2012) 102 (2) *Journal of Criminal Law and Criminology* 397–440.
124 P Waddington and M Wright, 'Police Use of Force, Firearms, and Riot Control' in T Newburn (ed.), *Handbook of Policing*, 2nd edn, London: Routledge, 2011.
125 J Jackson, A Huq, B Bradford, and T Tyler, 'Monopolizing Force? Police Legitimacy and Public Attitudes toward the Acceptability of Violence' (2013) *Psychology, Public Policy, and Law*, Advance online publication.
126 Ibid.
127 A Cebulla and M Stephens, 'Public Perceptions of the Police: Effects of Police Investigations and Police Resources' (2010) *Internet Journal of Criminology*, available at www.internetjournalofcriminology.com

6 Recommendations and conclusion

Police interrogation in India is in dire need for reform. This volume has brought to light gaps in Indian legislation and Supreme Court jurisprudence, and the risks for suspects' rights arising at police interrogation as a result of these gaps. Previous police reforms have failed to orientate custodial interrogation in India towards a more rights-based approach, with the use of force at the police station remaining a perennial issue. In the light of an analytical comparative study of custodial interrogation in England, this volume concluded that effectively implementing the right to legal assistance and introducing audio-visual recording of different aspects of police interrogation would be two very important steps forward for the Indian criminal justice system. But taking these steps would require breaking with a culture of lawlessness at the police station. Any solutions borrowed from England and Wales, and the jurisprudence of the ECtHR for that matter, would not exist in a vacuum. There should rather be a clear realisation of the specific conditions required for these foreign solutions to be effectively transplanted into India.[1] Institutional and cultural change should go hand in hand with legislative reforms providing rights that might theoretically protect the suspect and guarantee the fairness of the proceedings.

6.1 Can PACE work for India?

The grossly outdated procedural and evidentiary legislation in India means that the rights of the suspect are given secondary importance and that the abuse of police powers at the police station goes unchecked. Supreme Court jurisprudence has made admirable efforts to provide clarification of, and help enforce, police duties and suspects' rights, but it has failed to work in practice.[2] Problems with notifying the suspect of his right to legal assistance or, more importantly, ensuring the suspect is not interviewed in the absence of a lawyer are two illustrations only of the significant deficiencies of police interrogation in India. Custodial interrogation in India shares many characteristics with the pre-PACE regime of custodial interrogation in England and Wales. It is therefore logical to expect that as PACE has worked for England and Wales, so it is likely to work for India.

DOI: 10.4324/9781003213024-6

6.2 Need for national legislation

The present police legislation in India is a state responsibility as each state has its own police manual, containing provisions relating to police duties and their breach. It is observed from the standpoint of the empirical research undertaken here that there is a gap in the interrogation process between the big cities and the rural areas. It is suggested that the present state police governance and state legislations in the form of manuals may be the reason for this gap in practice. The lack of a national legislation as opposed to state legislation has been one of the reasons why police reforms have failed to work. While commissions made efforts in establishing the Model Police Act, this has not been implemented in practice.[3] Now, as this volume suggests, there are important comparative lessons to learn from the English custodial interrogation framework, as encapsulated in the Police and Criminal Evidence Act 1984, as well as from the increasing focus of the ECtHR jurisprudence on the right to custodial legal assistance.

6.3 Police training

Police officers in India receive no specific training for carrying out an interrogation. Police training has always been a subject of police reforms in various law commission reports and jurisprudence. There is an urgent need to cast a positive duty on police officers to inform the suspect of their rights and this can be delivered through training. Police training may benefit if police officers in India are provided with a manual such as the PACE codes of practice, which provides specific training relating to police interrogation. PACE also casts a positive duty on police officers to inform the suspect of his rights during an interrogation. It is suggested that police officers in India may be entrusted with providing a caution to the suspect at the time of arrest and before an investigation commences. Police training in India may also benefit from periodic training updates rather than the present two-year training.

6.4 Caution

As observed, PACE requires police officers to caution a suspect at the time of arrest and at other times during interrogation.[4] This caution informs the suspect of three main rights: the right to legal assistance, the right to legal aid and the right to silence and adverse inference from silence. In the absence of any current provision in India requiring police officers to inform the suspect of their right, the use of caution may help to fill this gap.

6.5 Mandatory right to custodial legal assistance

The provision of the right to legal assistance at the trial stage in India is well documented in the Indian Constitution and the criminal codes. The right to legal assistance is therefore a constitutional right; however, the constitution makes it the responsibility of the suspect to request a lawyer, not the duty of police officers to notify suspects of their right. In practice, therefore, suspects rarely exercise their right. Supreme Court jurisprudence has attempted to clarify that the right to legal assistance begins from the time a suspect is arrested. The courts in India have made reference to important ECHR cases such as *Salduz v. Turkey* to highlight the importance of the right to legal assistance.[5] However, mere judicial interpretations have failed to effectively implement this seminal right. The empirical survey undertaken in this volume provides support to these observations, and to similar accounts offered by international human rights NGOs. Modern European jurisprudence on right to legal assistance shows the way forward. National legislation is required to ensure effective implementation in practice. The presence of a lawyer at the police station is paramount because it ensures that the suspect is interrogated fairly and that there is a counterweight to the police.

An interrogation may be conducted only in the presence of a lawyer and anything that has been obtained in the absence of a lawyer should be held inadmissible in evidence. This is what *Salduz* and its progeny mandate, and their impact has been felt strongly in many European jurisdictions. Stringent legislative measures similar to those in England and Wales, and in line with Strasbourg jurisprudence, can act as a compass for the adoption of similar practices in India. Ensuring that a lawyer is present can also help do away with a culture of "justice for the rich," which the empirical survey also pinpointed as a reason obstructing the effective delivery of procedural fairness at the pretrial stage.[6] Ensuring access to a lawyer nationally and to each suspect irrespective of their financial means would reflect universal standards.[7] This could also allow for a more flexible approach to using confessional evidence obtained at the police station, moving away from the existing absolute ban towards a position of admissibility upon respecting fundamental safeguards for the suspect.

6.6 Legal aid

The concept of legal aid in India has gained momentum in the past few years, but this has been restricted to the trial stage. Legal aid at the police station in India for those suspects who cannot afford a lawyer is unheard of. The absence of legal aid at the police station deprives the suspect of legal assistance at a vital stage. Provisions of legal aid may be transplanted from the system in England and Wales. With the increasing number of qualified lawyers in India, the resources required are present, though the cost might of course be restrictive. National legislators need to take proactive steps towards providing legal aid and may take a lesson from other jurisdictions. However, it may be pointed out that the increasing legal aid cuts in England and Wales, resulting from mismanaged legal aid allocation to law firms, may be taken as a lesson. Effective management of manpower and funds allocation may assist Indian legislators in learning from the mistakes of others.[8]

6.7 Adverse inference from silence

With the provision of a lawyer at the time of police interrogation, it may be suggested that if the suspect exercises his right to silence on advice by the lawyer, the court may draw adverse inferences. This may provide a basis for the police officer to interrogate and not hit a dead-end in an investigation with the use of silence, which is justified when used after obtaining legal advice. Similar provisions are contained in PACE and CJPO and may be adapted by the Indian legislators after ensuring the rights of a suspect mentioned above are complied with.

6.8 Tape-recording of police interrogation

As observed, there is no written evidence of the interrogation in India apart from the FIR, which is usually, in practice, not issued by the interrogating police officer. In the lack of any written evidence, it is essential that there exists a safeguard which monitors the interrogation. The Bombay High Court has made an attempt to install CCTVs in police stations. The importance of using CCTV at a police station was also highlighted by the police personnel interviewed for the present research. However, as observed in the empirical research, this has not been complied with in practice even after a year of the passing of the judgement. An important practice such as this may be assisted in detail if a reference is made to the practice of recording police interrogation from England and Wales. Not only should the Indian police interviews be tape-recorded, but the records of these interviews should also be in possession of an independent body in India. This ensures transparency in the recording procedure also demonstrating it to the general public. In cases of conflict arising from an interview, this independent organisation may also assist in an enquiry.

6.9 Independent body such as IPCC

The present complaints commission represented by the NHRC and the SHRCs in India have contributed very little towards resolving issues around police complaints. The dormancy of these institutions is criticised by academics in India, which leads to police officers being unaccountable for their actions. These commissions have been criticised for not being transparent as it does not allow public access to its judgement. Adopting legislative procedures in creating a body similar to the IPCC may assist in rectifying the gaps left by the NHRC and the SHRCs. This independent organisation may be entrusted with the records of the taped interrogation in India. Such an organisation must be a governmental body ensuring the protection of suspects' human rights and holding police officers accountable for their actions.

6.10 Admissibility of confessions

Confessions given to a police officer in India are inadmissible in evidence; however, as observed in the present empirical research, police officers still interrogate with the aim to obtain a confession. Even the confessions made before a magistrate in India are later retracted. As observed, even if a confession is made before a magistrate, the suspect may be granted police custody. Thus, confessions made to a magistrate are not entirely credible, which makes it no different from a confession made before a police officer. There is very little enquiry into the inadmissibility of confessions other than for the fear of the police using force and torture to obtain a confession. It is also criticised that academics in India and legislators have failed to identify other reasons for inadmissibility of confessions. It is an assumption that confessions are inadmissible in evidence only due to the fear of the use of force. However, the use of force and torture by the police negates this reason given for inadmissibility of confessions made to a police officer. If the provision of two essential safeguards such as legal assistance and tape-recording of police interrogation is ensured, there may be merit in the admissibility of confessions made to a police officer. This may be in continuation of the current practice of confessions made to a police officer which are admissible in certain cases.[9] The absence of safeguards may be the reason why confessions given to a police officer have never been admissible in evidence. This may have a considerable impact on the backlog of court cases before a magistrate. Provisions relating to admissibility and inadmissibility of confessions may be incorporated in legislation. Relevant provisions in PACE may be taken as a precedent to investigate if they may be adopted in legislation and to check their practicability.

6.11 Putting an end to the use of force and torture

Latest jurisprudence and various human rights organisations in India have highlighted the use of force and torture during police interrogation in India even today. It is argued that in the absence of safeguards mentioned above, it is easy for police officers to continue using force and torture. The provision of the above safeguards may therefore help in reducing the use of force and torture during police interrogation in India. It is suggested that the presence of a lawyer may discourage police officers from using force and torture and thereby safeguard the suspects' rights. Along with the presence of a lawyer, a tape-recorded interrogation may further discourage the use of force. It is suggested that signing of international conventions by the Indian government has failed to reduce the use of torture by the police. Along with signing and ratifying international conventions, the government needs to take proactive steps by implementing measures to reduce the use of force in domestic legislation.

6.12 Reducing police bureaucracy

Political interference in the functioning of the police is another factor affecting police interrogation in India. This interference has restricted police reforms due to the lack of training and resulted in the lack of police accountability. There is alleged vested political interest in keeping these reforms so as to use the police force for personal use. This interference may be restricted by a separation of the investigation department from the miscellaneous duties of the police. A specific department for investigation may help rectify the current situation where police officers are entrusted to carry out all duties along with investigation. This was reflected in the present empirical research where police officers highlight the impact of political interference in investigative duties. The system in England and Wales which distinguishes the investigative role of a police officer and the role played by the CPS may be adopted.

6.13 Public faith in police officers

This volume has concluded that the general public have little or no faith in police officers, which hinders the investigative process. Among various reasons highlighted for this lack of faith, the lack of safeguards such as right to legal assistance and tape-recording of interrogation is the most important. In the absence of such safeguards, the public may view the police as unaccountable in their use of wide investigative powers. If these basic safeguards are made mandatory during each police investigation, public faith in the police might be restored. This has clearly been observed in England and Wales where public faith in police officers has increased after the implementation of PACE and codes of practice.[10] Legislators in England and Wales also considered the public outcry during various cases of miscarriage of justice. This is one of the main reasons that a legislation such as PACE was introduced. Similar action needs to be taken by Indian legislators in order to improve police interrogatory practices as there have been various cases of miscarriages of justice.

6.14 Corruption

For a long time, the non-implementation of police reforms has been attributed to corruption in the police force and at various levels in governmental organisations. While it is recognised that corruption exists in every country and in all the systems, it is endemic in India. Various efforts are being made by human rights organisations and NGOs to curb corruption from the police organisation but these have not been recognised by the government. Various anti-corruption organisations have been set up in place but have made little difference towards reducing corruption. This presence and ever-growing rate of corruption in the police organisation is one of the main reasons why the public has little faith in the police and why they refuse to cooperate. It is recommended that if police accountability is maintained through the above safeguards, it may assist in reducing corruption.

6.15 Conclusion

This volume has benefitted from the empirical research carried out with police officers and lawyers in India. New empirical surveys, wider in geographical scope and the range of methodological tools used, and in particular including observations at the police station would facilitate a deeper understanding of the law in action and pinpoint appropriate solutions. This volume has demonstrated the need for such work, which, it also suggests, should be modelled upon extensive empirical work in England and Wales and, more recently, in other European countries. It has been pointed out by this volume that there are inherent flaws even in the criminal justice system in England and Wales, but it may be used as a working example by the Indian criminal justice system. Even more importantly, this volume concludes that the role of a lawyer at the custodial police interrogation stage is vital and needs to be implemented in practice in India. It must also be made the duty of the police officer to inform the suspect of his right to legal assistance and associated rights. The reduction of bureaucracy from policing may ensure the implementation of police reforms. In the light of no action being taken by the legislators or the government to implement these police reforms, the above recommendations may be considered. The only criticism that can be made towards the present recommendations is the lack of availability of funds in India. However, it is argued that this lack of funds has been used as an excuse for non-implementation of police reforms for a long time. Legislators and the national government must take proactive steps towards arranging such funds in order to make the process of police interrogation fair. This volume has looked at ways to protect suspects' rights while improving police interrogation through training. This may be a step towards attaining the balance in crime control and due process values.

Notes

1 P Legrand, 'The Impossibility of Legal Transplants' (1997) 4 *Maastricht Journal of European and Comparative Law* 111.
2 This has reference to the Seven-Point Directive made by the Supreme Court discussed in Chapter 3.
3 Commonwealth Human Rights Initiative Analysis of the Sorabji Commission, available at http://www.humanrightsinitiative.org/index.php?option=com_content&view=article&catid=35%3Apolice-reforms&id=600%3Athe-police-act-drafting-committee&Itemid=98, accessed on 2 April 2015.

4 Code of Practice G, para 3.
5 *Ajmal Amir Kasab v. State of Maharashtra* (2012) 9 SCC 234.
6 Interview transcript PO4.
7 L Fuller, *Morality of Law*, revised edition, New Haven: Yale University Press, 1969.
8 S Tromans, 'Some Comparative Reflections' in B S Markesinis (ed.), *The Gradual Convergence: Foreign Ideas, Foreign Influences, and English Law on the Eve of the 21st Century*, Oxford: Clarendon Press, 1994.
9 Chapter 5 discusses the admissibility of confessions made to a police officer in cases relating to terrorism offences and possession of narcotic drugs.
10 This has been dealt with elaborately in Chapter 2.

Bibliography

Books

A Ashworth, 'The Exclusion of Evidence Obtained by Violating a Fundamental Right: Pragmatism before Principle in the Strasbourg Jurisprudence' in P Roberts and J Hunter (eds), *Criminal Evidence and Human Rights: Reimagining Common Law Procedural Traditions*, Hart Publishing, 2012.

A Ashworth and M Redmayne, *The Criminal Process*, 3rd edn, OUP, 2004.

A Choo, *Evidence*, 4th edn, OUP, 2015.

A Choo, *Evidence*, 5th edn, OUP, 2018.

A Fontana and J Frey, 'The Interview: From Structured Questions to Negotiated Texts' in N Denzin and Y Lincoln (eds), *Handbook of Qualitative Research*, 2nd edn, Thousand Oaks, CA: SAGE, 2000.

A Ganesan and P Grossman, *Police Abuse and Killings of Street Children in India*, Human Rights Watch, 1996.

A Goldsmith, 'Necessary but not Sufficient: The Role of Public Complaints Procedures in Police Accountability' in C Stenning (ed.), *Accountability for Criminal Justice*, Toronto: University of Toronto Press, 1995.

A Griffiths and B Milne, Will It All End in Tiers? Recent Developments in Police Interviews with Suspects in Britain' in T Williamson (ed.), *Investigative Interviewing: Rights, Research, Regulation*, Cullompton: Willan, 2006.

A Hucklesby and A Wahidin, *Criminal Justice*, 2nd edn, OUP, 2013.

A Mehra, *Police, State and Society: Perspectives from India and France*, Dorling Kindersley (India) Publishing Pvt Ltd., 2011.

A Mehra and R Levy, *The Police, the State, & Society: Perspectives from India and France*, Pearson Publication, 2011.

A Riles, 'Comparative Law and Socio-Legal Studies' in M Reimmann and R Zimmerman (eds), *The Oxford Handbook of Comparative Law*, OUP, 2006.

A Sanders and R Young, *Criminal Justice*, OUP, 2007.

A Shawyer, R Milne, and R Bull, 'Investigative Interviewing in the UK' in T Williamson, B Milne, and S Savage (eds), *International Developments in Investigative Interviewing*, Cullompton: Willan, 2009.

A Verma, *The New Khakhi: The Evolving Nature of Policing in India (Advances in Police Theories and Practice)*, CRC Press, Taylor and Francis Group, 2012.

A Watson, *Legal Transplants*, 2nd edn, University of Georgia Press, 1993.

A Watson, *Legal Transplants: An Approach to Comparative Law*, Edinburgh: Scottish Academic Press, 1974.

A Wright, *Policing: An Introduction to Concepts and Practice*, Willan Publishing, 2002.

A Zuckerman, *The Principles of Criminal Evidence*, OUP, 1989.

B Bradford, J Jackson, and M Hough, 'Police Legitimacy in Action: Lessons for Theory and Policy' in M Reisig and R Kane (eds), *The Oxford Handbook of Police and Policing*, Oxford: Oxford University Press, 2008.

B Emmerson, A Ashworth, and A Macdonald, *Human Rights and Criminal Justice*, 3rd edn, Sweet and Maxwell, 2012.

B Loftus, *Police Culture in the Changing World*, 1st edn, OUP, 2012.

B Uma Devi, Arrest, Detention, and Criminal Justice System: A Study in the Context of the Constitution of India, OUP, 2012.

C Kothari, *Research Methodology: Methods and Techniques*, 2nd edn, New Age International Publishers, New Delhi, 2004.

C Phillips, *Royal Commission on Criminal Procedure, the Investigation and Prosecution of Criminal Offences in England and Wales*, The Law and Procedure, 1981.

C Walker, *Miscarriages of Justice: A Review of Justice in Error*, OUP, 2004.

C M Upadhyay, *Human Rights in Pre-trial Detention*, APH Publishing, 1999.

D Anderson and D Killingray, *Policing the Empire: Government, Authority and Control, 1830–1940*, Manchester: Manchester University Press, 1991.

D Arnold, *Police Power and Colonial Rule: Madras 1859–1947*, Delhi: OUP, 1986.

D Bayley, *Changing the Guard, Developing Democratic Police Abroad*, OUP, 2006.

D Bayley, 'Police Brutality Abroad' in W Geller and H Toch (eds), *Police Violence: Understanding and Controlling Police Abuse of Force*, New Haven, CT: Yale University Press, 1996.

D Bayley, *The Police and Political Development in India*, Princeton, NJ: Princeton University Press, 1969.

D Beetham, *The Legitimation of Power*, London: Macmillan, 1991.

D Carlson, *When Cultures Clash: Strategies for Strengthening Police-Community Relations*, 2nd edn, Upper Saddle River, NJ: Pearson/Prentice Hall, 2005.

D Dixon, *Law in Policing: Legal Regulation and Police Practices*, Oxford Clarendon Press, 1997.

D Dixon, 'Revising 'Police Powers': Legal Theories and Policing Practices in Historical and Contemporary Contexts' in L Noaks, M Levi, and M Maguire (eds), *Contemporary Issues in Criminology*, 1995.

E Cape, 'Defence Services: What Should Defence Lawyers Do at Police Stations?' in M McConville, and L Bridges (eds), *Criminal Justice in Crisis - (Law in its Social Setting)*, 186–199, Aldershot: Edward Elgar, 1994.

E Cape, *Defending Suspects at Police Station, Practitioner's Guide to Advice and Representation*, 6th edn, LAG Publication, 2012.

E Cape and R Young, *Regulating Policing: The Police and Criminal Evidence Act 1984 Past, Present and Future*, Hart Publishing, 2008.

E Cape, Z Namoradze, R Smith, and T Spronken, *Effective Criminal Defence in Europe*, Antwerp: Intersentia, 2007.

E Durkheim, *Suicide: A Study in Sociology*, New York: Free Press, 1897.

E Orucu, 'A Project: Comparative Law in Action' in E Orucu and D Nelkin (eds), *Comparative Law: A Handbook*, Oxford: Hart Publication, 2007.

E Orucu, *The Enigma of Comparative Law*, Leiden/Boston: Martinus Nijhoff Publishers, 2004.

E Stokes, *The English Utilitarians and India*, OUP, 1959.

F Inbau, J Reid, and J Buckley, *Criminal Interrogation and Confessions*, 5th edn, Jones and Bartlett Publishers, 2011.

F Nariman, *India's Legal System: Can It Be Saved?*, India: Penguin Publishers, 2006.

F Pakes, *Comparative Criminal Justice*, 2nd edn, Willan Publishing, 2011.

G Gudjonsson, *The Psychology of Interrogation and Confessions: A Handbook*, Chichester: Wiley, 2003.

G Gudjonsson, *The Psychology of Interrogations, Confessions, and Testimony*, New York: John Wiley & Sons, 1992.

G Pelly, *State Terrorism: Torture, Extra-Judicial Killings, and Forced Disappearance in India*, Human Rights Law Network Publication, 2009.

G Slapper and D Kelly, *The English Legal System*, 16th edn, Routledge Publishers, 2015.

G Valentine, '"Tell Me about"...: Using Interview as a Research Methodology' in R Flowerdew and D Martin (eds), *Methods in Human Geography: A Guide for Students Doing a Research Project*, Edinburgh: Longman.

G Vogt and J Wadham, *Deaths in Police Custody: Redress and Remedies*, London: Civil Liberties Trust, 2003.

H Davies, *Human Rights and Civil Liberties*, Willan Publishing, 2003.

H Dobhal, *Writings on Human Rights, Law, and Society in India: A Combat Law Antholo: Selections from Combat Law, 2002–2010*, New Delhi: Human Rights Law Network, 2011.

H Gutteridge, *Comparative Law: An Introduction to the Comparative Method of Legal Study and Research*, 2nd edn, London: Wildy & Sons, 1949.

H Packer, *The Limits of the Criminal Sanction by Herbert L. Packer*, Stanford University Press, 1968.

H Quirk, 'The Right of Silence in England and Wales: Sacred Cow, Sacrificial Lamb or Trojan Horse?' in J D Jackson, and S J Summers (eds), *Obstacles to Fairness in Criminal Proceedings: Individual Rights and Institutional Forms*, Oxford: Hart Publishing, 2018.

H Quirk, *The Rise and Fall of the Right of Silence*, Routledge, 2016.

H Quirk, and J Robins, 'The Right of Silence and Undermining Legal Representation at the Police Station' in *No Defence: Miscarriages of Justice and Lawyers*, 2013, 48–51.

H L A Hart, 'A New Conception of Law' in J Feinberg and H Gross Belmont (eds), *Philosophy of Law*, 1986.

J Belur, *Permission to Shoot: Police Use of Deadly Force in Democracies*, New York: Springer Publications, 2010.

J Blackstock, E Cape, J Hodgson, A Ogordova, and T Spronken, *Inside Police Custody- An Empirical Account of Suspects' Rights in Four Jurisdictions*, Intersentia, 2014.

J Cotterill, *Language and Power in Court, A Linguistic Analysis of the O J Simpson Trial*, Basingstoke: Palgrave Macmillan, 2003.

J Hodgson, *French Criminal Justice: A Comparative Account of the Investigation and Prosecution of Crime in France*, Oxford: Hart Publishing, 2005.

J Jackson, B Bradford, B Stanko, and K Hohl, *Just Authority, Trust in the Police in England and Wales*, Routledge Press, 2013.

J Jackson, M Langar, and P Tillers, *Crime, Procedure and Evidence in a Comparative and International Context, Essays in Honour of Professor Mirjan Damaska*, Hart Publishing, 2008.

J Kleinig, *The Ethics of Policing*, Cambridge: Cambridge University Press, 1997.

J Lokaneeta, *Transnational Torture: Law, Violence, and State Power in the United States*, New York University Press, 2011.

J Rosenberg, 'Miscarriages of Justice' in E. Stockdale and S. Casale (eds), *Criminal Justice under Stress*, 1993.

J Sidanius and F Pratto, *Social Dominance: An Intergroup Theory of Social Hierarchy and Oppression*, Cambridge University Press, 1999.

J Stephen, *A Digest of the Law of Evidence*, New York Publishers, 1829–1894, available at https://archive.org/details/chasedigestoflawof00step, accessed 23 March 2015.

J Umrishankar, *A Sisyphean Saga, Functional Review of the Indian Police- A Step towards Good Governance*, India: Ameya Inspiring Books, 2009.

J Vadackumchery, *Indian Police and Equal Justice under Law*, India: APH Publishing House, 1999.

J Vadackumchery, *Indian Police and Miscarriage of Justice*, India: APH Publishing House, 1997.

J Wigmore, *A Treatise on the Anglo American System of Evidence in Trials at Common Law*, Boston: Little Brown Company, 1940.

K Davis, *Discretionary Justice*, Baton Rouge, LA: Louisiana State University Press, 1969.

K Dhillon, *Police and Politics in India: Colonial Concepts, Democratic Compulsions: Indian Police 1947–2002*, New Delhi: Manohar Publications, 2005.

K Dunn, *Interviewing in Qualitative Research Methods in Human Geography*, 2nd edn, Oxford: Oxford University Press, 2005.

K Kalra, *Be Your Own Layer: Book for Layman*, New Delhi: Vij Books Publication, 2013.

K Zweigert and H Kotz, *An Introduction to Comparative Law*, 2nd edn (trans. Tony Weir), Oxford: Oxford University Press, 1993.

L Campbell, A Ashworth, and M Redmayne, *The Criminal Process*, 5th edn, 2019.

L Fuller, *Morality of Law*, revised edn, New Haven, CT: Yale University Press, 1969.

L Palmier, *The Control of Bureaucratic Corruption: Case Studies in Asia*, New Delhi: Allied Publishers, 1985.

M Graziadei, 'The Functionalist Heritage' in P Legrand and R Munday (eds), *Comparative Legal Studies: Traditions and Transitions*, Cambridge University Press, 2003.

M Haberfeld and I Cerrah, *Comparative Policing: The Struggle for Democratisation*, SAGE, 2008.

M McConville, A Sanders, and R Leng, *The Case for the Prosecution*, London: Routledge, 1991.

M Monir, *Textbook on the Law of Evidence*, New Delhi: Universal Law Publication, 2011.

M Punch, *Police Corruption, Deviance, Accountability, and Reform in Policing*, Willan Publishing, 2009.

M Weber, *Economy and Society*, Volume Two, Berkley: University of California Press, 1978.

N Madhava Menon, 'Towards Making Criminal Justice Human Rights-Friendly – Policy Choices and Institutional Strategies' in C Raj Kumar and K Chockalingam (eds), *Human Rights, Justice and Constitutional Empowerment*, New Delhi: Oxford University Press, 2007.

N Shah and M Ganguly, *Broken Systems- Dysfunction, Abuse, and Impunity in the Indian Police*, Human Rights Watch, New York Publication, 2009.

N Unnithan (ed), *Crime and Justice in India*, SAGE, 2012.

P Alexander, 'Governance, Policing, and Human Rights' in K Rustamji (ed) *Policing India in the New* Millenium, 2002.

P Alexander, *Policing India in the New Millennium*, New Delhi: Allied Publishers, 2002.

P Cane and H Kritzer, *The Oxford Handbook of Empirical Legal Research*, OUP, 2010.

P Cruz, *Comparative Law in a Changing World*, 3rd edn, Routledge-Cavendish Publications, 2007.

P Devlin, *The Criminal Prosecution in England*, Oxford: Oxford University Press, 1957.

P Manning, *Police Work*, Cambridge, MA: MIT Press, 1977.

P Roberts and A Zuckerman, *Criminal Evidence*, 2nd edn, OUP, 2010.

P Scott, *The Jewel in the Crown*, New York: William Morrow Publications, 1966.

P Waddington and M Wright, 'Police Use of Force, Firearms, and Riot Control' in T Newburn (ed), *Handbook of Policing*, 2nd edn, London: Routledge, 2011.

R Bull, 'Police Investigative Interviewing' in A Memon and R Bull (eds), *Handbook of the Psychology of Interviewing* (pp. 279–292), Chichester: John Wiley & Sons Ltd, 2000.

R Card and R Ward, *The Criminal Justice and Public Order Act 1994*, Bristol: Jordans, 1994.

R Cotterrell, 'Seeking Similarity, Appreciating Difference: Comparative Law and Communities' in E Örücü and A Harding (eds), *Comparative Law in the Twenty-First Century*, The Hague: Kluwer, 2002.

R Crawshaw, *Police and Human Rights: A Manual for Teachers, Resource Persons, and Participants in Human Rights Programme*, Martinus Nijhoff Publishers, 1999.

R Dworkin, *Taking Rights Seriously*, Cambridge, MA: Duckworth Press, 1977.

R Kumar, A Singh, A Agrawal, and J Kaur, *Reduced to Ashes: The Insurgency and Human Rights in Punjab*, Nepal: South Asia Forum for Human Rights, 2003.

R Milne and R Bull, 'Interviewing by the Police' in D Carson and R Bull (eds), *Handbook of Psychology in Legal Contexts*, Chichester, UK: Wiley, 2003.

R Milne and R Bull, *Investigative Interviewing; Psychology and Practice*, Chichester: John Wiley & Sons, Ltd., 1999.

R Mittal, *Legal Aid: Catalyst for Social Change*, Delhi: Satyam Law International, 2012.

R Reiner, *The Politics of the Police*, 2nd edn, OUP, 1992.

R Reiner, *The Politics of the Police*, 3rd edn, OUP, 2000.

Ashworth, A. (1994), Reiner, R. and L. Leigh (1994), A Sanders and P. Young (1994), D Dixon, (1997).

R Vogler, *A World View of Criminal Justice*, Ashgate Publishers, 2005.

R Yin, *Case Study Research: Design and Methods*, 2nd edn, Newbury Park, CA: SAGE, 1994.

S Karthikeyan, 'Foreword' in A Reddy (ed.), *Dimensions of Crime and Corruption in India*, New Delhi: Serial Publication, 2005.

S Krishnamurty, *Human Rights and the Indian Police*, 2nd edn, Bangalore: R.R. Publishers, 1996.

S Singh, *Fundamentals of Interrogation Techniques*, Kalpaz Publications, New Delhi, India, 2008.

S Tromans, 'Some Comparative Reflections' in B S Markesinis (ed.), *The Gradual Convergence: Foreign Ideas, Foreign Influences, and English Law on the Eve of the 21st Century*, Oxford: Clarendon Press, 1994.

S K Chaturvedi, *Good Governance: Police and Human Rights' in Public Governance and Decentralisation*, Sweta Mishra et al. (eds), New Delhi: Mittal Publications, 2003.

T Hobbes, *Leviathan*, R Flathman and D Johnston (eds), New York Press, 1997.

T Macaulay, J Macleod, G Anderson, and F Millet, *A Penal Code Prepared by the Indian Law Commissioners*, Pelham Richardson (ed.), 1838 Millennium 337, ed., 2002.

T Metcalf, *Imperial Connections: India in the Indian Ocean Arena, 1860–1920*, University of California Press, 2007.

T Williamsons, *Investigative Interviewing: Rights, Research, Regulation*, Devon: Willlan Publishing, 2006.

U Baxi, *Socio-Legal Research in India-A Programschrift* (New Delhi: Indian Council of Social Science Research (ICSSR), 1975). Reprinted in S Verma and M Afzal-Wani (eds), *Legal Research and Methodology* (New Delhi: Indian Law Institute, 2nd edn, 2001).

U Baxi, *The Crisis of the Indian Legal System: Alternatives in Development Law*, New Delhi: Vikas Publications, 1982.

U Baxi, *The Future of Human Rights*, 2nd edn, Oxford University Press, 2006.

V Hoecke and M Warrington, 'Legal Cultures, Legal Paradigms and Legal Doctrine: Towards a New Model for Comparative Law' (1998) 47 International and Comparative Law Quarterly.

V Karan, 'A Case for a "Cultural Revolution" of India's Police' in J Guha Roy (ed.), *Policing a District*, Delhi: IIPA, 1992.

V Sithannan, *Police Investigation: Powers, Tactics, and Techniques*, Chennai: Jeywin Publication, 2013.

W Blackstone, *Commentaries on the Laws of England*, San Francisco, CA: Bancroft Whitney, 1916.

W Geller and M Scott, 'Deadly Force: What We Know' in C Klockars and S Mastrofski (eds), *Thinking about Police: Contemporary Readings*, New York: McGraw-Hill, 1991.

W Menski, *Comparative Law in a Global Context*, Cambridge: Cambridge University Press, 2006.

Z Mody, *10 Judgements that Changed India*, Penguin India, 2013.

Reports

180th Report, Law Commission of India, May 2002, available at http://lawcommissionofindia.nic.in/reports/180rpt.pdf

(2005), available at http://ipc498a.files.wordpress.com/2008/03/ti-india-police-corruption-study-

2008 Country Reports on Human Rights Practices: India, available at http://www.state.gov/g/drl/rls/hrrpt/2008/sca/119134.htm

47th Report of the Law Commission of India on The Trial and Punishment of Social and Economic Offences, New Delhi: Ministry of Law and Justice, Government of India, 1972.

A Leigh, G Johnson, and A Ingram, *Deaths in Police Custody: Learning the Lessons*, Home Officer Police Research Series Paper 26, London Home Office, 1998.

A Noorani, 'Teaching Human Rights to the Police' (October 1993) XXVIII(42) *Economic and Political Weekly* 2252.

ACHR, *Actions against Torture and Other Forms of Human Rights Violations in India*, New Delhi: ACHR, 2009, all reports, available at http://www.achrweb.org/, accessed 15 July 2014.

ACHR, *Torture in India 2009*, New Delhi: Asian Centre for Human Rights, 2009.

ACPO, *National Investigative Strategy, NPIA*, Briefing Paper, HMSO, 2009.

Amnesty International, *Amnesty International's Concerns and Consequent Recommendations for Reform in This Area Are Comprehensively Set Out in Its Report, India – Words into Action: Recommendations for the Prevention of Torture*, January 2001, AI Index: ASA 20/003/2001.

Amnesty International, *India: Report of the Malimath Committee on Reforms of the Criminal Justice System: Some Observations*, 19 September 2003, ASA 20/025/2003, available at http://www.unhcr.org/refworld/docid/3f914cba4.html

Annual Report of the Inter-American Commission, 1985–1986, OEA/Ser.L/V/II.68, doc. 8 rev. 1, 1986, p. 154, El Salvador.

'Article 6: The Right to a Fair Trial' *Human Rights Review*, 2012, available at http://www.equalityhumanrights.com/sites/default/files/documents/humanrights/hrr_article_6.pdf, accessed 12 November 2015.

Broken System: Dysfunction, Abuse and Impunity in the Indian Police, 2009, Human Rights Watch Report, available at http://www.hrw.org/sites/default/files/reports/india0809web.pdf, accessed 24 January 2013.

Bucke et al. 'The Right of Silence: The Impact of the Criminal Justice & Public Order Act 1994' 2000, HORS 199 Home Office, available at http://www.homeoffice.gov.uk/rds/pdfs/hors199.pdf, accessed 11 March 2015.

Bureau of Democracy, Human Rights and Labour, U.S. Dept of State, *Country Reports on Human Rights Practices: India 19*, 2010, available at http://www.state.gov/documents/organization/160058.pdf

Buyse, 'Evidence Obtained through Violation of Article 3 ECHR', *ECHR Blog*, July 2008, available at http://echrblog.blogspot.co.uk/2008/07/evidence-obtained-through-violation-of.html, accessed 2 August 2015.

Canada: Immigration and Refugee Board of Canada, India, *First Information Reports (FIRs)*, including procedures and time frames followed by police to inform complainants that an investigation will not be conducted, 22 March 2011, IND103687.E, available at http://www.refworld.org/docid/50b48d9d2.html, accessed 16 March 2015.

College of Policing, *Investigation Process*, 2013, available at https://www.app.college.police.uk/app-content/investigations/investigation-process/, accessed 10 April 2015.

Commonwealth Human Rights Initiative, *Analysis of the Ribeiro Commission*, 1998–1999, available at http://www.humanrightsinitiative.org/index.php?option=com_content&view=article&catid=91%3Ashiva&id=753%3Asummary-of-ribeiro-committees-recommendations&Itemid=100, accessed 12 March 2015.

Commonwealth Human Rights Initiative, *Police Organisation in India, Delhi, India*, 2011, available at http://www.humanrightsinitiative.org/index.php?option=com_content&view=article&id=88&Itemid=99, accessed 1 April 2015.

Commonwealth Human Rights Initiative, *Police Reforms India: Police Structure and Organisation*, 2005, Retrieved on 19 August 2005 from: https://humanrightsinitiative.org/old/publications/police/PRDebatesInIndia.pdf

Commonwealth Human Rights Initiative, Police Complaints Authority in India, *A Rapid Study*, 2011, available at http://www.humanrightsinitiative.org/index.php?option=com_content&view=article&id=182&Itemid=511, accessed 20 March 2015.

Confidence in the Police Complaints System: A Survey of the General Population in 2008, IPCC, 2008, available at http://www.ipcc.gov.uk/public_confidence_survey_2008.pdf

Corruption in the Police Services in England and Wales: Second Report - A Report Based on the IPCC's Experience from 2008 to 2011, May 2012, London.

Criminal Justice Reform in India, *Review of the Recommendations Made by the Justice Malimath Committee from an International Human Rights Perspective*, available at http://www.docs-archive.com/view/fa8ac0be9f7951d55b7f83c572efdf05/Criminal-Justice-Reform-in-India%3A-ICJ-Position-Paper.pdf

D Brown, *PACE: 10 Years on - A Review of the Research*, available at library.npia.police.uk/docs/hors/hors155.pdf, accessed 24 February 2015.

D Eby, J Metcalfe, J Richardson, and D Singhal, *Towards More Effective Police Oversight*, September, 2004. A report by PIVOT, available at http://www.pivotlegal.org/pdfs/Effective_Police_Oversight-Sept2004.pdf

http://www.humanrightsinitiative.org/programs/aj/police/India/history/default.htm.

http://www.humanrightsinitiative.org/publications/police/rtc_report_trivandrum.pdf.

http://www.ipcc.gov.uk/news/pr150709_murderofnasarhussain.htm.

http://www.outlookindia.com/fullprint.asp?choice=1&fodname=20090615&fname=Police+reforms+(F)&sid=1

Human Right Watch, *"We Have no Orders to Save You": State Participation and Complicity in Communal Violence in Gujarat*, Vol. 14, No. 3 (c), 2002; Concerned Citizens Tribunal – Gujarat 2002, Crime against Humanity: An Inquiry into the Carnage in Gujarat- Findings and Recommendations, 2002.

Human Rights Watch interview with Srikumar, Director General of Police in 2008, Bangalore, December 9, 2008.

Independent Police Complaints Commission, *Corruption in the Police Service in England and Wales – First Report*, London: IPCC, 2011.

Indian Corruption Study to Improve Governance: Volume 9, Corruption in Police Department 1, July 2005, available at https://ipc498a.files.wordpress.com/2008/03/ti-india-police-corruption-study-2005.pdf

J Berry, *Reducing Bureaucracy in Policing, Final Report*, October 2010, available at https://www.gov.uk/government/uploads/system/uploads/attachment_data/file/117162/reduce-bureaucracy-police.pdf

K Saxena, *Report on Prevention of Atrocities against SCs and STs*, 2002, report available at http://www.ambedkar.org/NHRCReport/prelim.pdf, accessed 20 May 2015.

L Hempel and E Topfer, *Urban Eye: Final Report to the European Commission, 5th Framework Programme*, Berlin: Technical University of Berlin, 2004, available at http://www.urbaneye.net/results/ue_wp15.pdf, accessed 2 February 2015.

L Scarman, *The Brixton Disorders 10–12 April 1981*, Cmnd 8427, London: Her Majesty's Stationary Office, 1981.

L Sherman, *Controlling Police Corruption: The Effects of Reform Policies*, Summary Report, Washington: US Dept of Justice, 1978.

Law Commission of India, *152nd Report on Custodial Crimes*, 1994, http://lawcommissionofindia.nic.in/101-169/Report152.pdf

Law Society, *Use of Interpreters in Criminal Cases*, 2012, available at http://www.lawsociety.org.uk/support-services/advice/practice-notes/interpreters-in-criminal-cases/, accessed 12 April 2014.

M McConville and Hodgson, *Custodial legal advice and the Right to Silence, RCCJ Study 16*, London, HMSO, 1993.

M Punch, 'Police Corruption and Its Prevention' (2000) 8(3) *European Journal on Criminal Policy and Research* 301–324.

Malimath Committee Report: Committee on reforms of Criminal Justice System, Government of India, 2003, mha.nic.in/pdfs/criminal_justice_system.pdf, accessed 12 February 2013.

Mehta, *Police Complaints Agencies in the Commonwealth*, available at http://www.humanrightsinitiative.org/programs/aj/police/papers/police_complaints_agencies_in_cw.pdf

Mohanty: Let Us First Reform Ourselves, The Indian Police Journal, Jan-March 2013, Vol LX, No. 1.

National Police Commission, *Third Report*, para. 22.24, quoted in the Law Commission of India, *177th Report on Law Relating to Arrest.*

NHRC, *Manual on Human Rights for Police Officers*, 2011, available at www.nhrc.nic.in/.../Manual_On_Human_Rights_for_Police_Officers.pdf, accessed 14 November 2015.

Opinion of the Commissioner for Human Rights Concerning Independent and Effective Determination of Complaints against the Police (12 March, 2009), available at https://wcd.coe.int/ViewDoc.jsp?id=1417857&Site=CommDH&BackColorInternet=FEC65B&BackC

P Softley, et al., *Police Interrogation: An Observational Study in Four Police Stations*, Home Office Research Study No. 61, April 1980, available at http://library.npia.police.uk/docs/hors/hors61.pdf, accessed 10 January 2015.

PACE, *Code C*, 1984, available at https://www.gov.uk/government/uploads/system/uploads/attachment_data/file/252903/2013_Code_C.pdf

PACE: 10 Years On, 1997, www.lawteacher.net/PDF/PACE%2010%20Years%20On.pdf

Police (Rupees 46,390.26 Crore), 2014, available at indiabudget.nic.in/ub2014-15/eb/npe.pdf, accessed 2 April 2015.

Police Accountability and Governance Structures, Public Attitudes and Perceptions, Ipsos MORI/Association of Police Authorities (APA), 2009, http://www.apa.police.uk/Admin/uploads/attachment/docs/Members/Police_Reform/APA-Ipsos_MORI_Police_accountability_report.pdf

Police Reform Act 2002. See also IPCC website at http://www.ipcc.gov.uk/index/about_ipcc/guardianship.htm.

Professional Policing, National Human Rights Commission, available at http://nhrc.nic.in/Documents/Publications/ProfessionalPolicing.pdf, accessed 2 March 2015.

Report of the Roundtable Conference on Police Reforms (26–27 June, 2003, CHRI), available at

Report of the Special Rapporteur on Torture, Sir Nigel Rodley, submitted in pursuant to the Commission on Human Rights Resolution No. 2000/43, UN Doc E/CN.4/2001/66.

Report on the Mission of the Special Rapporteur to the United Kingdom, UN Doc. E/CN.4/1998/39/add.4, 5 March 1998.

Report on the Situation of Human Rights of a Segment of the Nicaraguan Population of Miskito Origin, OEA Ser.L/V/11.62, doc.10, rev. 3, 1983, at 100.

Review of IPCC's Involvement in Relation to Cases Involving Death, available at https://www.ipcc.gov.uk/page/review-ipccs-work-relation-cases-involving-death, accessed 18 April 2015.

S Datta, 'Change Resistance: A Committee Sans Commitment Delays Reform of our Police' *Outlook*, June 15, 2009, available at http://www.outlookindia.com/article/change-resistance/240681, accessed 7 April 2014.

S Soukara, R Bull, A Vrij, M Turner, and J Cherryman, 'What Really Happens in Police Interviews with Suspects?: Tactics and Confessions' (2009) 15 Psychology, Crime & Law 493–506.

Second Administrative Reforms Report, Fifth Report, June 2007, Government of India.

See generally A Elson, "The Rushcliffe Report" (1946) 13(2) The University of Chicago Law Review; S Hynes and J Robins, *The Justice Gap* (2009, LAG); T Bingham, *The Rule of Law* (2010, Penguin), 86–89; Lord Justice Jackson, 'Review of Civil Litigation Costs: Preliminary Report Volume One' May 2009, http://www.judiciary.gov.uk/Resources/JCO/Documents/jackson-vol1-low.pdf

Seven Steps to Police reform: September 2010, Commonwealth Human Rights Initiative, http://www.humanrightsinitiative.org/programs/aj/police/india/initiatives/seven_steps_to_police_reform.pdf

Sir Henry Fisher, *Report of an Inquiry by the Sir Henry Fisher into the Circumstances Leading to the Trial of Three Persons on Charges Arising Out of the Death of Maxwell Confait and the Fire at 27 Doggett Road, London SE6*. HMSO, 1977.

Soli Sorabji Committee Report on Model Police Act, Chapter XI, 2005 available at http://www.humanrightsinitiative.org/index.php?option=com_content&view=article&catid=35%3Apolice-reforms&id=600%3Athe-police-act-drafting-committee&Itemid=98, accessed 2 April 2015.

T Newburn, *Understanding and Preventing Police Corruption: Lessons from the Literature*, Police Research Series paper 110, London: Home Office, 1999.

The Criminal Law Revision Committee, 1972, available at http://www.ncbi.nlm.nih.gov/pubmed/5076843, accessed 13 August 2014.

The Indian Police Journal, Vol LX, No. 1, January-March, 2013, available at http://www.bprd.nic.in/writereaddata/mainlinkFile/File1093.pdf

The National Police Commission, *Government of India, Fourth Report*, June 1980.

The Padmanabhaiah Committee on Police Reforms Report, Human Rights Initiative, 2000, available at http://www.humanrightsinitiative.org/index.php?option=com_content&view=article&catid=91%3Ashiva&id=687%3Apolice-india-padmanabhai-committee&Itemid=100, accessed 12 May 2015.

The Right to a Fair Trial: Part 1 - From Investigation to Trial, Chapter 6, October 2014, available at http://www.ohchr.org/Documents/Publications/training9chapter6en.pdf, accessed 20 August 2015.

The Runciman Committee Report, 1993, available at https://www.gov.uk/government/uploads/system/uploads/.../2263.pdf.

Three Lakh Rupees Monetary Relief in a Case of Death in Police Custody (June 5, 2009) available at http://nhrc.nic.in/dispArchive.asp?fno=1759

Transforming the CJS: A Strategy and Action Plan to Reform the Criminal Justice System, 2013, https://www.gov.uk/government/publications/transforming-the-criminal-justice-system

UNODC, *Handbook on Police Accountability, Oversight, and Integrity*, available at www.unodc.org/documents/.../Valrie_Lebaux_UNODC_-_DO.pdf, accessed 20 April 2015.

V Kemp and N Balmer, 'Criminal Defence Services: User's Perspectives' (2008) *Research Paper* No. 21. London: Legal Services Research Centre.

W Macpherson, *The Stephen Lawrence Inquiry*, Cm 4262-I, London: The Stationary Office, 1999.

Articles

A Ashworth, 'Case Comment: Human rights: Article 3 - Torture or Inhuman and Degrading Treatment - Whether Applicant Was Still a "Victim" after Other Remedies Pursued' (2010) 11 Criminal Law Review 865.

A Bewicke, 'Asian Developments in Access to Counsel: A Comparative Study' (2011) 10(2) Northwestern Journal of International Human Rights, at http://scholarlycommons.law.northwestern.edu/cgi/viewcontent.cgi?article=1124&context=njihr

A Cebulla and M Stephens, 'Public Perceptions of the Police: Effects of Police Investigations and Police Resources' (2010) Internet Journal of Criminology 1–19.

A Edwards, 'Do the Defence Matter?' (2010) 14 International Journal of Evidence & Proof, 119–128.

A Gavirneni, 'Measuring Police Efficiency in India: An Application of Data Envelopment Analysis' (2006) 29(1) Policing: An International Journal of Police Strategies & Management 125–145.

A Goldsmith, 'New Directions in Police Complaints Procedures: Some Conceptual and Comparative Departures' (1988) 11(1) Police Studies 60–71.

A Kalhan, 'Colonial Continuities: Human Rights, Terrorism, and Security Laws in India' (March 2007) 20 Columbia Journal of Asian Law 2006; Fordham Law Legal Studies Research Paper No. 970503. Available at SSRN: http://ssrn.com/abstract=970503

A Kalhan, G Conroy, M Kaushal, S Miller, and J Rakoff, 'Colonial Continuities: Human Rights, Terrorism, and Security Laws in India' (2006) 20(1) Columbia Journal of Asian Law 93–234.

A Papachristo, T Meares, and J Fagan, 'Why Do Criminals Obey the Law? The Influence of Legitimacy and Social Networks on Active Gun Offenders' (2012) 102(2) Journal of Criminal Law and Criminology 397–440.

A Qadri, 'Police Corruption: An Analysis' (1994) 22(1) Indian Journal of Criminology 5–8.

A Shinar, 'Accountability for Indian Police: Creating an External Complaints Agency' (2009), http://indiagovernance.gov.in/files/police_reforms.pdf

A Verma, 'A Uniform Betrayal' *India Together*, June 2004, available at http://indiatogether.org/betray-government, accessed 12 June 2015.

A Weisburd, 'Customary International Law and Torture: the case of India' (2001) 1 Chicago Journal of International Law Article 6.

A D E Lewis, 'Bentham's View of the Right to Silence' (1990) 43 Curr Legal Probs 135.

B Bradford, J Jackson, and E Stanko, 'Contact and Confidence: Revisiting the Impact of Public Encounters with the Police' (2009) 19(1) Policing and Society: An International Journal of Research and Policy 20–46.

B Bradford, J Jackson, and M Hough, 'Police Futures and Legitimacy: Redefining "Good Policing' in J Brown (ed.), *Future of Policing*, Oxon: Routledge, 2014. doi:10.2139/ssrn.2171394, accessed 12 January 2015.

B Fortman, 'Adventurous' Judgments: A Comparative Exploration into Human Rights as a Moral-Political Force in Judicial Law Development' (2006) 2(2) Utrecht Law Review 22–43.

Bureau of Democracy, Human Rights, and Labour, U.S. Dept of State, *Country Reports on Human Rights Practices: India*, 2010, available at http://www.state .gov/documents/organization/160058.pdf

C Clarke, R Milne, and R Bull, 'Interviewing Suspects of Crime: The Impact of PEACE Training, Supervision and the Presence of a Legal Advisor' (2011) 8 Journal of Investigative Psychology and Offender Profiling 149–162.

C Meissner, A Redlich, S Bhatt, and S Brandon, 'Interview and Interrogation Methods and Their Effects on True and False Confessions', (2012–2013) Campbell Systematic Reviews, Campbell Collaboration.

C Murphy, 'Lon Fuller and the Moral Value of the Rule of Law' (2005) 24 Law and Philosophy 239–262.

Council of Europe, *Human Rights Education for Legal Professionals*, 2012, available at http://www.coehelp.org/mod/glossary/showentry.php?courseid=75&concept= Positive+obligation

D Bayley, 'Law Enforcement and the Rule of Law: Is There a Tradeoff?' (November 2002) 2(1) Criminology and Public Policy 133–154.

D Bayley, 'The Police and Political Change in Comparative Perspective' (1971) 6(1) Law & Society Review 91–112.

D Bayley and C Shearing, 'The Future of Policing' (1996) 30(3) Law and Society Review 585–606.

D Giannoulopoulos, 'North of the Border and across the Channel': Custodial Legal Assistance Reforms in Scotland and France' (2013) Criminal Law Review 369.

D Giannoulopoulos, 'Strasbourg Jurisprudence, Law Reform and Comparative Law: A Tale of the Right to Custodial Legal Assistance in Five Countries' (2016) 16 Human Rights Law Review 1.

D Narby, B Cutler, and G Morgan, 'A Meta-Analysis of the Association between Authoritarianism and Jurors' Perceptions of Defendant Culpability' (1993) 78 Journal of Applied Psychology 34–42.

D Rea, D Donnelly, and J Fitzsimons, *International Comparison Research: Models of Police Governance and Accountability*. London: Association of Police Authorities/Northern Ireland Policing Board, 2009.

D Roberts, 'Legal Advice, The Unrepresented Suspect and the Courts: Inferences from Silence under the Criminal Justice and Public Order Act 1994' (1995) Crim. L. Rev., 483–484.

D Sharp, 'Who Needs Theories in Policing? An Introduction to a Special Issue on Policing' (2005) 44(5) Howard Journal of Criminal Justice 449–459.

D Skuy, 'Macaulay and the Indian Penal Code of 1862: The Myth of the Inherent Superiority and Modernity of the English Legal System Compared to India's Legal System in the Nineteenth Century' (1998) 32 Modern Asian Studies 513–557. doi:10.1017/S0026749X98003035.

D Wolchover, 'Serving Silent Suspects-Part 1' (2011) Criminal Law and Justice Weekly 71.

E Banakas, 'Some Thoughts on the Method of Comparative Law: The Concept of Law Revisited' (1981) 67 ARSP.

E Cape, 'Improving Pretrial Justice: The Roles of Lawyers and Paralegals' (2012) Open Society Foundations, New York. Available at http://www.soros.org/initiatives/justice/articlespublications/publications/cape – ptj –20120416

E Cape and T Smith, *The practice of pre-trial detention in England and Wales: Research report*, 2016, available from https://uwe-repository.worktribe.com/output/917566

E Goldstein, 'Using Videotape to Present Evidence in Criminal Proceedings' (1985) 27 Criminal Law Quarterly 369.

E Orucu, 'Critical Comparative Law: Considering Paradoxes for Legal Systems in Transition' (2000) 4 Netherlands Comparative Law Association, 133.

E Shepherd, A Mortimer, V Turner, and J Watson, 'Spaced Cognitive Interviewing: Facilitating Therapeutic and Forensic Narration of Trauma Memories' (1999) 5 Psychology, Crime & Law 117–143.

E L Nickels and A Verma, 'Dimensions of Police Culture: A Study in Canada, India and Japan' (2008) 31(2) Policing: An International Journal of Police Strategies & Management 186–209.

F Leverick, 'The Right to Legal Assistance during Detention' (2011) 15(3) Edinburgh Law Review 352–380, ISSN 1364-9809. Available at http://eprints.gla.ac.uk/54994/

G Gudjonson, 'False Confessions and Correcting Injustices' (2012) 46 New England Law Review 689–710.

G Sadasivan Nair, 'Fair Trial as a Human Right' (1998) 1 and 2 Indian Journal of Human Rights, 77–90.

G Singh, '"Bill of Rights" in the Constitution of India', 2009, available at http://www.newenglishreview.org/print.cfm?pg=custpage&frm=42164&sec_id=44259, accessed 20 November 2015.

H Kelsen, 'What is Justice? Professor Stone and the Pure Theory of Law' (1965) 17 Stanford Law Review 1128.

H Quirk, 'Twenty Years on, The Right to Silence and Legal Advice: The Spiralling Costs of an Unfair Exchange' (2013) 64 Northern Ireland Legal Quarterly 465.

H Sommerlad, 'Researching and Theorizing the Processes of Professional Identity Formation' (2007) 34 Journal of Law and Society 190–217.

I Clare, G Gudjonsson, and P Harari, 'Understanding of the Current Police Caution (England and Wales)' (1998) 8 Journal of Community & Applied Social Psychology 323–329.

J Baldwin, 'Police Interview Techniques: Establishing Truth or Proof?' (1993) 33(3) British Journal of Criminology 325–52.

J Baldwin, 'Police Interviews on Tape' (1990) 11 New Law Journal 662.

J Belur, 'Why Do the Police Use Deadly Force? Explaining Police Encounters in Mumbai' (2010) 50 British Journal of Criminology 320–41.

J Belur, N Tilley, D Osrin, N Daruwalla, M Kumar, and V Tiwari, 'Police Investigations: Discretion Denied yet Undeniably Exercised' (2015) 25(5) Policing and Society 439–462. Available from: 10.1080/10439463.2013.878343

J Black, 'Managing Discretion' (2001) Published as: ARLC Conference Papers - Penalties: Policy, Principles and Practice in Government Regulation, available at http://www.lse.ac.uk/collections/law/staff/julia-black.htm, accessed 20 January 2015.

J Chalmers, 'Recording of Police Interviews' in J Chalmers, F Leverick, and A Shaw (eds), *Post-Corroboration Safeguards Review Report of the Academic Expert Group*, Edinburgh: The Scottish Government, 2014.

J Courvoisier, 'Procedural Changes in Switzerland: The Lawyer Goes into the Interrogation Room' (2017) 19(1) The Journal of Forensic Practice 2–13.

J Gammon, 'A Meek, Weak NHRC' (July-August 2007) 6(4) Combat Law, 72.

J Hodgson, 'Conceptions of the Trial in Inquisitorial and Adversarial Procedure' in A Duff, L Farmer, S Marshall, and V Tadros (eds), *The Trial on Trial*, Vol. 2 Judgment and calling to account. Oxford, UK: Hart Pub, 2006, pp. 223–242. ISBN 9781841135427.

J Hodgson, 'The Role of Lawyers During Police Detention and Questioning: A Comparative Study'. Published in Justitiele Verkenningen (Judicial Explorations), March 2014, Warwick School of Law Research Paper No. 2014/06. Available at SSRN: http://ssrn.com/abstract=2433562, accessed 23 April 2015.

J Jackson, A Huq, B Bradford, and T Tyler, 'Monopolizing Force? Police Legitimacy and Public Attitudes toward the Acceptability of Violence' (2013) Psychology, Public Policy, and Law, Advance online publication.

J Jackson, B Bradford, M Hough, J Kuha, R Stares, S Widdop, et al., 'Developing European Indicators of Trust in Justice' (2011) 8(4) European Journal of Criminology 267–285.

J Mathivanan, *Legal Aid-Issues, Challenges, and Solutions*, available at https://www.google.co.uk/url?sa=t&rct=j&q=&esrc=s&source=web&cd=1&cad=rja&uact=8&ved=0CCEQFjAA&url=http%3A%2F%2Fwww.hcmadras.tn.nic.in%2Flegalaid-issues.pdf&ei=CxHaVOiGNsLwatbzgqAI&usg=AFQjCNHP1JZBdzPtO-z-ttRa64kia2qH7Q&sig2=SNMzaWnhnvLuJpp0r9pEiw&bvm=bv.85464276,d.ZWU

J Miller, 'Police Corruption in England and Wales: An Assessment of the Current Evidence', *Home Office Online Report*, 11/03, available at http://www.belui.ru/Doc/Mejdunar/Angl/33.pdf, accessed 20 April 2015.

J Pearse and G Gudjonnson, 'A Review of the Role of the Advisors in the Police Stations' (1996) 6 Criminal Behaviour and Mental Health 231–239.

J Pearse and G Gudjonsson, 'Police Interviewing and Legal Representation: A Field Study' (1997) 8(1) The Journal of Forensic Psychiatry 200–208.

J Varghese, Police Structure: A Comparative Study of Policing Models (2010), available at SSRN: http://ssrn.com/abstract=1605290 or doi:10.2139/ssrn.1605290

J Waldron, 'The Torture and Positive Law: Jurisprudence for the White House' (2005) 105(6) Columbia Law Review 1681–1750.

K Balagopal, 'Terrorism of the Police Kind' (July-August, 2007) 6(4) Combat Law, 69.

K Bottomley, C Coleman, D Dixon, and M Gill, 'The Detention of Suspects in Police Custody: The Impact of the Police and Criminal Evidence Act 1984' (1991) 31(4) British Journal of Criminalogy 347–364.

K Madan and G Swapti, 'Legal Aid in India, Legal Services India' (October 2008), available at http://www.legalserviceindia.com/article/l261-Legal-Aid.html, accessed 12 March 2015.

K Mathur, 'Social Deviance and Marginal Crime in Police Organisations- How to Control the Police?' (1994) in compilation of the lectures delivered at XXVI All India Police Science Congress, Hyderabad.

K Murphy, Lyn Hinds, and Jenny Fleming, 'Encouraging Public Cooperation and Support for Police' (June 2008) 18(2) Policing and Society 136–155.

K Reid, 'Current Developments in Police Accountability' (2002) 66(2) Journal of Criminal Law 172–195.

K Roberts, 'Police Interviewing of Criminal Suspects: A Historical Perspective' (2012) Internet Journal of Criminology, available at http://www.internetjournalofcriminology.com/, accessed 14 April 2015.

K Tummala, 'Corruption in India: Control Measures and Consequences' (2010) 10 (2) Asian Journal of Political Science 43–69.

L Griffin, 'Correcting Injustice: Studying How the United Kingdom and the United States Review Claims of Innocence' (2009) 41 University of Toledo Law Review 107.

M Ahmad, *Law as to Information in and Investigation into Non-Cognizable Cases as per S.155 of the Code of Criminal Procedure*, 1898 (January 12, 2012). Available at SSRN: http://ssrn.com/abstract=1984372 or doi:10.2139/ssrn.1984372

M Bussani, 'Current Trends in European Comparative Law: The Common Core Approach' (1998) 21 Hastings International and Comparative Law Review 785.

M Coulthard, 'Suppressed Dialogue in a Confession Statement' in M Coulthard, J Cotterill, and F Rock (eds), *Dialogue Analysis VII: Working with Dialogue*, Tübingen: Max Niemeyer Verlag, , 2002, 417–24.

M Damaska, 'Structures of Authority and Comparative Criminal Procedure' (1975) Faculty Scholarship Series, Paper 1590.

M Daruwala, G Joshi, and M Tiwana, 'Police Act, 1861: Why We Need to Replace It?' CHRI, July 2005, available at www.humanrightsinitiative.org/.../police/.../advocacy_paper_police_act_.., viewed on 12 January 2014.

M Foucault, 'Discipline & Punish', (1975) Panopticism, available at http://dm.ncl.ac.uk/courseblog/files/2011/03/michel-foucault-panopticism.pdf

M Hartwig, P Granhag, and A Vrij, 'Police Interrogation from a Social Psychology Perspective' 2005, 15 Policing and Society 379–399.

M Seneviratne, 'Policing the Police in the United Kingdom' (2004) 14(4) Policing and Society: An International Journal of Research and Policy 329–347.

M Weber, 'The Theory of Social and Economic Organization' (1948), by A. M. Henderson, Talcott Parsons Review by S. E. Thorne, 57(4) The Yale Law Journal 676–678.

M Zander, 'PACE (The Police and Criminal Evidence Act, 1984): Past, Present, and Future' LSE Legal Studies Working Paper, 1–14.

N Deslauriers-Varin, P Lussier, and M St-Yves 'Confessing Their Crime: Factors Influencing the Offender's Decision to Confess to the Police' (2011) 28(1) Justice Quarterly 113–145.

O Kahn-Freund, 'Comparative Law as an Academic Subject' (1966) 82 Law Quarterly Review, 40.

P Legrand, 'On the Singularity of Law' (2006) 47 Harvard International Law Journal 517–530.

P Legrand, 'The Impossibility of Legal Transplants' (1997) 4 Maastricht Journal of European and Comparative Law 111.

P Mirfield, 'The Future of the Law of Confessions' (1984) Criminal Law Review 70.

P Pleasence, V Kemp, and N Balmer, 'The Justice Lottery? Police Station Advice 25 Years on From PACE' (2011) Criminal Law Review 3–18.

R Leng, *The Right to Silence in Police Interrogation: A Study of the Issues Underlying the Debate*, Royal Commission on Criminal Justice Research Study No. 10, London: HMSO, 1993.

R Merton, 'Insiders and Outsiders: A Chapter in the Sociology of Knowledge' (1972) 78(1) American Journal of Sociology 9–47.

R Merton, 'Social Structure and Anomie' (1938) 3(5) American Sociological Review 672–682.

R Schlesinger, 'The Past and Future of Comparative Law' (1995) 43 American Journal of Comparative Law 477.

S Culhane, H Hosch, and C Heck, 'Interrogation Technique Endorsement by Current Law Enforcement, Future Law Enforcement, and Laypersons' (2008) 11(3) Police Quarterly 366–386.

S Fenner, G Gudjonsson, and I Claire, 'Understanding of the Current Police Caution (England and Wales) among Suspects in Police Detention' (2002) 12 Journal of Community and Applied Social Psychology 83–93.

S Jon and T Quah, 'Curbing Corruption in India: An Impossible Dream?' (2008) 16(3) Asian Journal of Political Science 240–259.

S Jones, 'The Police and Criminal Evidence Act, 1984' (November 1985) 48 The Modern Law Review 679–693.

S Kassin et al., 'Police-Induced Confessions: Risk Factors and Recommendations' (2010) 34 Law and Human Behaviour 3.

S Kassin and G Gudjonsson, 'The Psychology of Confessions: A Review of the Literature and Issues' (2004) 5 Psychological Science in the Public Interest 33–67.

S Moston, G Stephenson, and T Williamson, 'The Effects of Case Characteristics on Suspect Behaviour during Police Questioning' (1992) 32 The British Journal of Criminology 33.

S Moston and G M Stephenson, 'Changing Face of Police Interrogation' (1993) 3(2) Journal of Community & Applied Social Psychology, 101–115.

S Moston and T Engelberg, 'Police Questioning Techniques in Tape Re-corded Interviews with Criminal Suspects' (1993) 3 Policing and Society 223–237.

S Sarangi and A Wright, 'Human Rights is not Enough: The Need for Demonstrating Efficacy of an Ethical Approach to Interviewing in India' (2008) 13 Legal and Criminological Psychology 89–106.

Sheela Barse v. State of Maharashtra (1988) 1 S.C.R. 210 (India).

T Endicott, 'The Impossibility of the Rule of Law' (1999) 19 Oxford Journal of Legal Studies 1.

T Kaye, *Unsafe and Unsatisfactory? Report of the Independent Inquiry into the Working Practices of West Midlands Police Serious Crime Squad*, London: Civil Liberties Trust, 1991, available at https://www.ncjrs.gov/App/Publications/abstract.aspx?ID=134391, accessed 13 April 2015.

T May, H Warburton, and I Hearnden, 'Appellants', Complainants', and Police Officers' Satisfaction with the Independent Police Complaints Commission', The Institute of Criminal Policy Research, available at www.nao.org.uk/wp-content/uploads/2008/11/ipcc.pdf, accessed 22 April 2015.

T Smith and E Cape, 'The Rise and Decline of Criminal Legal Aid in England and Wales' in A. Flynn and J Hodgson (eds), *Access to Justice and Legal Aid: Comparative Perspectives on Unmet Legal Need*, Hart Publishing, 2017, available from https://uwe-repository.worktribe.com/output/899612

T Tyler, 'Legitimacy and Criminal Justice: The Benefits of Self-regulation' (2009) 7 Ohio State Journal of Criminal Law 307–59.

T Tyler, 'Trust and Legitimacy: Policing in the USA and Europe' (2011) 8 European Journal of Criminology 254–256.

T Williamson, *Strategic Changes in Police Interrogation: An Examination of Police and Suspect Behaviour in the Metropolitan Police in Order to Determine the Effects of New Legislation, Technology, and Organisational Policies*, unpublished thesis, University of Kent, Faculty of Social Sciences.

U Rao and A Khurana, 'Proactive Policing Approach: What is It?' (1999) XLVI–XLVII(4&1) The Indian Police Journal 90–95.

V Grover, 'Recipe for Impunity' (July-August, 2007) 6(4) Combat Law Journal.

V Hoeke and Warrington, 'Legal Cultures, Legal Paradigms, and Legal Doctrine: Towards a New Model for Comparative Law' (1998) 47 International and Comparative Law Quarterly 495–536.

V Kemp, "No Time for a Solicitor": Implications for Delays on the Take-Up of Legal Advice' (2013) 3 Criminal Law Review 184–202.

W Twining, 'Cosmopolitan Legal Studies' (2002) 9(2) International Journal of the Legal Profession 99–108.

W Twining and P Twining, 'Bentham on Torture' (1973) 24 Northern Ireland Legal Quarterly 305.

Y Vijay, *The Adversarial System in India: Assessing Challenges and Alternatives*, 2012. Available at SSRN: http://ssrn.com/abstract=2147385.

Cases

Indian Cases

Abhay Nath Dubey v State of Delhi, 2002 (2) Chand Cri 354 (Delhi).

Agnou Naagesia v The State of Bihar, 1966 Crim L J 100 SCC.

Ajmal Amir Kasab v. State of Maharashtra (2012) 9 SCC 234.

Alok Nath Dutta v State of West Bengal, 2007 (12) SCC 230.

AmolakRam v Emperor, AI.R. 1932 Lah 13.

Anant Brahmachari vs Uoi & Others, W.P. (CRL) No. 55/2011.

Anil K Khandelwal v Maksud Saiyed 2006 CRI LJ 3180.

Ariel v The State, AIR 1954 SC 15.

Arnesh Kumar vs State Of Bihar & Anr, Criminal Appeal No. 1277 of 2014 on 2 July, 2014.

Ayyub v State of U.P., AIR 2002 SC 1192.

B S Sundaresh v State of Karnataka, 2012 (3) PLJR (SC) 258.

Babubhai Parmar v State of Gujarat, 2007 Cri LJ 786.

Badkujoti v State of Mysore, AIR 1966 SC 1746.

Bharosa v Emporer, 1941 Nag 86.

Bodh Raj v State of Jammu and Kashmir, AIR 2002 SC 16.

Brij Lal Bhar v State of UP, 2006 CRI LJ 3334.

Centre for Legal Research and Another v The State of Kerela, AIR 1986 SC 2196.

Chattar Singh v State of Haryana, AIR 2009 SC 378.
Court on its Own Motion v. The State (2010) 175 DLT 110 (DB).
Dagdu v. State of Maharashtra, AIR 1977 SC 1579.
Dalbir Singh v The State of Uttar Pradesh, W P Crim 193 of 2006.
Dara Singh v Republic of India 2011 (2) SCC 490.
DK Basu v State of West Bengal (1997) 1 SCC 216.
Forest Range Officer, Changathara II Range v Aboobacker, 1989 Crim LJ Kerela 2038.
Francis C Mulin v The Union Territory of Delhi, AIR 1981 SC 746.
Gauri Shankar v State of Bihar, AIR 1972 SC 711.
Gian Singh v. State (Delhi Admn.), 1981 Cri.L.J. 100.
Gurdeep Singh v State (Delhi Administration), AIR 1999 SC 3646.
H N Rishbud and Inder Singh v The State of Delhi, 1995 (1) SCR 1150.
Hans Raj v. State, AI.R. 1956 All 641.
Hanumant Nargendkar v State of MP, 1952 SCR 1091.
Harichandra Kurmi v. State of Bihar, AIR. 1964 S C 1184.
Husen Bhenu Malad vs State of Gujarat, 2003 Cri L J 5070.
Inspector of Police, Tamil Nadu v Bala Prasanna, 2008 11 SCC 645.
Jameel Ahmed v State of Rajasthan, 2003 (9) SCC 673.
Janardhan Reddi v. State of Hyderabad, A.I.R. 1951 S.C. 217.
Jitender Kumar v State of Haryana (2012) 6 SCC 204.
K Veeraswami v Union of India, 1991 3 SCC 655.
Kamalanantha v The State of Tamil Nadu, 2005 5 SCC 194.
Kanhayalal v Union of India, AIR 2008 SC 1044.
Kartar Singh v The State of Punjab 1994 (3) SCC 569.
Khatri v. State of Bihar, A.I.R. 1981 S.C. 928 or 1981 SCR (2) 408.
Kuldip Singh v The State of Punjab, AIR 1997 SC 82.
Lalan Choudhary v State of Bihar, 2007 (1) BBCJ 205.
Lalita Kumari v Govt. of U.P., (2014) 2 SCC 1.
Leonard Valdaris v The Officer in Charge Writ Petition No. 2110 of 2014.
Llewelyn Evans A.I.R., 1926 Born. 551.
Mabarak Ali Ahmed v State of Bombay, AIR 1957 SC 857.
Madhu v The State of Kerela, 2012 (2) SCC 399.
Maneka Gandhi v Union of India, 1978 (1) SCC 248.
Md. Sukur Ali v State of Assam (2011) CRIMINAL APPEAL NO. 546 of 2011.
Mohammed Khalid v The State of West Bengal, 2002 (7) SCC 334.
Mohindro v The State of Punjab, 2001 Crim L J 2587.
Mothi Bhai v State of Rajasthan, 1954 CriLJ 1591.
Nandini Satpathi v. Dani, A.I.R. 1978 S.C. 1073.
Niranjan Singh v Prabhakar, AIR 1980 SC 785.
Omprakash v State of UP, AIR 1960 SC 409.
Pakkirisamy v The State of Tamil Nadu (1997) 8 SCC 158.
Palvinder Kaur v. The State of Punjab (1953) SC 94.
People's Union for Civil Liberties v Union of India, 2004 SCC 580.
Prakash Singh v Union of India, Writ Petition (civil) 310 of 1996.
Prakash Singh v. Union of India (2009) 17 SCC 329.
Pyare Lal v. State of Rajasthan, AIR 1963 SC 1094.
R. v. Babulal, 1884 (6) A 509, at 523.
Rahim Beg v The State of UP, 1972 3 SCC 759.

Rajkumar Kanwal v Union of India, AIR 1991 CRI LJ SC 97.
Raju Premji v Customs, 2009 16 SCC 496.
Ram Chander v State of Rajasthan, 2003 Cri LJ 2485.
Ram Singh v Sonia, 2007 2 SCC (Crl) 1.
Ram Singh v The State, AIR 1959 Crim L J 1134.
Ram Singh v. State of Maharashtra, 1999 Cr LJ 3763 (Bom).
Ramdev Food Products Private Limited v State of Gujarat, Criminal Appeal No.600 of 2007.
Ramesh Kumari v State of U.P., 2006 (1) Crimes 230 (SC).
Ravindra Sharma v Santosh Kumar, H.C.P., Dasarath on 2 February, 2007.
Rudul Shah v The State of Bihar 1983 4 SCC 141.
Sakiri Basu v State of U.P., 2007 (8) SCC 226.
Sampath Kumar v Enforcement Directorate AIR 1998 SC 6.
Sandeep v The State of UP, 2012 6 SCC 107.
Sansar Chand v The State of Rajasthan, (2010) 10 SCC 604.
Satpathy v P.L. Dani, AIR 1978 SC 1025.
Satyawan Pagi v The Union of India, 2006 Cri L J 2181.
Selvi v. State of Karnataka 2010 (7) SCC 263
Sheela Barse v Union of India, A.I.R. 1983 S. C. 378.
State (NCT of Delhi) v Navjot Sandhu, 2005 (11) SC 600.
State of Delhi v Ashok Kumar Jain; Delhi High Court; 07 February 2014.
State of Gujarat v. Kishanbhai, 2014 Indlaw SC 11.
State of Haryana v Ch. Bhajan Lal AIR 1992 SC 604.
State of Haryana v Dinesh Kumar AIR 2008 SC 1083.
State of Punjab v Surinder Singh 1965 Cri.L.T. 161 (P & H).
Sube Singh v. State of Haryana and Others, AIR 2006 SC 1117.
Sube Singh v State of Haryana (2006) 3 SCC 178: AIR 2006 SC 1117.
Sukhveer Singh v State of U.P., 2006 CRI LJ 4816.
Sundeep Bafna v The State of Maharashtra, Criminal Appeal No 689 of 2014.
Surendra Koli v The State of Uttar Pradesh, 2011 4 SCC 80.
Surinder Kumar v The State of Punjab, AIR 1999 SC 215.
Surjit Singh Chandra v Union of India, 1996 (8) Supreme 374.
The Inspector of Police, P. Saravanan v/s K.C. Palanisamy CRL.O.P.(MD). No.13615 of 2011.
The State (NCT) of Delhi v Navjot Sandhu, 2005 (11) SCC 600.
The State of Andhra Pradesh v G Satya Murthy, 1997 CRI LJ 744 (SC).
The State of Bombay v Kathi Kalu AIR 1961 1808.
The State of Punjab v Barkatram, AIR 1962 SC 276.
The State of Rajasthan v Raja Ram, 2003 (8) SCC 180.
The State of Uttar Pradesh v Mohammad Naim, AIR 1964 SC 703.
Vikram v The State 1996 Crim LJ 1536.
Vineet Narayan v Union of India 1998 (1) SCC 226.

English Cases

AT&T Istel Ltd v Tully (1993) AC 45.
Cadder v HM Advocate (2010) UKSC 43.
Castorina v Chief Constable of Surrey (1988) 138 NLJ 180.

Dickson v HM Advocate (2001) SLT 674.
Hayes v CC Merseyside Police (2011) EWCA Civ 911.
Howarth v Metropolitan Police Commissioner (2011) All ER (D) ECtHR 8 February 1996.
Imran and Hussain (1997) Crim.L.R. 754, CA.
John Murray v UK No. 18731/91; ECtHR 18 February 2010.
Murray v DPP 1993 Cr. APP. REP. 151.
Murray v UK 1996 (22) EHRR, 29.
Paton v Ritchie (2000) SLT 239.
R v Absloum (1989) 88 Cr. App. R. 332.
R v Alladice (1987) Cr. App. R. 380.
R v Argent (1997) 2 Cr App R 27.
R v Betts and Hall (2001) EWCA Crim 224.
R v Brown 2011 EWCA Crim 1606 (Eng).
R v Bryce 1992 4 All E R 567.
R v Delaney (1988) 86 Cr App R 18.
R v Delany (1989) 88 Cr. App. R. 338.
R v Farrell (2004) EWCA Crim 597.
R v Fulling 1987 2 All E R 65.
R v Howell (2003) EWCA Crim 1.
R v Imran and Hussain (1997) Crim L.R. 754 CA.
R v Jones (2002) UKHL 5.
R v Keenan (1990) 90 Cr App R 1.
R v Mackenzie (1993) 96 Cr. App. R. 98.
R v McGovern (1991) 92 Cr. App. R.
R v Paris, Abdullahi and Miller (1992) 97 Cr App R 99.
R v Quinn (1990) Crim. L.R. 581.
R v Roble (1997) CLR 346.
R v Sang (1980) AC 402.
R v Voison (1918) 1 KB 531.
R v Walsh (1990) 91 Cr. App. R. 161.
R v. Crampton (1990) 92 Cr App R 369.
R v. Emmerson (1991) 92 Cr App R 284.
Regina (EO and others) v Secretary of State for the Home Department (2013) EWHC 1236.
Richardson v CC West Midlands Police (2011) EWHC 773.
Zaichenko v Russia No. 39660/02; ECtHR 13 October 2009.

European Cases

Aboufaied v. Libya, HRC No. 1782/2008 (2012).
Aksoy v. Turkey (1996) 23 EHRR 553.
Chitti v Zambia, CCPR/C/105/D/1303/2004.
Commonwealth v DiGiambattista, 2004 813 N E 2d 516.
Condron v UK (2000) 31 EHRR 1, 60.
Dayanan v Turkey 7377/03; ECtHR, Grand Chamber, 27 November 2008.
Demirkaya v. Turkey, 13 October 2009, No. 31721/02.
Gafgen v Germany, 2011 52 EHRR 1 (Grand Chamber).

Gerasimov v. Kazakhstan, CAT 433/2010 (2012).
Hooper v. the United Kingdom (2005) 41 EHRR 1.
Ibrahim and the Others v The United Kingdom (2016) ECHR 75.
Imbroscia v Switzerland (1994) 17 EHRR 441.
Ireland v United Kingdom (1978) 2 EHRR 25.
McCann and Others v United Kingdom, 1996 21 EHRR 97.
Nechiporuk and Yonkalo v Ukraine Application no 420/04 (2011), 175.
Pishchalnikov v Russia, 7025/04 [2009] ECHR 1357 .
Salduz v Turkey 36391/02 (2008) ECHR 1542; (2009) 49 EHRR 19.
Tomasi v. France (1992) 15 EHRR 1.

Other Cases

Miranda v Arizona, 384 US 436 (1966).

Laws

Indian Legislation

The Code of Criminal Procedure, 1872.
The Constitution of India, 1950.
The Evidence Act, 1875.
The Indian Penal Code, 1860.
The Police Act, 1861.
The Prevention Of Terrorism Act, 2002.
The Terrorism And Disruptive Activities Act, 1995.
Unlawful Activities of Act, 1967.

English Legislation

The Police and Criminal Evidence Act, 1984.
The Criminal Justice and Public Order Act, 2004.

Foreign Legislation

The European Convention on Human Rights, 1950.

Miscellaneous

As reported by the Times of India, 'Businessmen Held 'Improperly': Court Sees Red, available at http://timesofindia.indiatimes.com/city/mumbai/Businessmen-held-improperly-court-sees-red/articleshow/45862067.cms, accessed 24th March 2015.
K Marx, 'The British Rule in India' (25 June 1853), *New York Daily Tribune*.
S Khurana and U N B Rao, *Impact of Proactive Approach on Attitude of Students towards Police in India*. Paper presented at the 38th Annual Program of Academy of Criminal Justice Sciences, Washington, DC, 2001.

S Mukhopadhyaya, *Conceptualising Post-Colonial Policing: An Analysis and Application of Policing Public Order in India*, 1997, Unpublished PhD thesis submitted to the University of Leicester.

Times of India, 'Police Still Reluctant to Register FIRs' July 26, 2008.

Internet Search Engines and Websites

AHRC, http://www.humanrights.asia/

Human Rights Watch Interview with Dr. U.N.B. Rao, Consultant for Delhi Police, Delhi, December 3, 2008.

Sir Robert Peel and the New Police Act 1829, available at http://www.nationalarchives.gov.uk/education/candp/prevention/g08/g08cs2.html and http://content.met.police.uk/Article/The-Metropolitan-Police-how-it-all-began/1400015336362/1400015336362, accessed 6 April 2014.

Law Commission Reports, India

152nd Law Commission Report.

177th Law Commission Report.

Police Manuals, India

Delhi Police Manual, available at http://www.delhipolice.nic.in/home/rti/rti.aspx, accessed 12 September 2015.

Index

For Product Safety Concerns and Information please contact our EU representative GPSR@taylorandfrancis.com
Taylor & Francis Verlag GmbH, Kaufingerstraße 24, 80331 München, Germany

www.ingramcontent.com/pod-product-compliance
Lightning Source LLC
LaVergne TN
LVHW021122300926
849160LV00010B/825